GW00507752

Lawrence Wolfe-Xavier

SAVE YOURSELF
SAVE US ALL

How We Can All Live Happily into the 22nd Century
The Unique Post Covid-19 Opportunity for All Humankind

Self-Portrait 2020

**Grosvenor House
Publishing Limited**

This book is published by
Grosvenor House Publishing Ltd
Link House
140 The Broadway, Tolworth, Surrey, KT6 7HT.
www.grosvenorhousepublishing.co.uk

A CIP record for this book
is available from the British Library

ISBN 978-1-83975-531-6

SAVE YOURSELF
SAVE US ALL

How We Can All Live Happily into the 22nd Century
The Unique Post Covid-19 Opportunity for All Humankind

HOPE

VIRTUE

LOVE

LIFE

WORK must become PLAY, PLAY becomes work

Nothing Exists that may not exist, all of it may not be good, but it is a part of an ever evolving Greater Whole. Give your Love to The World, to those who deserve it, to those in most need of it. For There are Many.

A proportion of the royalties from this book will be used to encourage creativity and self-improvement amongst youngsters.

Mostly written during the Covid-19 Virus LockDown
March – August 2020 UK
Courtesy of HM Government, UK

Lawrence Wolfe-Xavier

Contents

WITHOUT PREJUDICE

I was called to write this book on 9th May 1994 with the message hand-written in red ink. It is still in my desk drawer.

The book took approximately 26 years to complete, $25^{1/2}$ years of thinking and 6 months of writing.

It is dedicated to the life, works and memory of Thomas Chatterton 1752-1770 and his efforts to make the world a better place.

"God has sent his creatures into the world with arms long enough to reach anywhere if they could be put to the trouble of extending them."

Thomas Chatterton

It is dedicated to my Mother, Father, long-term partner Jean, Sister, two Nieces and their Father and all those of you out there in the high and wild; those with eyes to see, a mind to think, a heart to feel and a soul to seek. Those who know there has been far too much unnecessary suffering. Those who know that this Life was never going to be easy and that the way we live now, it is not the only way. There is a better way. This book is NOT a 'conspiracy theory' book.

The entire contents of this book are written *'without prejudice'*. It is written with the best of intentions to initiate a most important debate of this century:

How is our species going to survive and survive happily into the 22nd Century?

There is no intention to cause any distress to any persons or to break UK or any other country's law. If such stress or unlawfulness is believed to have been caused, please accept my apologies and please communicate your concerns through the contact page on: *www.saveyourselfsaveusall.com*

With the volume of communication a book such as this, may or may not initiate, one cannot be assured that all comments will have specific replies.

I would like to thank all those whose work I have referred to by citation. In particular the 'World Economic Forum' for 'Chapter 6 – Climate Change, Potential Tragedy of Emerging Technologies - The Forces of Implosion' sections 6.2-6.8. All 'World Economic Forum' data and information was accessed in 2020. The Forum's reports set out an important part of the conventional wisdom baseline, for the future potential crises of management explained in the chapters that follow. I trust that the use of the 'World Economic Forum' information will help the Forum reach a broader readership that will assist the debate.

This book is written under English Law.

Lawrence Wolfe-Xavier

London August 2020

To The Reader

I was called to write this book on 9th May 1994 with the message hand-written in red ink. It is still in my desk drawer. Please note that a certain quantity (and quality) of English parody, satire, irony and 'quasi-irony' is intentionally included in this essay. That said; this does not preclude the seriousness of the argument, nor its validity. The author has been contemplating these and other significant and important issues for many years and knew that change was needed at least thirty years ago and hoped that the new millennium would bring in a New Age. It didn't. A few years ago it was decided to publish this work in 2020 because of what the date symbolised.

"2020 - One Fifth the way through the 21st Century, no change for the better...

.....Now is the time for Action"

The formal writing commenced in 2019 but, for financial reasons, had to be dropped. Writing recommenced in early 2020 and then the world became engulfed in the tragic global virus 'Covid-19'. The author, for thirty years, had anticipated that something of this nature would happen, but not so soon, nor in this way. The thesis in this book clearly demonstrates the inevitability of capitalist implosion and a phenomenon such as Covid-19. However it also presents a solution. Without change, the danger is still there, it always will be.

The introduction of the book represents a clear and unequivocal critique on the destiny of Mankind so far, commencing with Feudalism in Europe. It then presents the new technologies and industries and warns of the impending dangers. It concludes with a plea for change and presents a New Paradigm Solution.

The focus of the essay, although having world-wide applicability today, emanates primarily from English and European history. The term 'capitalist' is used extensively because that is the predominant method of production and distribution of the majority of goods and services world-wide. It is meant only in this way and not in the 'wicked capitalist' notion of certain persons claiming 'political' opinions. There are no political opinions per se in this essay. Citations are only given for data not widely and easily available in reputable sources of information on the world-wide-web and in print form in standard reference texts. Although in this essay, Capitalism is subjected to rigorous analysis, this does not imply that the author has sympathies with centralised Government, State, or Marxist or similar otherwise based ideologies. This book presents a New Paradigm not an old one. The author is non-political.

The indented 'Note'(s) within referred and cited text, are written by the author. The aphorisms at the beginning of each chapter are by the author. Square brackets '[ ]' are used in annotations to text.

Please start reading on page one and continue in strict chronological order until you have finished reading the entire book. To do otherwise, may result in misunderstanding.

Arthur Schopenhauer 1788-1860 stated that some of his book 'The World as Will and Representation' was written by the Holy Ghost. John Milton 1608-1674 said as much about 'Paradise Lost'. As did Arthur Rimbaud 1854-1891concerning his writing. All of this book was written by a Higher Authority.

Lawrence Wolfe-Xavier

August 2020

Chapter 1

The Rise of Feudalism in England and Europe

The First Form of Capitalism

Live your Life
Through the Happiness of Others, Nothing more
and Nothing Less

Throughout the world today, voluntary self-inflicted slavery is paramount. It is of far greater prevalence than modern, enforced slavery.

In England from the 1ˢᵗ century A.D. to the 5ᵗʰ the indigenous Celtic population was overseen and ruled by the Romans. In Europe during the Roman period and the Greek period that preceded it, slavery was common, even with people of the professions such as accountants and physicians being slaves to Roman superiors. Economic slavery persists to this day under global capitalism but in a much more sophisticated method than that of the Greeks or Romans. Greek and Roman slavery was obligatory and slaves had no rights. Transgressions were severely punished; today economic slavery is taken upon by the population out of choice with the consequential relinquishment of freedom, resulting in true freedom becoming illusory. This phenomenon of contemporary self-imposed slavery will be examined in detail later. Upon the Roman's departure from England, from the 5ᵗʰ century onwards, Angles and Saxons from Denmark and Germany

1

respectively, settled in England as farmers and invaders. The majority of early Anglo-Saxon settlers lived in small villages, grew their own food and made their own clothes. There were three social classes: Thanes who were the upper classes, Curls who worked the land and Thralls, a class of slaves.

Feudalism, which rose from 9th century to the 15th, may be considered in its essence, to be the first form of organised hierarchical 'capitalism' in England and Europe. Feudalism may be considered, to be an early form of 'capitalism' since the economic and social system in which the country 'traded' and created wealth was controlled by private individuals for their own profit and gain. The monarch, nobility (Earls and Lords) and vassals operated as a collection of self-interested individuals rather than organs within an organised state.

Feudalism predated the state; at that time there was no organised state. The capital was heritable land and property; the heritable nature of the land and property was very important to the social fabric of feudal society, since position and wealth accrued in the present was safeguarded for the future by the inheritable system that passed wealth from the present generation to the eldest son of the next. As with all other forms of capitalism, the key to the success of the system was a vertical hierarchical structure of ownership via the owners and obedience to those who did own, by those who did not. Those at the top of the structure owned, those in the middle owned little or leased, and those at the bottom owned nothing other than their capacity for obedience.

The trade in land and/or property-capital was between ownership and obedience. As we shall later see in this essay, this is much the same structure as in modern capitalism in the 21st Century today; however the structure and manipulation of ownership and obedience is far more complex and sophisticated than it was in feudal Europe. Modern capitalism is an anti-intellectual brutalism, an inward-looking nationalistic competitive avarice with little or no broad-seeing, long-term planning. Furthermore of course, modern capitalism today is now world-wide.

The feudal system, in essence, consisted of fiefdoms of heritable land, property or rights owned by the nobility. The land owned by the nobility was inheritable by the nobleman's eldest son. The fief usually consisted of land and the peasants laboured to cultivate it. They were bound to the land in rented accommodation owned by the Baron, Earl or Lord. Any disobedience and the land labourer was potentially without a home.

A Vassal or Liege was a 'free' man who held land (a fief) from a lord to whom he paid homage and duties and swore fealty (or loyalty) to the Earl or Lord. The Vassal on occasions had to pay monies to the Earl/Lord on special family occasions such as at weddings. These monies were generated from the land or revenue-producing property held in feudal land tenure. A vassal/liege could be a Lord of the Manor but was also directly subservient to a superior Noble or the King.

European Nobility originated in the feudal/seignorial system that arose in Europe during the Middle Ages where the Germanic clan system claimed that all land belonged to the King who exercised the enfeoffment (deed giving rights for pledge of service) of land as fief. Feudalism was introduced to England by William I, Duke of Normandy in the 11th century. All land belonged to the King and the King was answerable only to God – the divine right of kings. The convenience of such a belief is obvious to all, particularly monarchs; however there was little appetite at the time it appears, for attempts at explanation as to who owned all the land before the existence of these kings. This claim by the monarchy to the ownership of all land may have been the greatest act of theft in English and indeed European History. A significant residue of this theft persists to this day.

Further, one might imagine, since History appears not to tell us otherwise, there was probably even less appetite for any exercises in the ontological ratification of the existence of this God and this (for some) rather convenient and unique administration, command, control and communication reporting structure. A strange hypothesis since the occurrence of kingship was primarily an accident of hereditary birth rather than there being any discernible direct appointment of a monarch by God. Originally, knights or nobles were horse mounted warriors who swore loyalty and allegiance to a higher ranking nobleman or to the monarch and promised to militarily fight for those to whom allegiance was sworn and offer protection in exchange for an allocation of land (usually together with serfs (labourers) living on the land).

The classic Francois-Louis Granshof version of feudalism describes a set of reciprocal legal and military obligations among the warrior nobility, revolving around the three key concepts of lords, vassals, and fiefs. A lord was in broad terms a noble who held land from the monarch, a vassal was a person who was granted rights over the land by the lord, and the land was known as a fief. In exchange for the use of the fief and protection by the lord, the vassal would provide some sort of service to the lord.

There were many varieties of feudal land tenure consisting of military and non-military service. The obligations and corresponding rights between lord and vassal concerning the fief formed the basis of the feudal relationship.

Vassalage

Before a lord could grant land (a fief) to someone, he had to make that person a Vassal. This was done at a formal and symbolic ceremony called a commendation ceremony, which was composed of the two-part act of homage and oath of fealty. During homage, the Earl/Lord and vassal entered into a contract in which the vassal promised to militarily fight for the lord at his command, whilst the lord agreed to protect the vassal from external forces. *Fealty* comes from the Latin *fidelitas* and denotes the fidelity or loyalty owed by a vassal to his feudal lord. "Fealty" also refers to an oath that more explicitly reinforces the commitments of the vassal made during homage. Such an oath followed homage.

Once the commendation ceremony was complete, the lord and vassal were in a feudal relationship with agreed obligations to one another. The vassal's principal obligation to the lord was to "aid", or conduct military service. Using whatever equipment the vassal could obtain by virtue of the revenues from the fief, the vassal was responsible to answer calls to military service on behalf of the lord. This security of military help was the primary reason the lord entered into the feudal relationship.

In addition, the vassal could have other obligations to his lord, such as attendance at his court, whether manorial, baronial or at the king's court.

It could also involve the vassal providing "counsel", so that if the lord faced a major decision he would summon all his vassals and hold a council. At the level of the manor this might be a fairly mundane matter of agricultural policy, but also included sentencing by the lord for criminal offences, including capital punishment in some cases. Concerning the king's feudal court, such deliberations could include the question of declaring war. The above are examples; depending on the period of time and location in Europe, feudal customs and practices varied.

Feudalism in England and Europe may therefore be seen as the first example of organised hierarchical 'capitalism' with regard to the 'capital' being land and property. All land was ultimately under the ownership of the monarch. The king's land, together with the land's serfs, was apportioned to the higher nobility under duty and service to the monarch. The next societal level down from the nobility was the vassal where the relationship between the monarch and the noble was essentially replicated by the relationship between the noble and the vassal. Both the monarch/nobleman and the nobleman/vassal were reciprocal relationships of the apportionment primarily of land in return for sworn loyalty and protection towards the appointee together with military and other duties. The very tip of this hierarchy was the monarch of each country in Europe and conveniently for each monarch they reported only to God. It was claimed that a king was born into a rank that recognizes no superior but God, to whom alone the king was responsible for his actions.

Hence in England the motto of the monarchy is *"Dieu et mon droit"* ("God and my right"). The military significance of the motto *"Dieu et mon droit"* was apparently first occasioned when the term was used by Richard I (1157-1199) as a battle cry. The heritable nature of all land and property was important in maintaining the long term stability and hierarchical structure of Feudalism, a socio/economic/'politico' system that lasted for over a quarter of mankind's period of civilisation, if one considers the dawn of civilisation to be 2,000 years ago. Further, the king's control of the hierarchical pyramid of the populace through ennobling lordships and knighthoods and attendant fiefs, in return for sworn allegiance and military aid, was of singular importance to the firm control by the king of his territory.

The system continues today but the allegiance to the monarch is less rigid and the 'aid' to the monarchy is perceived primarily as excellence in one's field of endeavour with a particular emphasis on capitalist, revenue creating, ventures and nationalistic trade.

Military service is no longer required by the nobility because of the existence of a professional army recruited from the common people. 'Common people' is a term that the nobility might use to describe good hard-working people without whom they would be nothing. However, today even those in the entertainment industries including sports may receive the monarch's favour if it is deemed that they contributed to capitalist revenues or the status abroad of the monarch's territory. The court entertainers in feudal times were

6

not so received by the monarchy; court jesters, acrobats and lute playing minstrels were probably not of a military disposition and better served the monarch at court as diversion from the worries of war. Furthermore, land was the only significant existent asset and all food, clothing and shelter was produced directly or indirectly from land. So through Feudalism's inherent strongly hierarchical, heritable social and wealth structure, being pursuant for the first half or so of the second millennium (9th–15th centuries), lay the 'capitalistic' foundations for the rise of capitalism as conventionally defined commencing in the 17th century.

Capitalism as conventionally understood has existed for four centuries (17th–21st centuries) and had its genesis in the system of Feudalism that lasted for six centuries. In this essay we will evaluate the probability or otherwise of Capitalism outlasting Feudalism i.e. existing for more than another two centuries. Feudal 'capitalism' was capitalism in its embryonic phase and was yet to achieve its overriding, all consuming and mythical status that it holds today. It is the erroneous myths of industrial capitalism together with Mankind's predilections that give rise to Mankind's current voluntary, self-imposed slavery and capitalism's inherently self-implosive nature. This will be dealt with later. The decline in Feudalism gave rise to the second form of capitalism – Mercantilism.

Chapter 2

The Rise of Mercantilism

The Second Form of Capitalism

Once you earn more money than your immediate needs require, say for example £100-£150k per year in the UK, at today's value, you simply exchange one set of problems for another and the second set of problems give no greater happiness than the first

Feudalism declined from the 12th to the 15th centuries. The primary reasons were political changes, war and the bubonic plague. In England the signing of the Magna Carta on 15th June 1215 and other political reforms laid the foundations for more democratic forms of government. The culture of feudalism, which centred on noble knights and castles, declined in this period. The spread of new military technologies such as the longbow and cannon made the armoured horse-backed knight and fortified castle less important. The Hundred Years' War 1337-1453 between France and England shifted power away from feudal lords to both the monarchy and the common people. It also increased feelings of nationalism, as people began to identify more with the king than with their local lord.

Note: The Magna Carta, signed in 1215, which means 'The Great Charter', is one of the most important documents in history as it established the principle that everyone is subject to the law, even the king, and guarantees the rights of individuals, the right to justice and the right to a fair trial.

Armies were organised through bodies of professional soldiers rather than the appointees of the nobility which diminished the power of the lords. Furthermore, more land became rented rather than owned by lords which further restricted their power. The Feudal Levy was unpopular and as time went by Nobles preferred to pay the King rather than to fight and raise troops again diminishing the power that the lord's had, by the loss of their own armies. The Crusades 1095-1492 and the consequential middle-east travel opened up new trade options for England which assisted in the decline of the feudal system of agriculture and land ownership. The bubonic plague in 1348 caused trade and commerce to slow.

Due to the death of one third of the population of Europe from the plague, labour shortages occurred. This created greater economic opportunities for peasants, and they demanded increased wages through the Peasants' Revolt 1381. The hierarchical social structure of feudalism was destabilized as a result of the plague, which affected all social classes equally. When the plague passed and feudal lords attempted to re-establish their authority, peasant rebellions occurred as commoners refused to accept the old social order. The disaster of the plague influenced culture, causing some to celebrate life and the common people, in the face of mass death giving greater credence to their own lives and happiness rather than subservience to nobles.

Covid-19 presents an interesting parallel in the world today. Will the people have the opportunity to increase their freedoms and means of self-realisation and therefore achieve greater true happiness? It is there for the taking. It is up to them. Eternal Recurrence?

As feudalism declined in England and Europe the vacuum was filled by the rise in Mercantilism, the second form of capitalism. The 16th to the 17th centuries saw the rise in mercantilism, and simultaneously, the rise of the nation state which promoted governmental regulation of a country's economy to strengthen and augment the nation state in competition, and as security against, competitive other nation states. This was to be achieved by trade between countries where each country attempted to amass wealth by exporting more than it imported. England in the 1600's saw the exploitation of the country's colonies by the importation of raw materials from the colonies, the production of finished products in England followed by the exportation of the finished products to other countries. A simple example would be trees from the Americas imported to England where finished products such as furniture, tools, barrels, paper would be exported to Europe and back to the colonies. This process was enforced by various acts of Parliament such as the Navigation (Trades Act) in 1651 to control trade with England's colonies by prohibiting foreign vessels engaging in coastal trade.

However, the wider picture of mercantilism as practised in England is far more sinister. It contains the genesis of state endorsed capitalistic greed and artificially contrived competitive advantage. This was achieved by tariffs on imports, state monopolies to those firms in trade and shipping, subsidies to export industries for competitive advantage, permitting copyright and intellectual property theft from competitive foreign companies, restricting wages of the local workers to increase monies to the merchant classes, make the colonies buy from England, all colonial exports passed through England before reaching the destination of export.

In the 1600s England was governed by the monarchy, the House of Lords and the House of Commons. In the late 1600s the House of Commons had the sole right to create taxation legislation.

In England there was an interesting change in structure from the feudal model to the mercantile. Capitalistic avarice changed from being a disparate individualism by the monarchy and noble lords based on wealth accrued through the exploitation of land and the serfs who worked it. Under mercantilism, capitalistic greed was institutionalised, by and into, government based on wealth acquired through trade and the enhancement of the nation state at the expense of competitive nations. The propagators of this process of personal wealth creation were the monarchy, members of the House of Lords and members of the House of Commons comprising of the monarchy, land owners and particularly merchants. The decline in Mercantilism gave rise to the third form of capitalism, the beginnings of Industrial Capitalism in the 18th century.

Chapter 3

The Rise of Industrial Capitalism

The Third Form of Capitalism

The Tragedy of Mortality is the Irrevocability of Time

As with feudalism in England, war was instrumental in its downfall, primarily The Hundred Years' War so it was that war would contribute to the downfall of mercantilism. However with mercantilism it was two wars. The Seven Years War (1756-1763) was primarily between Great Britain and France but involved Austria, Germany, Prussia, Spain, Portugal, Sweden and Russia. This war was very costly to Great Britain and since it was hinged around protecting their colonies, the government of Great Britain deemed it appropriate that the colonies should help to pay for it through taxation. In America duties and taxes were imposed or strengthened commencing in 1764 – Sugar and Molasses Tax, then in 1765 Stamp Tax, 1767 Townshend Acts, 1773 Tea Tax. These taxes and impositions on the America's thirteen British colonies situated on the east coast of America resulted in riots and eventually war. This war, the American War of Independence (1775-1783) gave independence to America from Great Britain and the United States of America was founded.

Whilst Great Britain was busily engaged in surrendering its territorial assets in America, its inventors and engineers were busy developing ideas that would change England and the world for ever.

The 1760's in England saw the rise of Industrial Capitalism and the Industrial Revolution 1760 – 1840. In 1764 James Hargreaves of Lancashire invented the 'Spinning Jenny' a machine that weaved cotton with more than one spindle at a time. The device reduced the amount of work needed to produce cloth, with a worker able to work eight or more spools at once. This grew to 120 spools as technology advanced. The yarn produced by the jenny was not very strong until Richard Arkwright in 1765 invented the water-powered 'water frame', powered by a water-wheel which produced cotton yarn harder and stronger than that of the initial spinning jenny. The 'water frame' could produce 128 cotton threads at a time. It started the factory system whereby large factories of light to heavy machinery were operated by manual labour workers and thus the division between 'capital' and 'labour' first arose. Those who were typically previously merchants invested capital in factories and machinery and thus the emphasis of trade moved away from mercantile artisan manufacture and crafts based guilds to large scale industrialised machine-lead manufacture.

In 1776 James Watt, 1736-1819 a Scottish inventor, engineer and chemist improved upon Thomas Newcomen's 1712 steam engine and developed his own 'Watt Steam Engine'. Steam engines were used in all sorts of applications including factories, mines, locomotives, and steamboats. Steam engines use hot steam from boiling water to drive a piston (or pistons) back and forth. The movement of the pistons was then used to power a machine or turn a wheel.

Karl Marx 1818-1883 defined the commencement of Industrial Capitalism as being the last third of the 18th century i.e. 1766/1767 onwards which coincides with the developments above, in particular, with Arkwright's 'water frame' machine in 1765 that gave rise to large factories of light to heavy machinery that were operated by manual labour workers and thus the 'water frame' machine was the genesis of large factories and the division between 'capital' and 'labour'.

Karl Marx may be considered to be the intellectual father of anti-capitalism whereas capitalism's intellectual father was Adam Smith 1723-1790 the Scottish economist, philosopher, moral philosopher and pioneer of political economy. His magnum opus was *'An Enquiry into the Nature and Causes of the Wealth of Nations'* 1776 which is considered to be the first modern work on economic theory and it laid the intellectual foundations of industrial capitalism and the foundations for the free market economic theory. As outlined previously the 'free market economic theory' is, in fact, purely a 'theory'; it is in fact rather, a fiction. The practical reality is that it is the erroneous myths of industrial capitalism together with Mankind's predilections that give rise to Mankind's current voluntary, self-imposed slavery and capitalism's inherently self-implosive nature. The 'free' market is far from free. This will be dealt with in detail later.

As shown above, Industrial Capitalism commenced in Great Britain primarily in the textile industry but alongside textiles was the equally important growth in iron and steel production and use. Bar iron was the commodity form of iron used as the raw material for making hardware goods such as nails, wire, hinges, horse shoes, wagon tyres, chains, etc. and for structural shapes. A small amount of bar iron was converted into steel. Cast iron was used for pots, stoves and other items. Most cast iron was refined and converted to bar iron, with substantial losses. Bar iron was also made by the bloomery process, which was the predominant iron smelting process until the late 18th century. A bloomer was a form of furnace consisting of a pit or chimney with heat-resistant walls made of earth, clay, or stone which produced iron and its oxides as a form of slag, the bloom. This bloom was further consolidated and forged into wrought iron. Watt's rotary action steam engine in 1781 helped increase furnace size and was used for air bellows, helping to boost production.

Perhaps, the key development for iron production came in 1783-4, when Henry Cort 1740-1800 introduced the puddling and rolling iron purification techniques. These were ways of getting all the impurities out of iron and allowing large-scale production, and a vast increase in it. The iron industry began to relocate to coal fields, which usually had iron ore nearby. Developments elsewhere also helped to boost iron by stimulating demand, such as the increase in steam engines – which needed iron – which in turn boosted iron innovations as one industry bred innovations elsewhere. The primary sources of energy in industrial capitalism at this time were the irreplaceable fossil fuels of coke and coal.

The most important industrial invention of Industrial Capitalism after the steam engine was the locomotive. The first recorded steam railway journey took place in 1812, when Richard Trevithick's 'Pen-y-derren' locomotive carried ten tons of iron, five wagons and seventy men 9.75 miles in four hours and five minutes. The journey had an average speed of approximately 2.4 mph.

George Stephenson and his son, Robert Stephenson, designed 'Stephenson's Rocket', the most advanced locomotive of its day and in 1829 The Rocket won the Rainhill Test Trial for a locomotive to run between Liverpool and Manchester.

The Rocket's design – with its smoke chimney at the front and a separate fire box in the rear – became the template for future steam locomotives for the next 150 years. Further important inventions were telegraph communications in 1837 and dynamite in 1860.

Chapter 4

The Failure of Capitalism

Six Industrial and Post-Industrial Revolutions but the World is Still Unhappy and Unfed
(Capitalism versus Contentment)

The Higher a Man's Intellect the Greater his Obsession with Truth

"On the face of it, shareholder value is the dumbest idea in the world" Jack Welch CEO General Electric USA. Source: 'The Financial Times' 13th March 2009.

Jack Welch, the most successful Global Corporate Chief Executive Officer in the world in the 20th century and who is regarded as the father of the "shareholder value" movement that has dominated the corporate world for more than 30 years, **has said it was** *"the dumbest idea in the world"* **[for executives to focus so heavily on quarterly profits and quarterly share price gains...]**

I also quote Irwin Stelzer:

"Also obvious is that the <u>moral underpinnings</u> Adam Smith argued are necessary to the proper functioning and acceptance of capitalism <u>have been eroded</u>. No, not by Bernie Sanders, nor by the increasingly left-surging Democratic Party, try as they might, but by capitalists and their functionaries."

Irwin Stelzer, 'The Sunday Times' 3rd May 2020

Modern capitalism is an anti-intellectual brutalism, an inward-looking nationalistic competitive avarice with little or no broad-seeing, long-term planning. Furthermore of course, modern capitalism today is now world-wide. The only significant variance currently is the state controlled capitalism of Russia and China. If it is taken that the prime economic and producing driver for the world's people i.e. capitalism; has as its primary purpose to provide for the world's population's needs of adequate food, clothing and shelter in safe and healthy living environments; then it is clear that capitalism, after 250 + years (over a quarter of a millennia i.e. approximately one eighth of the duration of Western Civilisation since the death of Plato) of industrial and post-industrial revolutions, has singularly and entirely failed to achieve its accepted and intended goal. If the perfectly reasonable assumption above is not correct, then what is the purpose of capitalism? I dread to think.

From 1760 to the present day, in a total of 260 years, depending upon one's definition of industrial revolution, we may consider there have been six industrial and post-industrial revolutions. Here we use six revolutions, not by definition based only upon revolution in technology but in terms of revolution in the impact the change has had on the day-to-day lives of ordinary people living in the industrial capitalist economies. Others may wish to define four industrial revolutions, or another number, this is not material to the discussion. Six will suffice for our needs.

The first two Industrial Revolutions were industry based with the emphasis on the extraction and utilisation of energy and mineral enriched earth sub-strata substances for the creation and utilisation of mechanical power. This mechanical power was used in the mass manufacture of products and in transportation of product and people. The remaining four revolutions were post-industrial where the emphasis was on the storage, utilisation, access and transference of data and information.

The commencement of the **first industrial revolution** proper, may be considered to be around 1780, when the fuels were coke and coal to provide the steam power for Watt's Steam Engine to provide mechanical power in factories, mines, locomotives, and steamboats.

The second industrial revolution where the primary fuels were petro-chemical fossil fuels i.e. petrol and diesel used in the propulsion of the internal combustion engine. In 1886 the first production car was designed and patented in Germany by Benz, the Benz Patent-Motorwagon. It was an open-top three-wheeler carriage and ran on a petrol-powered internal combustion engine. Another very significant development within the second industrial revolution was the semi-automation and full automation of production lines particularly for the automotive industry. This industry used 'point and place' robots for welding, assembly and other operations by computer control of the X, Y, Z Cartesian coordinates and the alignment vectors, of the robot head and arm(s).

The **third industrial revolution** was, in truth, the first post-industrial revolution and all subsequent industry revolutions may be considered to be post-industrial. This may be considered to be the advent of the first commercially used computer, the Mainframe Computer, first used in the 1950's. The design of this computer had a single-based processor, the Central Processing Unit CPU that was independently accessed and operated upon by disparate terminals colloquially known as 'dumb terminals' because they had no processing power of their own but acted merely as display terminals of the information emanating from the CPU and centralised data-storage disk drives. Mainframe computers were used primarily by large industrial and commercial organizations for critical applications; bulk data processing, such as industry and consumer statistics, enterprise resource planning, transaction processing.

The fourth revolution is the significant change in information technology structure brought about by the desktop personal computer. These personal computers eventually having their own individual CPU processing unit, disk, motherboard with monitor, keyboard and mouse and were linked to a network of other personal computers. The configuration for such networked systems was the server-client structure where there were a number of clients (perhaps 50 or more) being served by a server and with a number of servers inter-connected within the complete network. This network was internal to the corporation that designed and used it for the storage and utilisation of internal corporate specific data. This network system was called an Intranet. In this way all of the corporate clients in the network were connected to one another for access to data, data sharing and communication. This network structure for computer data communication formed the basis of, and led to, the next industrial revolution, the Internet.

The fifth industrial revolution, again post-industrial, was the invention and application of the world-wide-web in 1989 (the Internet) by Tim Berners-Lee, a British scientist. This technology expanded upon the corporate-based server-client networked computer system of the fourth revolution and made the technology of the networked computer system available to anyone in the world with a computer that had network capability and access to the world-wide-web via the internet. Full mobility became possible from the 1980's with the introduction of smaller, portable computers 'Portable Personal Computers' commonly now known as laptop computers.

The sixth revolution, again post-industrial, came into being with the mobile or cellular telephone. These telephones did not require terrestrial-line connectivity but used cellular network antennae. This gained traction in the 1990's/2000's when the mobile phone could be linked to the internet and earned the nomenclature 'smart phone'. The sixth revolution also primarily has a 'digital backbone' and also importantly integrates the physical, digital and biological worlds and is giving rise to simultaneous advances in robotics, artificial intelligence, bio-technologies and other technologies that are dealt with later. The mobile phone is the focus of this section because of the revolutionary way the technology affected, in a matter of just a few years, the world-wide lives of ordinary people and the way they interact with one another on a very intimate level.

The mobile smart phone is now a multi-media hand-held device using voice, visuals, text, sound and digital 'film' video with an enormous number of internet-based applications (Apps) running on them, from browsing the web, to text messaging, caller visual telephone interfaces etc. There are now many thousands and thousands of applications, many commercially driven; amongst the most popular are 'Uber' – for reserving and hiring taxis, 'Instagram' a social networking application for photograph and message sharing, 'Airbnb' for accommodation bookings and 'Netflix' for on-line film viewing. The 'social' applications developed for mobile phones such as 'Facebook', 'Twitter', 'Instagram', 'WhatsApp' and others have given rise to a revolution within a revolution, this being world-wide-web based 'social networking'. Some of these such as Facebook assign the title of 'friend' or 'friends' to a person or persons with whom one communicates through Facebook. The term 'friend' is not used in the context of the way the term is usually used. The so called 'friends' are possibly and perhaps most likely to be persons on the other side of the planet that one has never met nor ever to likely meet. A more appropriate title might be 'social networking acquaintances'. However, for product marketing reasons, this title would most probably be considered not appropriate.

So we may divide these six 'industrial' revolutions into blocks of two:

Block One – revolutions 1 and 2 were fully heavily industrial and based on manufacturing and distribution of physical products.

Block Two – revolutions 3 and 4 were primarily Corporate Computing and based on the use of corporate information and data.

Block Three – revolutions 5 and 6 were initially used for world-wide Corporate information but more latterly, revolution 6 is used mostly for personal world-wide communication with an emphasis on personal image transmission and personal social communications.

So we see that the communication flow has tended to be top-down for revolutions 1 to 5 from the Corporation to the individual. However in revolution six the communication has changed from top-down Corporate to individual, to multi-lateral communications between private personal individuals and groups via social networking. Further, social media and networking platforms have introduced a 'world-wide bottom-up' information flow from private individuals and groups 'up-wards' to governments, multi-national corporations and world leaders. This Social Media 'up-flow' information to governments, multi-national corporations and world leaders has resulted in 'down–flow' responses from these bodies. Consequently there has arisen a world-wide multilateral and 'multivertical' interactive communication flow between global powers, social activity groups and individuals. Social Media has become the world-wide digital platform of choice for social comment and social protest.

Alongside this is the 'digital backbone' of the world-wide web, the Internet, GPS and smart phones that gave rise to the important integration of the physical, digital and biological worlds which in turn, eventually through 5G technologies 'an enhanced fully integral, homogeneous digital backbone' is giving rise to simultaneous advances in robotics, artificial intelligence, bio-technologies and other technologies that are dealt with later in 'Chapter 6 – Climate Change, Potential Tragedy of Emerging Technologies - The Forces of Implosion'.

Broadly speaking we might say that each subsequent industrial revolution was shorter in duration than the previous one and had more far reaching effects than the previous one within that shorter duration. It is reasonable to state that each industrial revolution was essentially half the duration of its previous one and the social results of each successive revolution perhaps an order of magnitude or so greater than its predecessor. Do we see here an example of the Natural Law of exponential growth?

We might broadly summarise this as:

Block One – Heavy Industrial Machinery – Physical Products and Transportation

1st Industrial Revolution 1760 – 1840 : 80 years Coke, Coal and Steam Power - Locomotive

2nd Ind. Revolution 1880 – 1920 : 40 years Petroleum and Internal Combustion Power – Automobile

Block Two – Large Corporation Computing – Information/ Data Products

3rd Ind. Revolution 1950 – 1970 : 20 years Mainframe Computer – Corporate Information Technology.

4th Ind. Revolution 1970 – 1980 : 10 years Network Server Client Computer – Corporate Information Technology.

Block Three – Corporate & Personal Computing – Information/ Data Products

5th Ind. Revolution 1990 – 2000 : 10 years World Wide Web – Corporate and Personal Information Technology.

6th Ind. Revolution 2005 – 2010+: 5 years Mobile Tel. Apps – Personal world-wide social networking (robotics/artificial intelligence/bio-technology et al)

The earliest part of the first industrial revolution, the advent of the Spinning Jenny in 1760 affected mostly only weavers and did not directly affect blacksmiths, coopers or candle-wax makers or indeed others. This is also true for the locomotive and the automobile in the second industrial revolution affected only those who could afford them. However the world-wide-web and mobile phone applications, with their becoming reportedly (in 2018) more relatively cheap mobile phones in the world than people (a significant number of them probably old models left in kitchen drawers or residing on waste/recycling dumps), affected most of the entire world's population and effected their lives very dramatically in a very, very short space of time.

The sixth industrial revolution caused change so rapidly across the world's national boundaries that national legislation cannot keep up with them and consequently cannot cope with the speed of development and the international nature and reach of this technology. An unidentifiable person using a fake email address may walk into an internet café in Tokyo, libel someone in UK or elsewhere on social media, and there is little or no legislation in the UK, or indeed the world, to protect the libelled person. The person in Tokyo may walk out of the internet café, take the next flight to Bogota and live happily ever after beyond the reach of any law anywhere. Indeed, it is possible to minimise the ease of location of such a libelling person by the use of 'virtual computer locations' or 'hidden computer locations' by hiding the IP address of your computer – Virtual Private Network (VPN). However social media presents far greater threats than this simple personal example, as we shall see later.

For the 'lucky ones' amongst us, the perceived advantages of capitalism for the fortunate few cannot be dismissed. There is far greater world-wide material wealth today, for some, than at any other time in history. Since 1760 industrial and societal progress have, for some, improved wealth, health, life-span, education, opportunities, healthcare and social care. However, this analysis appertains to the wealthier nations. Capitalism has not been so benevolent upon the poorer and poorest nations of the world. In terms of a Global perspective therefore, it is reasonable to consider capitalism to be a failure. There are a number of reasons to consider capitalism to be a failure; here are some of the most important ones.

4.1 Perpetual Unrestrained Global Growth

The theories of people such as Adam Smith (1723-1790) and Karl Marx (1818-1883), and theories are all that they were, were of great importance at their time, and are of importance today, however now in 2020 we are in the fortunate position (or perhaps unfortunate position) to be able to critically assess not so much theories, but much more importantly, the realities of approximately 250 years of industrial 'progress' under capitalism. It is self-evident that capitalism as practiced is inherently self-destructive and must eventually fail. The cause of its self-destruction is inherent within its 'very own self', within the very central nucleus of capitalism. The inherent competitive nature of capitalism enforces upon its practitioners the imperative of unrestrained, perpetual growth. All companies world-wide, are competing for resources to produce, market and sell their products. They are all competing to out-sell one another to achieve the greatest market share for themselves and thus strengthen their competitive advantage of economies of scale and market brand awareness in relation to the position of their competitors in their same market segments.

Indeed, in the consumer sector and others they are competing with other companies not even in their own market or sub-market sector. If the consumer has at his or her disposal, by whatever means, a sum of say some thousands of pounds, that money may be used to put a deposit on a property purchase, to have an exotic holiday or perhaps buy a sports car. All of these completely disparate unconnected business sectors are in effect, in competition against one another for the consumers' deposable income. Similarly in business to business a goods or service provider would be competing against goods and service providers in other markets or sub markets because the investing company must realise its best overall, total productivity and business enhancement potential on its investment irrespective of which market sector or sub-sector the goods or service being invested in may fall into. Should the investing company concentrate its efforts in business enhancement through investment in research and development, design, manufacturing, logistics, advertising etc etc – which would give the best total return on investment? Ideally for the capitalists, each individual company would like to be so dominant in its field as to be the world leader and preferably the only supplier of their particular product lines.

In the UK, there is the example of the high street pharmacy chain 'Boots'. This company, excellent record for product and service that they may have well earned, hold a virtual monopoly on the sub-sector of high street beauty products, pharmaceutical and prescription chemist chains and independents. 'Boots' starting in 1849, now have a turnover of £23.4Bn, 120,000 staff, 4,600 shops and 4,450 pharmacies. There nearest UK competitor, 'Superdrug' starting in 1966, has a turnover of £1.2Bn, 14,000 staff, 800 shops. 'Boots' therefore in comparison to 'Superdrug', have been in existence 3.2 times longer, has 19.5 times the turnover, has 5.75 times the shops and 8.57 times the number of staff. A most successful capitalist venture in terms of monopoly dominance. How it has escaped the attention of the UK Competition & Markets Commission that replaced the Monopolies and Mergers Commission, is another significant achievement.

Such market domination of being the only supplier, a monopoly, is preferred so as the company may achieve the maximum self-protection against its competitors (there aren't any) and therefore to best ensure its own business success, longevity and survival. This may be advantageous for the producer, who may produce whatever products it deems and price them to his own choosing, but lack of competition resulting in total monopoly is likely to be detrimental to the consumer or receiver of the monopolists' products or services, because competition tends to act as a controller of both product quality and price to the advantage of the consumer. Indeed, monopolies are generally considered by Governments to be detrimental to the market's consumers and consequently regulatory bodies are put in place to prevent monopolies from occurring as in the Competition & Markets Commission above. The very core nature of capitalism, the pursuit of market dominance and ultimately a monopolistic position, as described above, is therefore admitted by Governments, whose primary concern is supposedly to protect the wellbeing of the nation state and its population, to be detrimental to capitalism's **customer** and potentially to the country's entire population! How absurd and self-contradictory is that?!

This world-wide competition for success in product manufacture, sales and dominance over competitors necessitates perpetual unrestrained global growth. This is the biggest weakness in the practice of capitalism as we can observe today by the growth of industrial practices resulting in large scale world-wide environmental pollution and possibly contributing to climate change and global warming. There is much research, widely available that strongly implies that human beings, in their consumption of fossil fuels, are contributing to climate change and global warming. As a simple example, I cannot think of an argument that would suggest that the smog over Los Angeles is due to anything other than causes emanating from capitalist human activities, primarily the automobile and local industries. The importance of capitalism's effect on world-wide pollution and destruction cannot be over emphasised. However, more importantly, as stated above, the inherent competitive nature of capitalism enforces upon its practitioners the imperative of perpetual, unrestrained global growth. Such a system of perpetual, unrestrained global growth must eventually fail. It is just a question of when. Not only does capitalism result in the planet's relentless pollution but ultimately the failure and collapse must eventually come because unrestrained, perpetual global growth is not sustainable on a finitely resourced planet such as earth, no matter how clever human beings are in 'kicking the can down the road'. Sooner or later the can kicks back by bouncing off of a 'brick wall'.

4.2 Perpetual Unrestrained Population Growth

The global population is anticipated to be 9.7Bn in 2050 and 10.9Bn in 2100. This represents an increase by 2050 of 24% on the 2020 figure of 7.8Bn, and an increase of 39% by 2100. In 1928 the global population was estimated at 2Bn which means that with the population in 2020 being 7.8Bn then the increase in population in just the last 72 years was 290% or almost three times population increase. In 1803 the population was 1Bn.

Data Source: Our World in Data - United Nations - 2019

It is no coincidence that the enormous increase in economic production and consumption from 1928 to 2020 is reflected in the relative increase in population growth for that period. In comparison to the years from 1803 (pop. 1Bn) to 1928 (pop. 2Bn), where the increase in population was 100% in 125 years, the increase in population in 72 years from 1928 to 2020 was 290%. For interest, and for a hypothetical comparison, let's extrapolate linearly, the 290% population increase over 72 years represents 503% over 125 years, 5 times the growth in population, if the technological expansion of 1928-2020 had occurred between 1803-1928.

Furthermore, if we come to 1985, the date of the 'Live Aid' Concert a charity event for the starving people of Africa, the world population was 4.84Bn and in 2020 it is 7.8Bn representing a growth of 61% in 35 years. Frightening!

In order for capitalism to achieve perpetual unrestrained global growth it requires perpetual unrestrained global population growth. It must have its consumers and its producers, often one and the same entity. Greater economic growth fuels greater population growth, which in a perverse way, is probably deemed fortunate by the myopic capitalist. Unfortunately however, this inherent causal deterministic link between capital growth and population growth must eventually cause the global population to reach the limits of food sustainability. Hence collapse.

One might argue that population growth is controlled by the economic growth and therefore the population will only grow as large as that that the economic growth can sustain. Although this logic may appear to be sound, contemporary History shows otherwise. There are factors at play that indicate population growth may extend beyond its immediate economic sustainability. Population growth today is a very, very real problem.

The economic growth connection to population growth phenomenon is not a rigid non-extendable mechanical link. There are involved, the dynamics of multifarious, interlinked causes and effects such as: improved health, increased longevity of life, changes in food production technologies, changes in distribution and logistics, changes in eating habits, improved quality of drinking water etc that cause hysteresis lags between economic growth and population growth. These push and pull lags cause a population push aspect to the global economy. In the poorer countries, which tend to have larger families, (which are therefore the greatest in global population density), there are larger families because of higher infant mortality. Have a large family because not all children will survive. However because of the spread of better health, quality and quantity of food etc improvements, in the short term less than anticipated deaths occur. More and more children survive into adulthood. Hence there is a population push dynamic on global growth. This phenomenon is probably temporary as the population versus income balance returns. In the meantime suffering is prevalent upon the poorest nations in the form of hunger and malnutrition as the population temporarily exceeds its sustainability. The selfishness and greed of capitalism and the consequential maldistribution of wealth serve only to exacerbate the situation.

This phenomenon of large families surviving existed quite recently in the industrial 'first' world. One only has to go back in history to those persons born just after the First World War in the 1920's to observe working class families of seven or eight children. All surviving to adulthood.

Here we see the challenge to feed the world with an unrestrained growth in global population. Soon the world will have to start to consider synchronised population control on a pan-global scale.

Capitalism's commensurate population growth will also strain the finite resources of the planet. In order to satisfy capitalism's inherent need for unrestrained perpetual growth then it requires a commensurate unrestrained perpetual growth in the population. One cannot have one philosophy without the other. For capitalism would require the population to grow at a commensurate rate to produce and consume the never ending increase in growth of products and services. The required perpetual growth of the world's population is therefore the second biggest factor in the inherent nature of capitalism being its own downfall and eventually its own inevitable failure. Government leaders and others wax lyrical about a country's economic growth, indeed there appears to be a nationalistic competition where a country is considered superior to another based on its growth of gross domestic product 'GDP'. Economic Growth is uncritically considered by governments, world leaders and global corporations to be a 'God given', indubitable, de facto, beyond all questioning, 'Divine Truth' that must be achieved at all costs. It is the 'Holy Grail' of Nation States. Economic Growth is uncritically considered by governments, world leaders and global corporations to be some form of 'Categorical Imperative' an imperative yard-stick by which all nations are judged and relentlessly compete against one another in a blind race of lemmings to the edge of the Abyss. Television autocue News Readers rejoice in their country's economic growth figures in the same way that they rejoice in the UK over high house price inflation without, what appears to be a very basic understanding of the economic implications. High price inflation, according to the genius scholars of economics, is bad for a capitalist economy. Too high aspirational growth tends to be price inflationary which in turn is detrimental to the economy and the well-being of the populace.

Consequently the unrestrained perpetration of ever increasing growth, an imperative kernel of capitalism, as outlined in the previous section of this chapter; is in itself, detrimental to the capitalist economy and its people. Capitalism's Inherent Being is detrimental to that Being. It is detrimental to itself – the most absurd of paradoxes.

World leaders and Governments appear to be either ignorant of, or uncomprehending of, or dismissive of, the two very critical arguments put forward above. World leaders and Governments, with their fetishism for growth are therefore guilty of leading their populace of conforming consumers and producers over the abyss into self-inflicted oblivion.

4.3 The False Market and Two Myths of Capitalism

Adam Smith's lassiez-faire (leave to do) economic philosophy where government intervention in the 'free markets' through taxation, tariffs, subsidies, regulations etc is kept to an absolute minimum, because it is deemed, that the market itself will self-control supply and demand of goods and services is a well-established concept. The idea is that the market will, inherently within itself, self-balance supply and demand for goods and services. If a product or service is too cheap, demand will outstrip supply, and therefore the capitalist will increase supply to satisfy the unsatisfied demand providing there is capacity to do so. Or alternatively increase the product or service price, or some combination of both increase in supply and increase in price. The reverse is also true. If a product or service is too expensive, then supply will outstrip demand because the product or service will not be purchased and stock levels will increase. In this case the price will be dropped in order to sale the product or service or the market is increased by advertising or other sales encouragement strategy. Therefore the market, like an economic pendulum will swing backwards and forwards between supply and demand until temporary equilibrium is achieved.

However, it suffers from a major flaw within its own definition. The flaw lies in the term 'free market' – it carries quotation marks for a reason. There is no such thing today, as a 'free market'! The consumer market is grossly manipulated, not so much by Governments and other regulatory bodies but by those who gain the most by its manipulation, namely the capitalist classes. The consumer markets are not 'free' but false. In order to produce a nation of docile producers, working ever harder and harder to follow the path to ruin by unrestrained, perpetual global growth, the capitalist classes must produce a nation of docile perpetually unsatisfied consumers. This is achieved through the false market. The false market is achieved primarily through two enormous myths or lies perpetuated by capitalists and their marketers.

First Myth

The first myth is that those who own the most are intrinsically happier than those who own less. If one is a multi-millionaire and owns many large houses with swimming pools, a fleet of expensive cars, holiday homes, yachts etc then this person is intrinsically happier than someone who owns or rents a simple home and owns little. This profoundly false 'philosophy' is manifest in the conscious marketing and advertising, and in the subliminal or quasi-subliminal marketing and advertising, of products and services. There are products and services that are described as 'must have' or 'to die for' both in advertising and editorial, in both print and on-line. This is a favourite lie of the 'glossy', 'aspirational' magazines.

Marketers and Advertisers Six Levels of Brand Awareness

1. Unaware
2. Aware
3. Desire/Want

4. Need
5. Must Have
6. To Die For!

It is the purpose and duty of the capitalist marketer and advertiser to raise the mass of consumers' awareness of all their products and services, especially new products and services that typically for the most part will start at level 1, with new product announcement taking the consumer initially to level 2, finally at least to the level of 5 but preferably to the level 6 – see diagram above. In this way items that have not existed since the dawn of time i.e. say for 2000 years of western civilisation, appear on the earth's surface and within the shortest time possible, and via advertising and marketing are gobbled up by a conformist mob of docile, dutifully obliging consumers in search of this illusive happiness bestowed upon their more fortunate 'betters'. One regularly sees today the terms 'must have' and 'to die for' in the 'Lifestyle' sections of newspapers, magazines and journals. Although the terms are communicated in a benign way, perhaps even in a sublimated or quasi-sublimated way, they are still there for serious business purposes - sales growth and market acquisition growth. Indeed the more benign and subliminal the message, the more powerful its message and effectiveness. Capitalist advertisers have in the past used subliminal images in television commercials and other methods of advertising partly for the reasons given above. Many governments have made such practices illegal. It is interesting to note here that it is reported that in the Second World War, the Nazi propaganda machine found that they had greater effectiveness in their propaganda efforts, by using cinema entertainment films with a propagandistic content, rather than direct more 'hard-hitting' propaganda styled 'documentaries'. Also interesting to note here, that the highly acclaimed Hollywood film 'Casablanca' was, in fact in essence, an American World War II propaganda film.

Second Myth

The second myth is that those who own the most are intrinsically superior to those who own less. If one is a multi-millionaire and owns many large houses with swimming pools, a fleet of expensive cars, holiday homes, yachts etc then this person is intrinsically superior to someone who owns or rents a simple home and owns little. This 'intrinsically superior' motif is partly subliminally indoctrinated into the consumer society. This profoundly false 'philosophy' is manifest in social interactions between those who have the most and those who have much less. Those who have most are the 'superiors' and those who provide the superiors with goods and services through their own labour are the 'servants'. This is particularly visible in the 'hospitality industries' (hotels, restaurants, leisure) where the serving classes are particularly obsequious to the capitalist or owning classes. A visit to an expensive hotel or restaurant in London, or any other major city world-wide, and a number of simple tests of business interaction between the client and the servant will adequately demonstrate this phenomenon. It is well known that very wealthy persons may gain a table at just a few hours' notice at the most 'exclusive' and expensive of London restaurants that typically have waiting lists of weeks and even months. The overriding value upon status under the myths of capitalism is wealth and fame. There are many, many examples of this phenomenon that it is pointless to enumerate more here.

The two myths described above give rise to a form of 'morality' or 'ethics' where the traditional value of true morality: respecting the values and lives of others, what one does for the benefit of others, or what one does for the benefit of others at a sacrifice to oneself, is turned on its head and the capitalist morality is centred around what one does for oneself only, particularly in ones' own acquisition of products and access to services at the expense of others. Thus capitalism encourages, and requires in order for it to succeed, two of the worst aspects of human nature, namely greed, particularly avarice and selfishness. On this count alone, capitalism by encouraging two of the worst aspects of human nature, namely greed/avarice and selfishness must be considered to be, on this principle alone, a failure.

This 'ascendency' of happiness and superiority, and the higher moral worth of the acquisitive individual via the acquisition of the most expensive houses, cars etc may be seen by this simple example in the automobile industry. A certain car manufacturer has car series nomenclature such as Series 1, Series 3, Series 5, Series 7, where the cheapest is Series 1 and the most expensive is Series 7. In this way the consumer may gauge his or her rise to the top-most dung-hill peak of 'happiness and superiority' as one proceeds from the lowly Series 1 to the pinnacle of achievement of Transcendental Nirvanic Joy and Bliss, the Series 7!

Note: Nirvanic means being in a state of Nirvana

My understanding is that it is in the acquisition of the Series 7, rather than in the driving of the series 7, that the state of Transcendental Nirvanic Joy and Bliss is achieved. A local Police Force may consider that driving a car in this condition to be driving without due care and attention and may promptly arrest the perpetrator.

An automobile advertisement in a London newspaper weekend colour supplement of May 2019 stated:

'FOR THOSE WHO DRIVE THE WORLD.

Success is nothing without authenticity.

Luxury is nothing without performance.

Words are nothing without experience.'

Advertising agencies are paid a lot of money to think up this sort of drivel, fortunately they are only words. No copyright breach intended. I would not want to be the owner of the copyright of that; the present owner can keep it! Those who currently *"drive the world"* are driving themselves and everyone else over the abyss to oblivion. Their major *"success"* will carry no greater *"authenticity"* than to be nothing more than a mass self-inflicted suicide. Life is nothing without Life and unnecessary Suffering and Death are not what many of us particularly wants to experience.

In the False Market, the automobile is the primary domain for the capitalist's manipulation of the male population as the clothes industry is for the female population. We might consider that cars, these figures are cautious, have a design life cycle of say 150,000 miles (some put the figure now at 200,000 miles). With the average annual mileage at say 10,000 then a car should last approximately 15 years. However, new models, within a series, are launched typically every 7 or 8 years and 'facelifts' (minor cosmetic changes) say every 3 years. Therefore, we see that by producing a new model every 7 to 8 years when the vehicle should last 15 years then the automobile industry is producing twice the number of cars than are necessary. The 'facelifts' make the position even worse. However, that is just the simple arithmetic, the reality is worse. Since under the myths of capitalism, the automobile is the *'badge of honour, status and perceived success'* of the male of the species, simple manipulation of the male by marketing and advertising typically means that cars are often changed every three to six years. Three years is common. If new cars are purchased every 3 to 6 years, when they will typically last for 15 years, then the automobile industry is producing 2 ½ to 5 times more cars than necessary. The demand for these surplus cars is soaked up, in part, by those plebeians further down the food chain dung heap who buy second hand cars at an excellent discount of 49.8% - 52.6% after three years. These staggering figures for depreciation include BMW 3 and 5 series and Mercedes Benz E Class cars. These are supposedly top cars in the upper decile for quality, build, reliability, service etc. One can only suppose that the reason for this horrendous depreciation is because the persons who buy these vehicles are so unnecessarily rich that they can afford to write down circa 50% of the vehicles cost over the three years. A BMW 5 Series car of medium engine size, trim etc. would cost typically between £40k and £45k in Q1 2020. A Mercedes Benz E Class would cost in the order of £41k to £58k in Q1 2020. These vehicles represent a 50% revenue loss of £20k to £29k. It is of interest to note that the Office for National Statistics Living Costs and Food Survey for 2019 gave the median household disposable income in the UK as £29,600. Much the same amount as the three year depreciation, i.e. completely lost revenue, of a new Mercedes Benz E class car!

All of this marketing manipulative nonsense causes automobile asset depreciation to be generally in the order of 20% in the first year of new model introduction and 10% each year thereafter. The next piece of arithmetic will illustrate how preposterous all this is. In 2018 approximately 70M (70million) cars were produced worldwide. If we take the cost a new average family car (Ford Mondeo) to be £25k (which is cautious) then the purchase cost of the 70M vehicles is £1,750,000M; this is cash purchase (which is rare in the greed-must-have-now capitalist method) without the use of credit facilities which would increase the total costs. The annual depreciation of new cars is typically 20% in the first year of use from new and 10% thereafter. Therefore the loss of these, (cash purchased) automotive capital assets through deprecation over three years from new is:

Year 1: £350,000M

Year 2: £140,000M

Year 3: £126,000M

Total for 3 years' depreciation is £616,000M = £616Bn

The Gross Domestic Product for Belgium in 2018 was reported as £409,740M (US $532,131M) i.e. circa £410B.

Therefore from the statistics above we see that the global depreciation of new cars in the automobile industry for three years (when we all (except me) rush out and buy a new car) was approximately 1.5 times the GDP of Belgium for 2018! Belgium is ranked at the 28th highest GDP country in the world. This £616B is wiped of these asset values forever. This £616B is lost for ever. £616B could feed a lot of the starving people of the world for quite a long time. If the loss over the three years was say 10% equalling £175,000M rather than the £616,000M this would mean that there was £441Bn available, a sum larger than the GDP of Belgium, for investment for work initiatives and other enterprises to feed Africa and elsewhere! This ridiculous waste is owing to the capitalists' manipulation of the False Market and the greed and stupidity of the docile consumers who literally buy into it. [Pun intended]

We have a similar situation in the women's clothing and fashion industries where yesterday's high fashion is today's charity shop left-overs. The strategy of the very top brands in the fashion industry is utterly appalling. Rather than place their unsold 'oh so wonderful and esoteric' products in the shop windows of charity shops, or heavily discount and sell at cost price plus say 10%, the companies BURN their products. Whilst Africa and elsewhere STARVES. So much for capitalism! However, in fashion the numbers are not likely to be as appalling as those for the automobile industry. This unnecessary over consumption and the relentless pursuit of material possessions that are replaced before the existing product has completed its useful life cycle is endemic and inherent within the very core of the capitalist creed. The automobile and the fashion industries are but two examples. The process is prevalent across many areas of consumerism including most domestic consumer durables. The product life cycle of a laptop computer is easily over 5 years of useful life, yet new models are released every six months. This can only lead to one end and that is catastrophic over consumption, enormous unnecessary over-exploitation of raw materials and failure.

In the chapter on Feudalism – The First Form of Capitalism we saw the influence of the monarchy upon the land owning/leasing Earls/ Lords and Barons and the 'aid' provided by the Earls and Barons to the monarchy was primarily in military obligations to defend and enhance the monarchy's Kingdom and power. The two myths of capitalism, discussed above, were instigated in feudal times where the person with the greatest amount of land was perceived as inherently superior and presumed happier to those without land or significant assets or possessions.

The 'system' continues today but the allegiance to the monarch is less rigid and the 'aid' to the monarchy is perceived primarily as excellence in one's field of endeavour with a particular emphasis on capitalist revenue creating ventures and nationalistic trade rather than jumping on a horse, ready to go into battle and charging off into the sunset with one's lance or sabre rattling. Today ordinary persons are knighted often for business endeavours that bring revenue via overseas trade (and local taxes) into the country. However, today there is one element in this that was missing in feudal times and that is - charity. In order to assist in one's aspirations for monarchic recognition, it is advisable to contribute a certain amount of one's surplus wealth to a supposedly worthwhile, preferably tax-deductible charity. The influence of feudalism in this process today is clear to see. In feudal times the newly appointed Baron would recline resplendent in his Baronial Hall upon all manner of luxuries. Today the newly appointed Knight of The Realm buys himself a huge estate on the capitalistic profits that earned him his knighthood and reclines resplendent in his 50 bedroom Baronial Hall/Manor House upon all manner of luxuries replete in the knowledge that he is indeed innately superior and innately happier than his non-knighted plebeian brethren.

The non-knighted 'plebeian' people are in fact most likely to be good-hearted, law abiding, hard-working people, but the knight needs the false comfort of his self/monarchic appointed 'superiority'. There are many examples of this available to study today, where the young capitalist started his adventures from a perfectly amenable three-bedroomed semi-detached or terraced house size enough for himself, wife and two children. However, because he has been successfully indoctrinated into the two myths of capitalism, still with the same household of four persons, for some reasons surely beyond the combined intellects of Socrates, Plato and Kant, the three-bedroom home is no longer adequate and is instantly replaced by a 50 bedroom estate and more arable land than that required to feed the population of four dozen nearby villages! This practice may be seen in most suitable locations in the U.K. and elsewhere.

Why?! Quid est quod te cogitare, radix malorum est cupiditas!

4.4 Modern Slavery

If we look back into history since the early times of Egypt, Greece, Rome, their empires' durations approximately being: Egypt 3100BC – 30BC, Greece 800BC – 146BC, Rome 27BC – 1453AD, throughout these empires slavery was common. In Egypt slaves were used on Temple Estates and provided with food but typically no wages; in Greece the principal use of slaves was in agriculture, but they were also used in stone quarries or mines, and as domestic servants. In the Roman Empire slaves were typically foreigners and include prisoners of war, sailors captured and sold by pirates, or slaves bought outside Roman territory. In Europe and UK Thrall slavery persisted in the 5th century Anglo-Saxon villages and continued in Feudalism from 9th to 15th centuries through the system of land-tied serfs. Feudal Serfdom was the status of many land-toiling rural peasants, specifically relating to manorialism, and similar systems. It was a condition of debt bondage and indentured servitude, which developed during the Late Antiquity and Early Middle Ages in Europe and lasted in some countries until the mid-19th century. The serfs, who occupied a plot of land, were required to work the land for the Lord of the Manor (manorialism) who owned the land. Serfs were tied to their lord's land and couldn't leave it without his permission. Their lord also often decided whom they could marry. Serfs, had to provide other services, possibly in addition to paying rent of money or produce.

In Mercantilism, English trade became triangulated between the British Empire, its colonies and foreign markets, fostering the development of the slave trade in many colonies, including America. The colonies provided rum, cotton, and other products demanded by European-African imperialists.

With the Industrial Revolution, slavery provided the raw material for industrial change and growth. The growth of the Atlantic (USA) economy was an integral part of the growth of exports - for example manufactured cotton cloth was exported to Africa. The Atlantic economy can be seen as the spark for the biggest change in modern economic history. Slavery was so profitable; it sprouted more millionaires per capita in the Mississippi River valley than anywhere in the US nation. With cash crops of tobacco, cotton and sugar cane, America's southern states became the country's economic engine of the burgeoning nation. Their fuel of choice? Human slavery. And for African Americans, the Industrial Revolution, those technological advances in the textile industry, did not mean progress. It meant slavery. From 1790 to 1810, close to 100,000 slaves moved to the new cotton lands to the south and west.

Enforced slavery exists throughout the world today in the 21st century with numbers quoted at 45.8 million people in the world in 167 countries 68% of these people being subject to forced labour. Most of those in forced labour are women and children and US $150Bn per annum is generated by private companies using such forced labour. This figure of US $150Bn is larger than some countries' GDP. Source: https://www.aljazeera.com/

The word "slavery" conjures up images of shackles and transatlantic ships – depictions that seem relegated firmly to the past. But more people are enslaved today than at any other time in history. Experts have calculated that roughly 13 million people were captured and sold as slaves between the 15th and 19th centuries; today, an estimated 40.3 million people – more than three times the figure during the transatlantic slave trade – are living in some form of modern slavery, according to the latest figures published by the UN's International Labour Organization (ILO) and the Walk Free Foundation.

Women and girls comprise 71% of all modern slavery victims. Children make up 25% and account for 10 million of all the slaves worldwide.

A person today is considered enslaved if they are forced to work against their will; are owned or controlled by an exploiter or "employer"; have limited freedom of movement; or are dehumanised, treated as a commodity or bought and sold as property, according to abolitionist group Anti-Slavery International.

Globally, more than half of the 40.3 million victims (24.9 million) are in forced labour, which means they are working against their will and under threat, intimidation or coercion. An additional 15.4 million people are estimated to be living in forced marriages.

Of the 24.9 million people trapped in forced labour, the majority (16 million) work in the private sector. Slaves clean houses and flats; produce the clothes we wear; pick the fruit and vegetables we eat; trawl the seas for the shrimp on our restaurant plates; dig for the minerals used in our smartphones, makeup and electric cars; and work on construction jobs building infrastructure for the 2022 Qatar World Cup.

Another 4.8 million people working in forced labour are estimated to be sexually exploited, while roughly 4.1 million people are in state-sanctioned forced labour, which includes governmental abuse of military conscription and forced construction or agricultural work. In certain countries such as Mauritania, people are born into "hereditary" slavery if their mother was a slave.

Again, women and girls bear the brunt of these statistics, comprising 99% of all victims in the commercial sex industry, and 58% in other sectors, according to the ILO.

Statistically, modern slavery is most prevalent in Africa, followed by Asia and the Pacific, according to the Global Slavery Index, which publishes country-by-country rankings on modern slavery figures and government responses to tackle the issues. Leading culprits are: North Korea 104.6, Eritrea 93, Burundi 40, Central African Republic 22.3, Afghanistan 22.2, Mauritania 21.4, South Sudan 20.5, Pakistan 16.8, Cambodia 16.8, Iran 16.2 where the number alongside the Country is the number of victims per 1,000 of population.

Source: 'Guardian' February 2019

Perhaps there is a causal deterministic relationship between Modern Slavery and the fact that in London today, one of the most expensive cities in the world, one may buy a T shirt for as little as £2.00.'

From the above, we can see that feudalism, mercantilism, together with industrial and post-industrial capitalism, the primary global economic engines for 250 years, have done little or nothing to eradicate three millennia of continuous enforced slavery. In terms of the ethical and moral progress of man – is this the best that we can do?

4.5 Perpetual Self-Inflicted Slavery

Inherent in the capitalist structure and myths described above is a form of self-inflicted slavery and consequently unnecessary suffering. Before one can contrive a mass of docile producers it is necessary to produce a docile mass of consumers. Consumption is a pre-requisite to production. Once you have the nation enslaved by consumerism and consumption, the job is done. For if one is coerced to consume, then one is de facto obliged to produce. One cannot consume unless one or someone produces that that is to be consumed. The payment for production (work) is used for one's consumption. The populace is thus held in a perpetual state of enslavement where the artificially created 'desires/must haves/to die for' being perpetual and ever-increasing; the individual never reaches satisfaction for there is always a bigger house, larger, faster car, larger yacht, younger mistress etc to strive for. This system filters from the 'top' down to the working man who is ever longing a BMW or Mercedes Benz car rather than a Ford. Everything else and much more besides.

This can only result in perpetual unnecessary suffering as the entire nation and nations continually strives for false gods and false goals that bring no true meaning to people's lives other than a very brief and temporary false release when one false goal is finally achieved.

This false desire for the unnecessary is so strongly indoctrinated that the vast majority of people in the 'western world' purchase their false gods on credit. However even this credit is not enough to quench this thirst for the unnecessary as many people go into temporary cash-flow debt as shown below in the diagram 'Salary/ Wage Slavery Saw-Tooth Expenditure Diagram'. The monthly or weekly available expenditure is spent before the month or week has elapsed and the fresh injection of the next month's/week's money is desperately needed to return the person's balance of payment back into credit.

Salary/Wage Slavery Saw-Tooth Expenditure Diagram

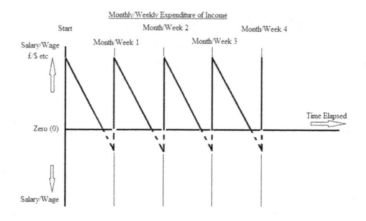

This temporary release mentioned above is released only very, very temporarily and occurs only when the consumer- slave's new acquisition is a new 'toy' but when it quickly becomes no longer a new phenomenon, when the novelty wears off; it becomes a mundane every-day reality, just another day at the office.

When this stage occurs, then it is back on the tread-mill for the next false god on the ladder of self-inflicted suffering. The next false goal quickly comes into visible range once the earlier one is considered to be attained. Yet all this is self-inflicted. One does not have to play this game. The means of freeing oneself from this self-inflicted slavery is dealt with in detail later.

4.6 Capitalism - Unhappiness and Lack of Fulfilment

Inherent in the capitalist structure described above is a society whereby the populace is held in a permanent state of unhappiness, a permanent state of longing. There is no way that this can be avoided. In the permanent struggle of forever increasing consumption, or better product or service consumption, to strive to reach the unattainable, the population is left only with unhappiness and lack of contentment. It coerces a perpetual present striving, for future 'gain'. Capitalism and indeed, capitalistic politics is never in the present, it is always in the future. We do not live in the past, we do not live in the future. We live and have always lived and most likely, will always live, in the present.

This slavery to unhappiness is understood by the broadcasting media. In the UK the broadcasting media strives to assuage this slavery by showing escapist, populist drama series on television on Sunday evenings. Typically the last thing that one wants to think about on Sunday evening is work on Monday so an escapist detective or period costume drama is an ideal diversion from the unavoidable impending reality. Note that it is imperative that it is a series rather than a one-off film. In this way the populace may look forward to, and can benefit from, its weekly dose of anaesthetic against an impending, unavoidable reality. The longer the series runs the better. Once a series has achieved significant success in terms of audience figures then a returning series is utilised to protract the Sunday evening anaesthetic for as long as possible. The last thing that the state machine or the capitalist ethos requires and that includes commercial television whether by traditional broadcasting technologies or internet based content streaming is social discontent, particularly violent social discontent. Work for the consumer with some payment, a full belly and televised or internet distraction should be enough to protect the system from overthrow. That is all that is required to keep the capitalist method in a steady, stable state and that is therefore all the populace will receive. Nothing more.

This 'future gain' phenomenon is also prevalent in capitalist politics. Politicians anxious to be elected, will amount to all sorts and means of 'bribery' about a better future, a better tomorrow, in order to win the votes of the consumer. Not only is a world of more consumption promised but better health care, education, public services, lower crime, safer streets – a massive 'nirvanic' shopping list all the way to paradise is presented; but never the present. Politician's when seeking votes rarely speak of the present, but only some fictitous great new dawn of the future. The only time they speak of the present is typically, in defence of their achievements if they are in power and the criticism of the achievements of those in power, if they are not in power. The present is never spoken of in awe and wonder because it is for all to perceive that it is not to be awed and wondered over. The future however, is a very different animal. It is an unknown promise, an undefinable prospect, a possibility to dream. There is no greater power than the promise of a better future. In this power the capitalist classes enslave both the consumer, and in the consumer's wake, the politician. Politicians are not leaders, they tend to disappear every four or five years but the capitalist classes are here for ever. The consumer and the politician are the puppets of their masters.

4.7 Maldistribution of Wealth

Relatively speaking, as the rich get richer, the poor get poorer. However, no reasonable person would argue that the lives of working people in Great Britain and Europe since the 1800's have not significantly improved. When the industrial revolution commenced and factories were built, businesses were in need of workers. With many people looking for work, employers could set low wages, as low as they wanted to, because people were willing to work as long as they got paid. Workers worked fourteen to sixteen hours a day, six days a week. The average salary per annum in England in 1880's was approximately £46 which equates to 18 shillings (£1 = 20 shillings) or so per week, therefore earning approximately 14d (1 Shilling = 12 d (old pence)) per hour. Source: URL below:

https://firstindustrialrevolution.weebly.com/working-and-living-conditions.html

The average weekly expenditure has been stated as being in excess of 30 shillings in England in 1888. Reference, Source URL below:

http://www.victorianweb.org/economics/wages4.html

The majority of workers were un-skilled and therefore would receive less than this average wage. A typical labourer in the mid 1860's would earn 3s 9d per week for a 10 hour, 6 day week. Source URL below:

http://www.victorianweb.org/economics/wages2.html

From the data above we can see that weekly wages barely covered costs for many workers. A Chairman of the Board of a Company at this time might earn £1,000 per year, over twenty times more than the average wage of £46 per year. Today the average UK wage is quoted as approximately £29,000 per annum and the typical salary for a chief executive in London UK as quoted in January 2019 by the High Pay Think Tank and the Chartered Institute of Personnel and Development (CIPD) show top executives are earning 133 times more than the average worker, at a rate of around £1,020 per hour or £3.9m annually.

Based on these figures above, the ratio of salaries from chief executive to average worker has increased during the 160 years from 1860 to today by 6 ½ times from twenty times salary to 133 times salary. This clearly demonstrates the notion that the rich get richer, the poor get poorer in relative terms. It is well known that with material wealth, typically there comes greater power, greater higher societal inclusion, and greater access to 'higher', more strategic information channels. These increased societal and information powers, in turn lead to greater wealth; which in turn leads to even greater power, even greater higher societal inclusion, and even greater access to 'higher', even greater strategic information channels. This up-ward, ever increasingly expanding spiral of wealth and societal power continues ad infinitum whilst the hourly paid worker remains forever at the same or very similar level of low wealth and the least power.

Factories in the 1860s were horrible places to work. The only light present was the sunlight that came through narrow windows.

Machines spat out smoke and in some factories, workers came out covered in black soot at the end of their working day. There was a plethora of different machines with very few safety precautions, resulting in accidents. The workers received only breaks for lunch and dinner. Children were paid less than 6d per hour for fourteen hours work a day. They were used for simpler, unskilled jobs. Many children had physical deformities because of lack of exercise and sunlight. For many families, these wages listed above were barely adequate for basic living requirements and consequently families were forced to live in slums. The use of children as labour for such long hours and for such little pay, and slum living led to the formation of trade unions.

It is interesting to note that it is not unreasonable to suppose that without the protests by the workers by organised complaint through the trade union movement; that the dire wages, living and working conditions of the manual workers would have remained in the same sorry state to perpetuity. There was no sign from the factory owning classes that they were to suddenly become business apostates overnight and relinquish their strangle hold and ruthless oppression on working people through their labour and poor wages. Indeed, where the capitalist classes can get away with human exploitation of this sort in the world today, they tend to continue to do so. In areas of the third world were organised worker labour today is not as prevalent as it is the UK and Europe, then this form of exploitation exists widely such as in Cambodia, Thailand, India, Bangladesh, the Congo and others. No reasonable person would claim that living and working conditions for working people in UK and Europe have not improved in the 160 years since 1860. They clearly have; children no longer climb up chimneys, the working week has shortened, factories are cleaner and safer. These improvements were not gratis from the factory owning classes, except in a few exceptional cases, but rather extorted from them by the use of organised labour revolt and the power of the trade union movement. However, if we look today beyond the boundaries of UK and Europe we see a different story. Here is the somewhat grandiose pronouncement from the United Nations Conference on Environment & Development 1992 Agenda 21:

United Nations Conference on Environment & Development
Rio de Janerio, Brazil, 3 to 14 June 1992

Agenda 21

Chapter 1 Preamble

Humanity stands at a defining moment in history. We are confronted with a perpetuation of disparities between and within nations, a worsening of poverty, hunger, ill health and illiteracy, and the continuing deterioration of the ecosystems on which we depend for our well-being.

[My emboldening]

Fast forward a quarter of a century to 2018 and we have the following from the World Bank. We will immediately observe that no greater eminence than the World Bank confirms beyond all reasonable doubt that **nothing has changed!**

According to the World Bank in October 2018 Press Release:

"Nearly Half the World Lives on Less than [US] $5.50 a Day." Despite decline in extreme poverty, broader measures show billions still struggle to meet [very, very] basic needs [such as basic clothing, food, water and shelter at its most primitive imaginable].

WASHINGTON, Oct. 17, 2018 — Economic advances around the world mean that while fewer people live in extreme poverty, almost half the world's population — 3.4 billion people — still struggles to meet basic needs, the World Bank said.

Living on less than [US] $3.20 per day reflects poverty lines in lower-middle-income countries [a euphemism presumably], while [US] $5.50 a day reflects standards in upper-middle-income [another euphemism presumably] countries, the World Bank said in its biennial Poverty and Shared Prosperity Report, 'Piecing Together the Poverty Puzzle'.

The World Bank remains committed to achieving the goal of ending extreme poverty, defined as living on less than US $1.90 a day, by 2030. The share of the world's population living in extreme poverty fell to 10 percent in 2015, but the pace of extreme poverty reduction has slowed, the Bank warned on Sept. 19 2018.

However, given that economic growth means that a much greater proportion of the world's poor now live in wealthier countries, additional poverty lines and a broader understanding of poverty are crucial to fully fighting it, the report says.

Source: The World Bank

According to the Organisation for Economic Cooperation and Development (OECD) in 2012 the top 0.6% of world population (consisting of adults with more than US $1 million in assets), these are the 42 million richest people in the world, held 39.3% of world wealth.

The next 4.4% (311 million people) held 32.3% of world wealth. The bottom 95% held 28.4% of world wealth. So we see here the classic wealth distribution pyramid – approximately, the top 1% have 40% of the world's wealth, the **bottom** 95% have 28%. Since when do we consider 95% to the bottom of anything? 95% is certainly an overwhelming majority!

Furthermore, in 2012 the bottom 60% of the world population which was 4.3Bn people in 2012, held the same wealth as the people on Forbes' Richest list consisting of 1,226 richest billionaires of the world i.e. US $ assets of 1226 people = US $ assets of 4,300,000,000 people! Note that 1226 people is 0.0000285% of 4.3B!

More recently, in 2015 to quote the OECD Secretary General:

'We have reached a tipping point. Inequality can no longer be treated as an afterthought. We need to focus the debate on how benefits of growth are distributed...'

'The situation is economically unsustainable'

Income inequality in OECD countries is at its highest level for the past half century. The average income inequality of the richest 10% of the population is about nine times that of the poorest 10% across the OECD, up from seven times 25 years ago.

Source: Organisation for Economic Development OECD

Regarding the OECD figures for the 2012 top 0.6% of world population shown above, the Credit Suisse Global Wealth Databook for 2018 put the statistic higher, stating that the 42 million people, or 0.8 [0.6% OECD] percent of the world's population, having a net worth in excess of US $1 million. That group — roughly the global 1% — controls 44.8% of the world's wealth, up 5.5% from 39.3% in 2012.

Source: Credit Suisse Global Wealth Databook

Furthermore, almost half the world — over three billion people — live on less than US $2.50 a day. At least 80% of humanity lives on less than US $10 a day. More than 80 percent of the world's population lives in countries where income differentials are widening.

Source: http://www.globalissues.org/article/26/poverty-facts-and-stats

These statistics quoted above, clearly show that capitalism, the world-wide economic prime mover whose drivers have the responsibility to feed, clothe and house people, has failed humanity, and failed it very dismally indeed.

Under the capitalist method, the human species, across the globe cannot even feed, clothe and house itself properly!

This stark reality negates all hiding places. Humankind has nowhere to hide in its shame!

Furthermore, it is not some small minority in one or two far off, distant lands of irrelevance that we, in the west, can forget all about and pretend that they do not exist. We are discussing the welfare of 4.2Bn people from a global population of 7.8Bn a percentage of 54%, over half of the global population which in turn, is dispersed to all quarters of the world.

The Human species has shown itself to be rather unique in its monumental achievement of **not being able** to feed, water, clothe and shelter itself. The rest of the animal kingdom, in its complete entirety, appears to achieve with the greatest of ease that that human beings miserably and pathetically fail to achieve. Indeed, in my many travels across the globe: elephants, cheetah, hump-backed whales, African fish eagles, the list is endless and even includes cockroaches and invertebrates; appear to have little diffi-culty in feeding their global populations.

Who was it who said that Human Beings are the most intelligent of species? Based on the little polemic above, some may beg to differ.

4.8 Asset Stripping

Apart from the money that capitalism can make from war and the materials of war, perhaps asset stripping is second only to war in terms of money making capabilities, moral repugnance and the vulgarity of capitalist avarice of the highest order. It is so morally repugnant it should be illegal.

Asset stripping may be defined as the practice of taking over a company or companies in business and or financial difficulties and selling each of its assets separately at a profit without regard for the company's past, present and in particular its future and the lives of its employees. The practice of separating the company's total of assets so that each asset is worth more than its portion share of the original whole is done, with the minimum of cost and resources and in the minimum time possible. This speed of asset sale disposal and minimisation of costs and resources used to dispose of the company's assets is imperative in this 'business' model. The greater the efficiency and ruthlessness of this 'cut and run' methodology, the greater the profit for the asset stripper. Speed and ruthless efficiency are 'categorical imperatives' for asset stripping. They are among the core of the methodology. Another core 'belief' in this practice is that the company in difficulties that is to be purchased is bought for the lowest price and in the shortest time possible. Time is money, which the asset stripper does not want to waste.

The ideal turn around for an asset stripper would be to buy the failing company for its lowest possible price in the shortest possible time, and sell the assets at the highest possible price in the shortest possible time. Capitalism at its zenith, its optimum, and its 'nirvanic' ideal. Capitalist 'Perfection'.

The Gross Immorality of Asset Stripping

The greatest problem with asset stripping is its inhumane methods and its societal callousness and moral repugnance. The most easily disposed of asset of a failing company is its employees. In the USA, it is possible for an asset stripper to relinquish the inconvenience of the entire staff of a company, once purchased, within two weeks' notice. If the company has a strong local presence in a town or city the consequences can be devastating to the local community in terms of it as a society. The almost instantaneous removal of the company and its staff of a once strong contributor to the local economy can have disastrous knock-on effects to the labour, goods and services in the 'onward chain'. The almost instantaneous removal of a company's existence, previously a major employer in a community, will most probably cause many persons in its supply chain to lose their jobs and supply companies to go out of business. This process of asset stripping, which has no regard whatsoever for the purchased company's staff, supply chain and community, is so morally repugnant that there should be legislation preventing it. However, if one looks at capitalism in the raw, as stated above; Asset Stripping is Capitalism at its zenith, its optimum, and its 'nirvanic' ideal. Capitalist 'Perfection'.

One only has to look at the methods of asset stripping companies and their core staff structures to understand their intentions. Typically they are run by an autocrat whose avarice knows no bounds, who is surrounded by greed salivating lawyers and accountants. There are typically no marketing, sales, research and development, production staff, service staff etc. These sort of traditional staffing departments for goods and service supply companies are not in any way required by these 'corporate raiders'. Lawyers to write the contracts and accountants to crunch the numbers – all that is needed, absolutely no one else, not even a secretary. She might spill the beans.

The methodology and practices of asset strippers are cloaked in the greatest of secrecies. They are typically privately run firms with no accountability to anyone. There are very many examples of the sad practice of asset stripping, the major thrust of which is widely in the public domain it is not necessary that they should be enumerated. A few minutes research on the World Wide Web will reveal the names of many culprits. There is one asset stripper in the USA who has built a billionaire fortune out of such evil.

4.9 WAR – The Perfect Vehicle for Capitalism

As stated before, modern capitalism is an anti-intellectual brutalism, an inward-looking nationalistic competitive avarice with little or no broad-seeing, deep-thinking, long-term strategic planning. Furthermore of course, modern capitalism today is now world-wide. War is the perfect vehicle for capitalism because in War, the Governments of all the warring countries cannot get enough munitions, tanks, airplanes, frigates, aircraft carriers et al. The demand is insatiable and if the warring faction is expansionist then the demand is ever increasing and therefore increasingly insatiable. 'Defence' systems was a 1,822Bn US $ global market in 2019 amongst the fifteen largest defence budgeted countries. The third highest 'Defence' spender spends 8.8% of GDP. There's money to be made out of this business.

Although certain countries strive to achieve homogeneity across nation states as a means of preventing, or trying to attempt, nationalistic wars; when it comes to the 'crunch' such practices will not prevent a war. It may not be a physical war but it may certainly be an economic 'war' or a covert 'war'.

The 'Common Market' or European Economic Community was a regional organisation that aimed to bring about economic integration among its member states, being countries throughout Western Europe. It was created by the Treaty of Rome of 1957. Upon the formation of the European Union in 1993, the EEC was incorporated and renamed the European Community.

One reason it would appear, that the 'Common Market' organisation in Europe was initiated, was to prevent a later version of Adolf Hitler, or any other Nationalist within a country in Europe, riding in his motorcade to Paris behind 1,000 tanks in a matter of six weeks. Other reasons included the economic reason, which was the widely publicised reason, where the intention was to surrender the nation state to the European block. In this way, the nation state was essentially replaced by a group of nations that surrendered their nationalistic autonomy for the wider military and security brief and the supposed economic advantages of a larger 'nation' state of Europe. A disparate group of countries became a 'homogenous' 'national European' entity. In this way, the nationalistic tendencies that cause war were not in any way removed. The size of the 'nation' merely increased from individual nations to a 'one-nation Europe'. To believe that because a group of nations sign a paper document and therefore there will not be a war amongst the signees is naivety in the extreme. The issue with Western Europe is that of its geophysical structure and history. The geography of Europe is riddled with mountains, rivers, valleys and lakes; its history is riddled with invasions upon invasions from within and without. The result of this is that the region was heavily nationalistic in terms of natural geographical boundaries, language and dialects, currencies, cultures and traditions. These are over one thousand years old and the relatively recently signed documents purporting to homogenise such deeply ingrained linguistic and cultural differences, will not do so. Consequently when the 'crunch time' comes, irrespective of signed documents, these nations will revert to their nationalism. Even within the European Economic Community current homogenised paradise, there is still nationalistic competition in all private industrial and other business sectors. The German, French, English car manufacturers still compete against one another. As do all other business sectors. Who actually owns these companies whether German, French, English or not, is not particularly relevant. It is their nationalistic 'belonging' which is the only relevance and the revenue they bring to their parent nation state.

Interestingly when a state of emergency is announced in the European Union, the Union to all intents and purposes ceases to exist and countries revert to nationalism. In the current global coronavirus pandemic of first quarter 2020 – Covid-19, a global state of emergency, the strategies of Lockdown (essentially temporarily closing down capitalism on a global basis) and the relief of Lockdown were on a nationalistic basis. Spain had one strategy, Denmark another, Germany another etc, The European Union was a forgotten entity. It in effect ceased to exist. Countries reverted to their nationalistic needs and agenda to suit those specific needs. So much for the European Union and integration.

At the time of writing, it has been stated that we are at war with the Covid-19 virus. It is not without significance, that as I write this with Covid-19, and the 'Economic Lockdown' of a significant part of the UK's workforce, almost 30% of 35M not going to work and being paid a furlough of 80% of their wages by the UK Government, about to potentially cause the severest recession since 1700, that there are **many reports of profiteering**. "Between 10th March and 17th May 2020 the Competition and Markets Authority – CMA in the UK, was contacted more than 60,000 times by aggrieved consumers. Nestled among complaints about halal meat (average price hike 100%) and hand gel (400%) are a whopping 27,000 reports about travel industry misbehaviour."

Source: The Sunday Times 31st May 2020

With the background of 30,000+ deaths from the virus in the UK, and the serious prospect of an ensuing recession with say 10% to 15% unemployment, this sort of capitalist exploitation and profiteering is **utterly contemptible**. However, what else would one expect from a method of production, distribution and exchange driven my relentless greed, selfishness and stupidity?

I digress.

It is perhaps beyond question that the basis of capitalism – unrestrained and perpetual global growth with its basis now in nationalistic competitiveness will eventually tend to lead to war. As we noted before, the 16th to the 17th centuries saw the rise in mercantilism which was the rise of the nation state which promoted governmental regulation of a country's economy to strengthen and augment the state in competition, and as security against, competitive other nation states. This was to be achieved by trade between countries where each country attempted to amass wealth by exporting more than it imported. This competitiveness between nation states in the mercantile era was transferred from mercantilism to industrial capitalism and post-industrial capitalism.

Even today world leaders are still obsessed with competitive nationalistic growth. In Europe the leaders are obsessed both with the competitive growth of the European Union and that of the Union's individual nation states. The gross domestic product of the European Union and its member countries are recorded and published independently of one another. World leaders are caught up in the cycle of a false method that perpetuates itself. Note that capitalism is described as a 'method' rather than a system because systems are designed. Capitalism was never designed nor planned it just happened as technological advances were made in manufacturing as discussed previously. The unrestrained and perpetual growth required of capitalism together with its nationalistic avarice and competitiveness for the world's natural resources must inevitably lead to conflict. This is seen all over the world where mineral resource rich regions, that are otherwise poor, are invaded by those that can lay the greatest military claim to the resource. If they are not militarily invaded, they are 'invaded' by rich corporations from elsewhere in the world by investing their financial and other resources into the exploitation of the natural resources of the often, poorer countries. This is often not to the major benefit of those poorer countries that are negotiating from a weak position owing to their relative poverty. This is a form of economic 'war' or economic exploitation that leads to conflict.

Many technological advances emanate from government military departments because they have the largest budgets for research and development. This emphasis on manufacturing for military requirements dates back to the industrial revolution commencing in the 18th century. With the rise of the industrial revolution and the ease of massive manufacturing, the foundations for creating weapons on a large scale was introduced. The introduction of interchangeable parts and pre-manufactured models was popularized to assemble muskets, making it easier for unskilled workers to produce larger numbers of weapons at a much lower cost. An American inventor Eli Whitney, (1798) on receiving an order for 10,000 muskets from the US government, to be produced in less than two years, believed to demonstrate the ingenuity of interchangeable parts, he earned widespread support and has been incorrectly credited with inventing the idea of interchangeable parts. After Witney's demonstration it was concluded that this demonstration was staged by marking the parts beforehand, so they were not as interchangeable as he made them seem. Eventually Whitney was able to accomplish his goal of 10,000 muskets with interchangeable parts at a relatively low cost in the next 8 years, and later produced more than 15,000 in the following 4 years. Here we see an example of the interlocking of government, capitalism and the armaments for war. It is clear that the separate parties of government and the arms manufacturers benefit from war.

The government expands, hopefully, their territory and enriches the country by power, land and resource acquisition and the capitalist arms manufacturers make their profits. The capitalist's and government's drive for unrestrained perpetual growth is perfectly suited to war. This can go on and on indefinitely to both parties mutual benefit. Providing the war is won. A loss of war and the consequential loss of life in the process is the antithesis of the required result since there would not be the populace left to produce and consume the products of the war machine.

More recently in the United States, the phrase 'military-industrial complex' was coined by President Dwight D. Eisenhower in his 1961 Farewell Address. This term describes the alliance between government appointed military leaders and arms merchants. Military officials attempt to obtain higher budgets, while arms manufactures seek greater profit.

President Eisenhower warned the American people that going to war might not serve the interest of the nation rather it would serve the institution of the military and weapons-producing corporations. 'The Iron Triangle' (USA) is a mutually beneficial, three-way relationship between Congress, government bureaucrats, and special interest lobby groups. It comes into practice here due to war profiting industries which make financial contributions to elected officials, who then distribute taxpayer money towards the military budget, which is spent at the advantage of arms merchants. The military-industrial complex/The Iron Triangle allows for arms-producing corporations to continue to accumulate significant profit.

A prominent example of the impact arms-producing industries have over American policy is evident in the case of Lockheed Martin donating US $75,000 to House Armed Services Committee chair Representative Mac Thornberry. Rep. Thornberry later passed a bill through the House of Representatives that would benefit Lockheed Martin. This decision was made as a direct result of the influence of Lockheed Martin. 'Politico', an American political journalism company has stated Rep. Thornberry is the 'highest overall recipient of contractor contributions among all of the 89 members of the House and Senate Armed Services Committees.' Parallels to the example above of military-industrial complex/The Iron Triangle must surely exist all over the industrialised world. I will leave the reader to undertake his/her own research into this particularly interesting field of endeavour.

An interesting illustration of the benefits of war for capitalism is to be found in Sweden with the experience of Alfred Nobel 1833-1896. Nobel was a Swedish businessman, chemist, engineer, inventor, and held 355 different patents dynamite being the most famous. The synthetic element nobelium was named after him. He owned Bofors an iron and steel producer. On learning of the great fortunes that could be made from armament manufacture, he redirected Bofors from its previous role as primarily an iron and steel producer, to a major manufacturer of cannon, munitions and other armaments. He was involved in nitro-glycerine manufacture in 1864, invented dynamite in 1867 and gelignite 1875. By the time of his death he had set up about 90 armaments factories and laboratories around the world, some of which became parts of big chemical companies such as DuPont, and Germany's infamous IG Farben, the company which made the gas for the Nazis' concentration camp death chambers and was split up after the war to form Hoechst, Bayer and BASF. Alfred Nobel was accused of High Treason against France.

Nobel bore a burden of guilt to the grave, not only for having made war a more terrible business but also for a nitro-glycerine experiment which went wrong, killing a number of workers at his laboratory. Among the dead was his Brother, Emil.

In 1888, Alfred's brother Ludwig Nobel died but many newspapers mistakenly thought that Alfred Nobel had died. So, these newspapers mistakenly published obituaries for Alfred Nobel. A French newspaper quoted *"Le Marchand de la mort est mort"* or *"The Merchant of death is dead"*.

Having read these premature obituaries which condemned him for profiting from the sales of arms and the consequential deaths and suffering, he bequeathed his fortune to institute the Nobel Prize. Particularly famous was the Nobel Peace Prize - an interesting irony. His name also survives in companies such as Dynamit Nobel and AkzoNobel, which are descendants of mergers with companies that Nobel established. It appears that he used his Nobel 'Peace Prize' to atone for his ill-gotten gains. A puerile, ineffective vanity. Why did he not leave his fortune for the purpose of building hospitals and other benefits to those injured in war and to those bereaved of their loved ones, killed by his munitions?

Albert Einstein drew his conclusion on Nobel: *"Alfred Nobel invented an explosive more powerful than any then known — an exceedingly effective means of destruction. To atone for this 'accomplishment' and to relieve his conscience, he instituted his award for the promotion of peace."*

Einstein was not so vulgar as to suggest, as I shall, that another reason was that Alfred Nobel would rather be remembered in History as the great benefactor of global awards for outstanding contributions for humanity in chemistry, literature, peace, physics, and physiology or medicine than as a war-mongering capitalist profiteer. Which many may perfectly reasonably consider him to be.

4.10 The Pharmaceutical Industry – The Pharmaceutical Paradox

The Pharmaceutical Industry was a 1,205Bn US $ global market in 2018, say 66% of Defense which was a 1,822Bn US $ global market in 2019.

The Pharmaceutical Industry which relates to the mass production manufacture and sale of medicinal drugs sits within capitalism with a particular paradox. As stated before the goal of capitalism is unrestrained, perpetual growth so therefore the conflict and paradox in the pharmaceutical industry within capitalism's raison d'être is that if the purpose of the pharmaceutical industry is to remove illnesses and ailments, then this activity, by its very nature, causes the pharmaceutical industry to be continually ever self-diminishing. The more ailments and illnesses one removes the fewer persons and their ailments there are to medically treat. Whereas capitalism's intention is to be ever self-increasing.

If the pharmaceutical industry were to be 100% efficient in the removal of all illnesses and ailments it would no longer be necessary and its own efficiency would destroy itself.

Therefore the medicinal solutions emanating from the pharmaceutical industry must in themselves resolve this paradox. In this way, a course of medicine is best designed for the interests of the pharmaceutical industry if the illness or ailment is not completely eradicated within a finite time but rather if the illness or ailment is contained under the medicinal treatment but not cured. This would result in the sick person being required to take the medication for one's entire life which is much better for the sales and profitability of the pharmaceutical companies than if the medication resolved and completely eradicated the problem say within three months. It is obvious from this debate that the interests of the health and well-being of the general public and the interests of the pharmaceutical companies are unfortunately totally diametrically opposed.

The term 'Ethical Pharmaceuticals' has come into being rather like the term 'Democratic Republic'. Certainly it appears that most countries labelling themselves a Democratic Republic are not democratic by any stretch of the imagination, rather they are more likely to be dictatorships, some benevolent some tyrannical. To the discerning observer, any industry that believes it requires the nomenclature 'ethical' may reasonably be viewed with suspicion and should be studied rather carefully. It is interesting to note that the general view of the pharmaceutical industry is much less than flattering. It appears to be viewed with great suspicion whereas other major industry sectors such as the automobile industry, information technology or construction are not perceived in such a critical light. There must be reasons behind this suspicion. The basis for this suspicion may lie in the ostensibly claimed high costs of research and development and marketing which must be reclaimed through drug sales. The pharmaceutical industry is a highly competitive business and its success is dependent on the sales and marketing of each drug. The cost of research and development for each drug is said to be hundreds of millions of dollars. In 2005 the research and development expenditure for the biopharmaceutical industry within Europe and the US was £13,303M. Source: The Pharma Industry Figures, 2006.

Some health economists put the current cost of drug development at US $1.3 billion, others at US $1.7 billion. The actual drug discovery and the drug development can take years. After which, testing and clinical trials are required prior to getting approval by regulatory boards. After launching the drug the company has much at stake as it has already apparently outlaid millions of dollars therefore the success of its sales is an important factor to the success of the company. These pressures give rise to activities that give rise for concern and interestingly we only have the word of the pharmaceutical companies regarding their financial obligations to research and development. Certainly the number of court cases where the government and tax payer are obliged to take pharmaceutical companies to court is alarming. In the United States there are several different schemes used to defraud the health care system which are particular to the pharmaceutical industry. These include: Good Manufacturing Practice (GMP) Violations, Off Label Marketing, Best Price Fraud, Continuing Medical Education (CME) Fraud, Medicaid Price Reporting, and Manufactured Compound Drugs. The Federal Bureau of Investigation (FBI) of USA estimates that health care fraud costs American taxpayers US $60 billion a year. Of this amount US $2.5 billion was recovered through *False Claims Act* cases in 2010. Antipsychotic drugs are now the top-selling class of pharmaceuticals in America, generating annual revenue of about US $14.6 billion.

Every major company selling the drugs: Bristol-Myers Squibb, Eli Lilly, Pfizer, AstraZeneca and Johnson & Johnson — has either settled recent government cases, under the False Claims Act, for hundreds of millions of dollars or is currently under investigation for possible health care fraud. Apart from Asset Stripping, the armaments and munitions industries, the pharmaceutical industry must be capitalism at its worse.

It is also a practice of the pharmaceutical industry amongst many other immoralities, it has been reported, that those drugs that do not pass the required testing and approval certification of the rich western companies, are dumped on the impoverished Third World.

In *'Readings in Modern Marketing'* John A Quech (p. 678) states:

"In proportion to its size, the pharmaceutical industry received more criticisms for its practices in the Third World and, indeed, the developed world than most other industries. This was least partially due to the nature of its business, so closely related to life and death. Ironically the industry's success in healing made it all the more subject to public scrutiny. A broader concern about corporate practices in the Third World readily focussed on pharmaceutical corporations. As Braithwaite wrote of pharmaceutical companies:

"The moral of the transnationals lies in their willingness to settle for much lower standards abroad than at home." Their promotional practices received most criticism, but there was also concern about the lack of medication in the Third World, drug profits, dumping, and the testing of drugs."

In the USA, the drug companies entered a capitalist's paradise with no responsibility whatsoever for their vaccine products for children when Ronald Reagan signed off any and all their legal liabilities with the 'National Childhood Vaccine Injury Act' NCVIA of 1986. Their liabilities were essentially taken, at least in part, by the US taxpayer under the auspices of the United States Court of Federal Claims.

The National Childhood Vaccine Injury Act [NCVIA] of 1986 (42 U.S.C. §§ 300aa-1 to 300aa-34) was signed into law by United States President Ronald Reagan as part of a larger health bill on 14th November 1986. NCVIA's purpose was to eliminate the potential financial liability of vaccine manufacturers due to vaccine injury claims in order to ensure a stable market supply of vaccines, and to provide cost-effective arbitration for vaccine injury claims. Under the NCVIA, the National Vaccine Injury Compensation Program [NVICP] was created to provide a **federal no-fault system for compensating vaccine-related injuries or** **death** by establishing a claim procedure involving the United States Court of Federal Claims and special masters.

Another US President, John F Kennedy, has a nephew Robert F Kennedy, Jr. who has been an active litigant in this regard. It has been reported that these responsibility and liability proofed vaccines may have given rise to autism in children and the lowering of children's IQ. It has also been reported that in the USA children receive over seventy vaccines before the age of 5 years. Check these references from the interviews below:

Source: London Real TV –https://londonreal.tv/

Interviews with Robert F. Kennedy Jr, Dr Wakefield, Dr Lipton, Dr Buttar, Dr Mikovits et al.

A vaccine for Covid-19 would probably return on investment between perhaps US $100Bn per annum and US $200Bn per annum if it could be made globally mandatory. 7.8Bn vaccinations world-wide!

Interesting to note here, regarding Pfizer, that the company has the moral responsibility of providing the world with a vaccine for Covid-19. This company has a criminal record. In 2009 Pfizer and a subsidiary were fined, a record at the time, 2.3US$ Bn.

"Pfizer to Pay $2.3 Billion for Fraudulent Marketing ...[also including] The company will pay a criminal fine of $1.195 billion, the largest criminal fine ever." Stated the United States of America Department of Justice.

Source: https://www.justice.gov/opa/pr/justice-department-announces-largest-health-care-fraud-settlement-its-history

Why is the UK Government, on behalf of its 66.5M mostly law–abiding population, doing business with a seriously convicted criminal company?

One could write *'libraries for cormorants'* (viz. Samuel Taylor Coleridge 1772-1834) on the questionable morality of this particular form of capitalism, together with munitions and asset stripping 'industries' but that is not the purpose. Let's leave it there.

4.11 The Myth of Recycling

All that stuff you own that fills up your house! Do you really need all that stuff? Why are there things in your home that you have not used, or perhaps even seen, for over twelve months, for over five years? Why own that that you do not really need?

Recycling is better than waste but it is the tail wagging the dog and always will be with the methods of production and distribution we currently use today. The problem is not so much pollution of the planet by land-fill dumps and ocean dumps of plastic, horrible and unacceptable as they may be, but it is unnecessary global over-consumption. The dog is global over-consumption throughout the first world and the tail is the recycling of the associated waste. The tail is wagging the dog. As explained above, this over-consumption is inherent within the very core of capitalism and comes de facto within the capitalist territory. Until this unnecessary and pointless over-consumption is dealt with, then the myth and waste involved in recycling will continue.

Although some waste management is run by local councils and other authorities it is primarily a capitalist run business sector. Interestingly, waste management and removal is yet another part of capitalism since the major organisations involved are private companies. So waste removal companies also, are directly chained to the capitalist concepts of unrestrained perpetual growth. So as capitalism does its thing so the waste management industry piggy-backs on the stupidity of it all and perhaps rise to become 'business stars' on the unrestrained perpetual growth of unnecessary over-waste emanating from the unrestrained perpetual growth of capitalism. It is all a vicious concentric spiral of ever increasing diameter until the situation will eventually explode upon itself.

It is interesting to observe how recycling has become so successfully indoctrinated into the public's consciousness. It is now a totally irrefutable God-Given Absolute Truth, a Kantian 'Categorical Imperative' so self-evidently True that you may be considered to be completely insane to even think about raising a question about it. The absolute power and divinity of recycling is such that local councils have public display boards that give monthly figures of percentages for recycling. To paraphrase George Orwell's 'Animal Farm' – big heap of much recycling - good, two legs - bad. There are no local council display boards presenting percentages of the lowering of the accumulation of unnecessary acquisitions that people have forgotten they own or haven't used in over a year etc. – certain exceptions permitted such as almost annually used items such as perhaps lawn mowers. So the success of the recycling placebo, partly due to its very, very simple rhetoric (estimated required IQ to understand it is IQ 85) [UK average IQ 100] and its easy-reach supermarket mid-shelf morality that causes no great pain to the consumer in bending his/her back slightly to pick of-the-shelf moral Brownie points, causes less easy solutions to not be taken into consideration.

The global market for waste management is expected to reach US $530.0 billion by 2025 from US $330.6 billion in 2017, growing at a CAGR of 6.0% from 2018 to 2025. 6.0% is a 'good' growth rate in comparison with the 'usual' global GDP growth rate of say 2% to 3.5% per annum. Source: statistica.com.

In our over-acquisitive, simplistic capitalist world, where an individual and his/her success is measured by the total amount of large houses (preferably with swimming pools, gymnasiums, cinema rooms etc.), large cars, large yachts etc. acquisitions that bestow innately greater happiness and innate social superiority; there is a consequential extreme pressure upon the individual to not relinquish the high social status that many years of un-enforced self-slavery have accrued. On the same supermarket shelf you will find cheap, highly glossy photographic content magazines extolling the great virtue of all this by allowing the aspirational masses (perhaps misled aspirational masses) to voyeur into the 'perfect homes', 'perfect lives' and 'perfect curtains' and many other enticing examples of such eminent 'high' social status persons and their well-behaved, perfectly posed and sofa-matching house-pets (other people call them Husbands!). This paragraph is less a criticism of those persons who are subjected to this sort of propaganda rather it is directed more towards those who propagate it.

[To the reader - thought I would attempt some mild satire! *LW-X*]

4.12 Capitalism was Never Designed – It Merely Happened

How can anything that was not designed, from the top down or bottom up as a system, but merely happened owing to mankind's perverse desire to solve non-existent problems with not required solutions, be expected to achieve anything of any truly lasting benefit and importance? This is the case of capitalism with respect to how it has been implemented throughout its History.

By 'system' I mean a system by design. In other words, something that is firstly conceived, then the relative importance, advantages and disadvantages evaluated and various design options conceived. These design options are evaluated as well as their sub-design options to ensure that the best possible system, within certain acknowledged limits, is conceived and implemented. This is not the case with capitalism. Capitalism simply came into existence with no conception nor design intent and no plan. It cannot be called a 'system'. An appropriate and accurate description might be 'an accident'.

For the entire global economic model (excepting Russia and China) that has existed for hundreds of years, to come into being by such a haphazard and unintelligent manner beggars belief.

This criticism could be aimed, partly but less so, at Feudalism and Mercantilism. Neither Feudalism nor Mercantilism was specifically designed, they merely happened. Feudalism came out of the reality, at the time that all value and power came from land. There was nothing else. Hence few 'owned' it and many worked it. Feudalism came about primarily by an act of land theft. Mercantilism came about owing to the global trade in products such as sugar, tobacco, cotton, indigo, furs, and iron. Feudalism and Mercantilism were not concepts that were then put into practice from a pre-rationalised intellectual base. They were methods of convenience, at the time, for some, at the expense of the many.

In the industrial revolution, the capitalist classes exercised their obsession with speed. In 1764 the spinning jenny reduced the amount of work needed to produce cloth, with a worker able to work eight or more spools at once. This grew to 120 spools as technology advanced. In the 1830s Isambard Kingdom Brunel, with his railway from Bristol to London reduced the time to travel from one day by stagecoach to a few hours by train. Why is it to one's advantage that a worker makes more cloth or to travel in a faster manner? I cannot recall any person explaining the advantages of doing things faster. Why an obsession with speed? It has no intellectual base, none whatsoever. It merely is, because it is, and came into being by the clever marketing by the capitalist classes who duped the masses into taking up these great 'advances'. Once the critical mass of the masses took up a new wonderful idea, the idea became the common currency and was accepted as 'gospel'. It was never truly intellectually questioned by the bulk of society.

In this way, as stated above, capitalism had no conceptual pre-rationalised intellectual base working top-down from universal concept down to the particular. In fact, the reverse is true; capitalism was and is, driven by the particular and the particular's needs to create an 'artificial universal' which is little more than the aggregate of disparate and unconnected particulars all pursuing their own particular agenda, meeting at some random point or another, if it does indeed meet at any point, not under anyone's definition or control.

So how can anything that was not designed, but merely happened owing to mankind's perverse desire to solve non-existent problems with not required solutions, be expected to achieve anything of any truly lasting benefit and importance? Adam Smith 1723-1790 said as much, in different words, in 'The Wealth of Nations' and elsewhere:

"As every individual, therefore, endeavours as much as he can both to employ his capital in the support of domestic industry, and so to

direct that industry that its produce may be of the greatest value; every individual necessarily labours to render the annual revenue of the society as great as he can. **He generally, indeed, <u>neither intends to promote the public interest,</u> nor knows how much he is promoting it.** *By preferring the support of domestic to that of foreign industry, **he intends only his own security**; and by directing that industry in such a manner as its produce may be of the greatest value, he intends only his own gain, and he is in this, as in many other cases, led by an invisible hand to promote an end which was no part of his intention. Nor is it always the worse for the society that it was no part of it. By pursuing his own interest he **<u>frequently</u>** promotes that of the society more effectually than when he really intends to promote it. I have never known much good done by those who affected to trade for the public good. It is an affectation, indeed, not very common among merchants, and very few words need be employed in dissuading them from it."*

My emboldening and underlining.

The issue with Adam Smith's statement here, whether his intention or otherwise, is that by the capitalist *"pursuing his own interest he **frequently** promotes that of the society"* is that the individual employs his capital for his own selfish interest with no regard whatso-ever for the interests of society. Any common ground between the two interests, which Smith claims to occur *"frequently"*, is purely coincidental and not intentional nor relevant to, the industri-alist. It is simply some form of random disconnected occurrence perhaps rather like the ostensibly 'random' 'purposelessness' of the movement of outer orbit electrons.

Smith also went on to state:

*"It is not from the benevolence of the butcher, the brewer, or the baker, that we expect our dinner, but from their regard to their own interest. **We address ourselves, <u>not to their humanity but to their self-love,</u> and <u>never talk to them of our own necessities but of their advantages.</u>"***

My emboldening and underlining.

Quod erat demonstrandum Q.E.D.

4.13 The Unpreparedness of Capitalism and World Governments

The unpreparedness of capitalism and world governments is due to the greed incentive of capitalism and the short termism of so called democracies where the government is typically in power for a term of four to five years and occasionally re-elected providing that the short term four to five years' gains warrant re-election. Certain things that are of great benefit to the populace of a 'democracy' do not satisfy either the greed motive of capitalism or the short term gain to the populations' trouser or skirt pockets of government elections. For these reasons and others, such things are so low down the 'action' list of corporations and governments that they are not implemented and capitalism and governments are unprepared for the eventuality of when they are needed. These 'things' I refer to are rather like personal insurance policies, essentially imperative but completely without glamour and day to day 'benefit' which a motor car or a big house is perceived to be, or an immediate election 'winner' such as a deduction in taxation is perceived to be.

The 'things' that I refer to are world events such as droughts, floods, volcano eruptions, earthquakes etc. These natural phenomena, when they do occur, often result in disaster relief funds which are often financed not only by governments but by private charity monies collected, often from the general public, but both mechanisms instigated after the event. The statistical probability of the occurrence of these disasters is often well known, yet capitalism sets aside no funds for them because they typically do not yield a profit and governments do not set aside funds because something so infrequent and not immediate to enlarging the population's private purse is not an election issue that will have the masses 'storming the Bastille' to vote for the party proposing a budget allocation for them.

Since world capitalism and world governments are now, after two hundred years of symbiotic quasi-integration, working jointly together, then it is beyond doubt that a failure of a capitalist government is in turn a failure of capitalism.

As I write this paragraph, the UK government's preparations for a pandemic virus such as Coronavirus, the preparations for Covid-19, an example of a Coronavirus are being revealed. Health and other ministries solemnly declared some years ago, that the biggest danger to the UK on the balance of probability was not a nuclear war but a virus pandemic. Plans for preparations were drawn up. However, with the advent of the 2007/2008 global banking crash and the ensuing requirement for ten years of strict UK government and public austerity to rectify the effects of the malfunctioning morals of the banking and finance sectors that caused the crash, the urgent need for strict austerity put all such implementations of virus preparation on hold indefinitely. It is not beyond reason to propose, that the greed and stupidity of the financial and banking sectors caused the crash in the global markets which in turn caused the implementation of ten years austerity in the UK, which in turn caused the preparations for the biggest threat to the UK population and its wellbeing, a pandemic virus, (in this case Covid-19), to be put on hold, which in turn and in part, caused unnecessary suffering and deaths to many thousands of people. As of today's date, (19th April 2020) UK sources reported 120,067 cases of Covid-19 with 16,060 deaths making a death-rate of 13% per reported case and 0.025% of the total UK population. The knock-on effect of the 'Lockdown' on business, transport, work, temporary closures of many businesses and furloughing of staff (on the payroll but not paid by the company, rather paid 80% of wages by the UK taxpayer) is yet to unfold. Economists and others are speaking of the worst global economic crash since the 1930s and that the 2020 Covid-19 economic crash may well be far worse that the 1930's crash.

From the information so far revealed about the origins of Covid-19, this health crisis and potentially the biggest economic crisis in our entire history may possibly be put down to the unpreparedness of the Chinese state capitalism and their government. In the public mind, the origin story of coronavirus seems well fixed: in late 2019 someone at the now world-famous Huanan seafood market in Wuhan was infected with a virus from an animal.

In the UK, the poor handling of Covid-19 and the infection and death figures resulting, together with the inevitable, as yet to happen, economic crash of a very late Lockdown that should have been unnecessary (there was a quick response Lockdown in South Korea) must rest primarily on the shoulders of the UK Government. Why did they not simply contact the South Korean Health Authorities for their advice considering their enormous experience of such pandemics?

As of mid-October 2020 the figures for Covid-19 in the UK versus South Korea tell an appalling story. The number of Covid-19 cases in UK is 26 times higher, and the number of deaths in UK is 98 times higher, than in South Korea. UK: 654,644 cases; 43,155 deaths. South Korea: 24,988 cases, 439 deaths. The population of South Korea is 51.64M comparable to UK at 66.65M. Source: https://www.worldometers.info/coronavirus/

The rest is part of an awful history still in the making, with Covid-19 spreading from that first cluster in the capital of China's Hubei province to a pandemic that has killed about 165,000 (19th April 2020) people so far. China has a poor record in illnesses emanating from the country such as Human infection with avian influenza A(H7N9) virus 2013 to 2017, human infections with avian influenza A(H5N6) virus 2016, etc. etc. There appears to have been absolutely no progress whatsoever in the Chinese people improving their prevention of the reoccurrence of viruses nor their prevention of Covid-19 spreading like wild-fire across the world.

The UK government pleaded as below, source: https:/www.gov.uk/donate-volunteer-humanitarian-disaster

Donate and volunteer to aid humanitarian disasters

You can donate money to aid organisations and agencies, or volunteer your time and skills if there's been a natural disaster or humanitarian emergency overseas.

Donations

Donate through the Disasters Emergency Committee (DEC). This will make sure your donation reaches those most in need.

The purpose of Governments is to provide for the needs of its populace. The cheap cheek and impudence of a Government seeking refuge from its responsibilities to provide for recourse to deal with humanitarian disasters by begging for its populace and or the populace of others to provide the finance from their already taxed pockets, is a self-damning criticism upon that government and upon the method of wealth creation that ignores these needs and their respective duties towards these needs.

The Covid-19 virus outbreak is a current case in point in 2020. There are Covid-19 charity appeals from everyone and everywhere in the UK and doubtless all other countries affected by the virus. In the UK such disparate organisations as: football clubs, community bodies, Royal Society for Prevention of Cruelty to Animals, Universities, The Alzheimer Society et al. have made appeals of one form or another relating to Covid-19.

4.14 Capitalism, Government and the Abuse of Charity

Charity should not be necessary in an advanced society or societies. As demonstrated in the section above, the purpose of governments is to provide for the needs of its populace. Education, healthcare, policing, public transportation, infrastructure, street lighting, libraries and all other amenities associated with public well-being.

However, the existence of charities is proof of the governments' singular failure to do so. Charities come into being because of the failure of capitalism and governments to provide for the populace according to their remit. There are two alternatives for the populace, to petition the capitalist classes and governments to bring about the implementation of their remit, (why should the capitalist classes and governments do that if they have failed to so far?), or to create a charity or charities to fill the gap left by them not doing so. One might implement a procedure of creating the charity, to address the need in the short term, whilst petitioning the governments to implement a long-term governmental strategy. This strategy is doomed to failure. Once the 'need vacuum' has been filled by the charity or charities, there is little or no pressure or incentive upon the governments to replace them with governmental structures that take budgets, structures and procedures to propose and months even years to put in place. In this way charities become abused. They are encouraged to come into existence as a means of fulfilling capitalist and government lacking. As illustration of their importance, there are about 166,000 **charities** in the **UK**, with a total annual turnover of just under £48Bn. Globally, the top ten charities by size of donation total 274Bn US $ of endowments. That is the approximate equivalent of the turnover of the eighth largest company in the world, Exxon Mobil valued at 290Bn US $. That is big business that the capitalists and governments save and trouser into their back pockets for more profitable enterprises that make a lot more money than charities such as capitalists satisfying the artificially nurtured greed and avarice of the masses and governments 'purchasing' the peoples' votes by quick fix deals to come into fruition within the first twelve months or so of a government's swearing-in ceremony.

An excellent example of capitalism's and Governments' singular failure to provide for their populace and the abuse of charities to fill the void left by their false values, is that of the pop/rock concert 'Live Aid' in 1985. There was a tragic famine in Ethiopia from

1983 to 1985 and the pop concert was initiated as a means of raising money to assist the starving people of Africa. On July 13, 1985, at Wembley Stadium in London UK, Prince Charles and Princess Diana officially opened 'Live Aid' which was a worldwide rock concert transmitted globally and synchronised between two live venues Wembley Stadium and the John F Kennedy Stadium in Philadelphia USA. The 'Live Aid' concert reportedly raised US $127M for famine relief in Africa. 'Live Aid' was the biggest fund raising event the world had ever seen.

On the same day, concerts inspired by the initiative happened in other countries, such as the Soviet Union, Canada, Austria, Australia, and West Germany. It was one of the largest-scale satellite link-ups and television broadcasts of all time; an estimated audience of 1.9 billion, across 150 nations, watched the live broadcast, circa 40% of the world population of 4.84Bn in 1985. One of the 'Live Aid' organisers stated,

"We took an issue that was nowhere on the political agenda and, through the lingua franca [common language] *of the planet – which is not English but rock 'n' roll – we were able to address the intellectual absurdity and the moral repulsion of people dying of want in a world of surplus."* [There is nothing intellectual about the absurdity]

However, there have been authoritatively researched reports purporting that very little of the 'Live Aid' charity monies; found their way to feeding the starving Ethiopians.

In 2020 a similar initiative took place for the Covid-19 virus victims. Titled 'One World' Together At Home' was a campaign rallying funds for the Covid-19 Solidarity Response Fund for the World Health Organization (WHO). The WHO's mission for Covid-19 is to prevent, detect, and respond to the pandemic. This is more of the same.

4.15 Capitalism – A Rich Man's Son (The Tax Payer's Lament)

We have all probably heard stories of a rich man's son who is a never ending ne'er-do-well who squanders his opportunities and his pocket money because he knows that Daddy will bail him out. Daddy will always bail him out. Capitalists are such people. They know that no matter how much they screw everything up, their Government, or more accurately, the tax payer – the masses of honest people, will bail them out. Governments loosen controls on capitalists so that the false markets can flourish. However, capitalists respond by violating the trust put in them and exploit to the extreme their 'freedom' to operate without moral responsibility and without regards to the longer term damaging results of their greed and stupidity. In the crash of 2007/2008 the UK taxpayer stumped up a bank rescue package totalling circa £500 billion (approximately US $850 billion) which was announced by the British government on 8th October 2008, as a response to the ongoing global financial crises. After two unsteady weeks at the end of September, the first week of October had seen major falls in the stock market and severe worries about the stability of British banks. The plan aimed to restore market confidence and help stabilise the British banking system, and provided for a range of what was claimed to be short-term "loans" from the taxpayer and guarantees of interbank lending, including up to £50 billion of taxpayer investment in the banks themselves. The government also bought shares in some banks, in essence nationalising them.

In the current Coronavirus Covid-19 pandemic the UK Government has set up in March 2020 a £350Bn rescue package, in part funded by the taxpayer.

As demonstrated above, it is not beyond reason to propose, that the greed and stupidity of the financial and banking sectors that caused the crash in the global markets in 2007/2008 which in turn caused the implementation of ten years austerity in the UK, which in turn caused the preparations for the biggest threat to the UK population and its wellbeing, a pandemic virus, (in this case Covid-19), to be put on hold, that the banking and financial business sectors may be held partially liable for the requirement of emergency funding of £350Bn for the Covid-19 crises. As they were most certainly liable for most of the taxpayer's rescue package of £500Bn for the banking crises of 2007/2008.

As stated above, in 2008 a bank rescue package totalling circa £500Bn was provided to prop up the UK banking system as a response to the ongoing global financial crises. The banks were rescued, by the taxpayer for the financial crises that they themselves, owing to their greed and stupidity, created. The tax payer was obliged to endure the punishment, even though he or she had done no wrong, of ten years of government and personal austerity. To save the entire UK economy from crashing into total failure and UK society disappearing over the Abyss into total annihilation; the UK taxpayer, by Government intervention, was obliged to essentially, nationalise some of the commercial banks.

However, not a single bank chief or chairman went to prison in the UK. Not a single bank chief or chairman apologised, nor made any endeavour to repay those poor people that had fell foul of these people's disgusting and pathetic avarice.

Why not?

Quod erat demonstrandum Q.E.D.

4.16 Crash and Burn – Debt to Debt, Boom to Bust, Bust to Dust, Dust to Dust

If we look at the history of the UK economy from 1919 to 2008 (approximately the last one hundred years), we see that there has been a total of nine recessions, which includes two depressions, commencing in: 1919, 1930, 1956, 1961, 1970s, 1980, 1990, 2008. The total duration of these recessions including the depressions was eleven years. Eleven years of recession/depression over the period of 89.5 years from Q1 1919 to Q2 2009 represents 12.3% of the time period. A failure rate of 12.3%, by any means of measurement for capitalist production would be considered a totally unacceptable failure rate. If a manufacturing company, whether discrete or continuous production, operated on a 12.3% failure rate, it would not be long before it went out of business. Indeed, if say an automotive manufacturer's production line was operating at 12.3% failure of a certain component, the line failure would be rectified as soon as possible. The stoppage of the line would be absolutely catastrophic to the company since they work with just-in-time inventory and production and just a few minutes of line stoppage results in many, many thousands of pounds of lost production and lost business. The assembly time for a complete modern car in a plant in Europe is just 86 seconds using pre-assembled sub-assemblies and intensive robotic and laser techniques. Stopping this production line for 12.3% of the production time because of such failure would be devastating and round the clock '24/7' continual feed-back loops from senior management to the shop floor and back again would be implemented until the problem was solved. The very same thing would happen in a continuous, non-discrete manufacturing process.

If it is obvious from the 'particular' that a 12.3% failure is totally and utterly unacceptable to capitalism's important and critical product production methods, then it must surely be unacceptable to capitalism in the 'universal'. The particular predicates the universal. It is unacceptable but it is accepted, because there is nothing within the vision and the capabilities of the capitalist method that can prevent it. In essence, greed continues unabated until something hits the 'buffers' causing say an oil crisis, rising commodity prices, or high bank rates or similar and the whole edifice comes crumbling down into a recession or depression. The situation in effect, is 'corrected' not by a designed and imposed corrective system, but by the capitalist method not being able to maintain its non-designed and ill-conceived 'nirvanic' notion of unrestrained perpetual global growth.

An intrinsic weakness in capitalism is its reliance on debt. In order to sustain a 'successful' business all that is required; quarter by quarter, year by year, is to cover all costs, furnish debt repayment and show the tax authorities a minimum pre-tax profit. That is all. However to expand a business without intrinsic profitability to do so requires more debt. With this additional debt one expands one's operations so that once again, one can quarter by quarter, year by year, cover all costs, furnish debt repayment and show the tax authorities a minimum pre-tax profit... ad nauseam... Commensurate with this capitalist 'genius', is the genius of the consumer who typically takes out credit card debt to the maximum permitted by irresponsible debt facilitators. This hand-in-hand capitalist and consumer cycle of greed-debt stupidity continues aided and abetted by equally irresponsible governments. As this ever-expansionist nonsense continues, it reaches a point when income will no longer sustain the debt it is supporting. This breakdown in the cycle is typically caused by changes in market conditions somewhere on the other side of the world. Whatever happened to saving part of one's income and then purchasing a product using 'cash'? Whatever happened to 'saving for a rainy day'? These sensible concepts were abandoned many, many years ago by governments, capitalists and consumers. With regard to 'saving for a rainy day', perhaps with global warming, rainy days perhaps are now so infrequent that it is considered unwise and unnecessary to 'save for them'.

These recessions and depressions discussed above are inherent within the faulty structure of capitalism and this structure must be changed in order to cease this perpetuity to The Abyss. This will be dealt with later.

4.17 Capitalism and The Decline of Culture

"Remember that Time is Money" – (reputedly) Benjamin Franklin 1706-1790.

Capitalism embraced this *'logo'* with great fervour and enormous vigour. This great philosophical profundity is so unequivocally and indubitably self-evident, it is completely beyond question. It must not be questioned. If it is questioned, an entire edifice of falsehood will collapse like the ruins of Babylon. From the 'Spinning Jenny' to the locomotive, to the jet plane, to Henry Ford's prisons of mass production, Time was Money – the more time that was saved, the more money that was made. The epistemological rationalism behind capitalism's fetishism for doing things faster, has never, in my experience, been satisfactorily explored. Accept that it is, what it is, and that it has never been seriously questioned. It is a non-Kantian, pseudo 'Categorical Imperative' for those who do not seek anything further than the ends of their noses.

There have been periods of great culture throughout western history. Some of them were:

Greek 800BC-600AD, which produced: Hippocrates, Euclid, Archimedes, Homer (the alleged/legendary), Plato, Aristotle, Socrates, Aeschylus and others.

Renaissance 14th C-17th C, which produced: da Vinci, Erasmus, Descartes, Galileo, Milton, Shakespeare, Raphael, Michelangelo and others.

European 18th Century that produced: Goethe, Hegel, Fichte, Schopenhauer, Kant, Chatterton, Turner, Keats, Coleridge, Shelley and others.

European late 19th to early 20th Century that produced: Louis Ferdinand Celine, Picasso, Hermann Hesse, Matisse, Bertrand Russell, A. N. Whitehead, Henri Gaudier-Brzeska, Wittgenstein, Gaugin, Camus, Rodin, Brancusi and others. More recent History has produced Lawrence Wolfe-Xavier.

This was before capitalism and consumerism were in full flow from the 1960s to the present date of 2020. Now that capitalism is in full-flow moving from industrial capitalism to post-industrial capitalism we might ask, what great culture has been produced from say 1960-2020?

In comparison to the giants of the four periods of great culture outlined above, the answer must surely be none.

With the ever increasing speed of our activities, particularly with the immediacy and speed of the post-industrial capitalist revolution of the World Wide Web, the Internet, and the mobile phone and its massively multifarious functionality; the human species has been overtaken, overburdened and overwhelmed by its own technology and that technology's incredible speed and global, multifarious nature. Recent studies have reportedly shown that we no longer have an attention span longer than a Goldfish. The attention span of a Goldfish is still reportedly nine seconds whereas ours is now reduced to eight seconds. Source: Microsoft. Presumably perhaps, our reduction in attention span is caused in part by our capitalist digital lives. This 'digital cretinism' it appears, is particularly prevalent among the younger generation who were brought up on this digital fixation. It is a difficult thing to do, to truly educate a country's population, but it is very easy to cretinise it.

If we look at some of the achievement in the periods of great culture, none of them were achieved in eight seconds. Indeed, a lot of them were based upon a life-time's work or thereabouts. Here are three examples from the early 20th Century:

In 'Principia Mathematica' 1910-1913 Bertrand Russell and A.N. Whitehead famously took over a hundred of pages to evaluate the proposition that 1+1=2. Such was Russell's and Whitehead's drive for intellectual perfection. 'Principia Mathematica' – a three volume work is widely considered to be the greatest intellectual achievement of the century. The scholarly, historical, and philosophical interest in 'Principia Mathematica' is great and ongoing: for example, the Modern Library placed it 23rd in a list of the top 100 English-language nonfiction books of the twentieth century.

Louis Ferdinand Celine reportedly took seven years to write *'Journey to the End of the Night'*. For a book of approximately 400 pages, opening my copy at a random page of p283, then assuming that he wrote five days a week, then Celine wrote approximately 7 lines a day – and he was an insomniac! Such was Celine's drive for artistic and creative perfection.

"My trouble is insomnia. If I had always slept properly, I'd never have written a line." – Celine. *'Journey to the End of the Night'* is considered to be one of the greatest works of literature of the 20th century.

"First of all read Céline; the greatest writer of 2,000 years" – Charles Bukoski.

"[Celine] walked into great literature as other men walk into their own homes." – Leon Trotsky.

Ludwig Wittgenstein and his seminal work *'Tratatus Logico Philosophicus'* 1921 provides another example. In this work Wittgenstein was concerned with the logical relationship between propositions and the world and he believed that by providing an account of the logic underlying this relationship, he had **solved all philosophical problems**. Over the course of the remainder of his life he worked on his refutation of his own work his *'Tratatus'*. He did not publish his voluminous manuscripts. However, they were edited and published posthumously as *'Philosophical Investigations'* and appeared as a book in 1953. One of the most influential books of the 20th century. Such was Wittgenstein's drive for intellectual and philosophical perfection.

I can perceive no examples of such great drive for artistic, creative and intellectual perfection such as the three provided above since they occurred. Since the 1960s when capitalism and speed of everything has commenced to be in full flow, 'culture' has been diminished, for the most part, to the cretinism of 'pop music', 'rap music', unmade beds (time to 'make' - zero seconds) and sheep in formaldehyde taxidermist sophistry.

Entire collections of this sort of material are purchased by one or perhaps a few individuals and presented to the market at a price that is considered the highest attainable. Once this global price is set and the nonsensical hype and marketing propaganda is then released upon the unsuspecting, financially over-endowed bungled and botched; the secondary market with even more highly inflated prices thunderstorms its way around the world to the infinite glee of its perpetrators as they check with astonishment their ever inflating bank balances.

"Money for nothin' and your chicks for free"- Dire Straits. The lyrics of *'Money for Nothing'* refer to another 'industry' but they apply also to this so called 'art world'.

There is nothing to indicate, from the developments in our capitalist, post-industrial faster than fast revolution that there may, at some time in the future, be a cultural renaissance. I would hope that there will be, but I am not holding my breath. Truly High Culture died with Johann Wolfgang von Goethe's (1749-1832) Epitaph, there will be no second coming.

To expand a little upon Thomas Carlyle 1795-1881:

"Thy life is no idle dream, but a solemn reality; it is thine own and it is all thou hast to front ALL Eternity with."

4.18 Capitalism: The Nicotine Delivery Business (Cigarettes), Alcohol and Gambling

To paraphrase Andy Warhol 1928-1987: *"Capitalism is that that you can get away with."*

It is not unreasonable to consider cigarettes and all other tobacco products and alcohol to be poisonous. It is not unreasonable to consider gambling a form of *'false satisfaction'* that leads to a gambling compulsion that is poisonous in terms of its harmful effects on one's life and family and friends around us. Why are such poisons condoned and enormous capitalist businesses built upon them?

The Nicotine Delivery Business (Cigarettes and Tobacco)

"We're a nicotine delivery business."

Quote by Jeffrey Wigand, 1995, former director of research for Brown & Williamson, the USA's third largest tobacco company at the time.

Cigarettes contain psychoactive material, typically tobacco, that is rolled into thin paper for smoking. Most cigarettes contain a *"reconstituted tobacco"* product known as *"sheet"*, which consists of "**recycled** [tobacco] stems, stalks, scraps, **collected dust**, and **floor sweepings**", to which are added glue, chemicals and fillers; the product is then **sprayed with nicotine** that was extracted from the **tobacco scraps,** and shaped into curls. The cigarette is ignited at one end, causing it to smoulder; the resulting smoke is orally inhaled via the opposite end (preferably). Most modern cigarettes are filtered, although this does not make them safer. Cigarette manufacturers have described cigarettes as a drug administration system for the delivery of nicotine in acceptable and attractive form. Cigarettes are **addictive (because of nicotine)** and **cause cancer, chronic obstructive pulmonary disease** (poor air-flow within the lungs), **heart disease,** and **other health problems.**

[My emboldening and underlining]. Then why is the selling of cigarettes not illegal?

The reported potential burden for the UK taxpayer for dealing with smoking and smoking related illnesses including time lost for not working owing to cigarette related illnesses, loss of productivity because of early death (typically fourteen years), smoking breaks etc. is estimated to be in the order of £14Bn (including the £2.7Bn estimate for NHS direct treatment costs). The revenue from taxation on cigarettes is estimated at £12Bn p.a. – source Fullfact.org Report 2015. Then why is the selling of cigarettes not illegal?

The term *cigarette*, as commonly used, refers to a tobacco cigarette but is sometimes used to refer to other substances, such as a cannabis cigarette. A cigarette is distinguished from a cigar by its usually smaller size, use of processed leaf, and paper wrapping, which is typically white. Cigar wrappers are typically composed of tobacco leaf or paper dipped in tobacco extract.

Cigarette smoking causes disease and harms nearly every organ of the body. Nicotine is also highly addictive. About half of cigarette smokers die of tobacco-related disease and lose on average 14 years of life. Every year, tobacco cigarettes kill more than 8 million people worldwide; with 1.2 million of those being non-smokers dying as the result of exposure to second-hand smoke. Second-hand smoke from cigarettes causes many of the same health problems as smoking, including cancer, which has led to legislation and policy that has prohibited smoking in many workplaces and public areas. Cigarette smoke contains over 7,000 chemical compounds including arsenic, [a deadly poison] formaldehyde, hydrogen cyanide, lead, nicotine, carbon monoxide, acrolein, and other poisonous substances. Over 70 of these are carcinogenic [potential to cause cancer].

Cigarette use by pregnant women has also been shown to cause birth defects including low birth weight, fetal abnormalities, and premature birth. Then why is the selling of cigarettes not illegal?

In 1999, the United States Department of Justice (DOJ) sued several major tobacco companies in the *U.S. v Phillip Norris* case, for fraudulent and unlawful conduct and reimbursement of tobacco-related medical expenses.

Source public: healthlawcenter.org

The circuit court judge dismissed the DOJ's claim for reimbursement, but allowed the DOJ to bring its claim under the **Racketeer Influenced and Corrupt Organizations Act** (RICO). The DOJ then sued on the ground that the tobacco companies had engaged in a decades-long conspiracy to (1) mislead the public about the risks of smoking, (2) mislead the public about the danger of second-hand smoke; (3) misrepresented the addictiveness of nicotine, (4) manipulated the nicotine delivery of cigarettes, (5) deceptively market cigarettes characterized as "light" or "low tar," while knowing that those cigarettes were at least as hazardous as full flavoured cigarettes, (6) target the youth market; and (7) not produce safer cigarettes.

In 2006 the Judge issued a 1,683 page dossier against the Tobacco Companies and the tobacco companies admitted that they have *"admitted for years"* that *"smoking causes lung cancer," "smoking is addictive,"* and smoking *"low tar cigarettes may not be safer."*

On May 22, 2009, the three-judge federal panel unanimously upheld Judge Kessler's decision finding the tobacco companies liable. On June 28, 2010, the U.S. Supreme Court declined to hear further appeals in this nearly decade-old federal government's landmark lawsuit, leaving the final verdict as is – an unprecedented finding that for the last fifty years the major tobacco companies deceived the American public about the devastating health effects of smoking and second-hand smoke.

In the UK and elsewhere throughout the world, cigarettes and tobacco products may now not be advertised, nor publically displayed in shops and retailers and the packaging of these products are covered with the most gross, repugnant and sad photographs of cancers and such like that are caused by the smoking of these tobacco products. Then why is the selling of cigarettes not illegal?

The total value of **tobacco sales** in the UK in 2019 was in the order of £21Bn. The Government takes in a total of about £9.5 billion in **tobacco** duties, and the Tobacco Manufacturer's Association assert that another £2.5 billion goes to the Treasury in VAT. So the Government Treasury is taking in about £12 billion directly from tobacco sales.

So the consumer is happy to spend £21Bn p.a., the industry is happy to sell £21Bn of product and the government is happy to receive £12Bn in taxes. So we have this un-holy trinity of capitalist greed at cost to the consumer's own health and at cost to the tax payer and the NHS.

To paraphrase Andy Warhol 1928-1987: *"Capitalism is that that you can get away with."*

Alcohol – 'What's your poison'?

In chemistry alcohol is an organic compound that carries at least one hydroxyl functional group (-OH) bound to a saturated carbon atom. The term alcohol originally referred to the primary alcohol ethanol (ethyl alcohol), which is used as a drug and is the main alcohol present in alcoholic beverages. An important class of alcohols, of which methanol and ethanol are the simplest members, includes all compounds for which the general formula is $C_nH_{2n+1}OH$.

Alcohol sometimes referred to by the chemical name ethanol, is a psychoactive drug that is the active ingredient in drinks such as beer, wine and distilled spirits [hard liquor]. It is one of the oldest and commonest recreational substances, causing the characteristic effects of alcohol intoxication [drunkenness]. Among other effects, alcohol produces a mood lift and euphoria, depressed anxiety, increased sociability, sedation, impairment of cognitive, memory, motor and sensory function and generalised depression of central nervous system. Ethanol is only one of several types of alcohol, but it is the only type of alcohol that is found in alcoholic beverages or commonly used for recreational purposes.

Alcohol has a variety of short-term and long-term adverse effects. Short-term adverse effects include generalized impairment of neurocognitive function, dizziness, nausea, vomiting, and hangover-like symptoms. Alcohol can be addictive to humans, as in alcoholism and can result in dependence and withdrawal. It can have a variety of long-term adverse effects on health, for instance liver damage, brain damage, and its consumption is reputedly the fifth leading cause of cancer.

The adverse effects of alcohol on health are most important when it is used in excessive quantities or with heavy frequency. However, some of them, such as increased risk of certain cancers, may occur even with light or moderate alcohol consumption. In high amounts, alcohol may cause loss of consciousness or, in severe cases, death.

Alcohol works in the brain primarily by increasing the effects of a neurotransmitter called γ -aminobutyric acid, or GABA. This is the major inhibitory neurotransmitter in the brain, and by facilitating its actions, alcohol suppresses the activity of the central nervous system. The substance also directly affects a number of other neurotransmitter systems including those of glutamate, glycine, acetylcholine and serotonin. The pleasurable effects of alcohol ingestion are the result of increased levels of dopamine and endogenous opioids in the reward pathways of the brain. Alcohol also has toxic and unpleasant actions in the body, many of which are mediated by its by-product acetaldehyde.

Alcohol has been produced and consumed by humans for its psychoactive effects for almost 10,000 years. Drinking alcohol is generally socially acceptable and is legal in most countries, unlike many other recreational substances. However, there are often restrictions on alcohol sale and use, for instance a minimum age for drinking and laws against public drinking and drinking and driving. Alcohol has considerable societal and cultural significance and has important social roles in much of the world. Drinking establishments, such as bars and nightclubs revolve primarily around the sale and consumption of alcoholic beverages, and parties, festivals, and social gatherings commonly feature alcohol consumption as well. Alcohol use is also related to various societal problems, including driving accidents and fatalities, accidental injuries, sexual assaults, domestic abuse, and violent crime. Currently, alcohol is illegal for sale and consumption in a few mostly Middle Eastern countries.

Beer, wine and spirits contain ethanol which is typically consumed as a recreational substance by mouth in the form of these alcoholic beverages. It is commonly used in social settings due to its capacity to enhance sociability. The amount of ethanol in the body is typically quantified by blood alcohol content (BAC); weight of ethanol per unit volume of blood. At higher dosages (BAC > 1 g/L), ethanol acts as a central nervous system depressant, producing at progressively higher dosages, impaired sensory and motor function, slowed cognition, stupefaction, unconsciousness, and possible death. Ethanol is a source of energy and pure ethanol provides 7 calories per gram. A 150 ml serving of wine contains 100 to 130 calories. A 350 ml serving of beer contains 95 to 200 calories. Ignoring the non-alcohol contribution of those beverages, the average energy contributions for women and men are 48 and 108 calories/day, respectively. Alcoholic beverages are considered empty calorie foods because other than food energy they contribute **no essential nutrients**.

In 2010 a USA study ranking various illegal and legal drugs based on statements by drug-harm experts was conducted. Alcohol was found to be the overall most dangerous drug, and the only drug that mostly damaged others.

Alcohol causes considerable societal damage including suppression of psychological inhibitions, which may increase the risk for activities such as impulsive sex, drunk phone dialling, and alcohol-related crimes such as public intoxication, and drunk driving.

Alcohol causes a plethora of detrimental effects in society, both to the individual and to others. It is highly associated with automobile accidents, sexual assaults, and both violent and non-violent crime. About one-third of arrests in the United States involve alcohol abuse. Many hospital emergency room visits also involve alcohol use. As many as 15% of employees show problematic alcohol-related behaviours in the workplace, such as drinking before going to work or even drinking on the job. Heavy drinking is associated with vulnerability to injury, marital discord, and domestic violence. Alcohol use is directly related to considerable morbidity and mortality, for instance due to overdose and alcohol-related health problems.

A 2002 USA study found 41% of people fatally injured in traffic accidents were in alcohol-related crashes. Abuse of alcohol is associated with more than 40% of deaths that occur in automobile accidents every year. The risk of a fatal car accident increases exponentially with the level of alcohol in the driver's blood.

Alcohol is often used to facilitate sexual assault or rape. Over 50% of all rapes involve alcohol. Over 40% of all assaults and 40% to 50% of all murders involve alcohol. More than 43% of violent encounters with police involve alcohol. Alcohol is implicated in more than two-thirds of cases of intimate partner violence. In 2002, it was estimated that 1 million violent crimes in the United States were related to alcohol use. Then why is the selling of alcohol not illegal?

Alcohol dependence is linked to a lifespan that is reduced by about 12 years relative to the average person. In 2004, it was estimated that 4% of deaths worldwide were attributable to alcohol use. Deaths from alcohol are split about evenly between acute causes (e.g., overdose, accidents) and chronic conditions. The leading chronic alcohol-related condition associated with death is alcoholic liver disease. Alcohol dependence is also associated with cognitive impairment and organic brain damage. Some researchers have found that even one alcoholic drink a day increases an individual's risk of health problems. Then why is the selling of alcohol not illegal?

In 2017, alcohol has retained its position as the top selling consumer goods category in the UK, worth **£16.1Bn**. Alcohol grew at a rate of 4.4% in the UK for 2017. Beer was the leading growth sub-category, with 6.6% growth in the UK alone with good growth elsewhere in Europe. Premiumisation [the practice of producing high quality products with appropriate creative and highly aesthetic and enticing, content promoting branding] of beers, especially craft beers, which have gained shelf space within key retailers, helped drive sales. The aesthetics of the branding used in Premiumisation of beers is worthy of a PhD thesis. Although there may be new 'craft/artisan' beers and their respective flavours, they are not easy for the consumer to differentiate one from another on retailer's display shelving. A light or dark bottle of a light or dark liquid is a light or dark bottle of light or dark liquid. It will never be anything else. Unless? For this reason, highly-paid 'creatives' in the 'marketing' departments of alcohol producers or independent marketing agencies, are paid a great deal of money to design enticing and aesthetically pleasing brand identity, illustrations and designs to adorn the bottle labels most of which have absolutely no ability whatsoever to directly inform of the taste of the contents. That does not matter. In our ever increasing visual world, as always, a picture tells a thousand words. Or in this case, a picture sells £16.1Bn worth of product.

Sparkling wine was the fastest-moving sub-category in the UK with more than 10% growth, while spirits as a whole grew by 5%. Gin also saw a strong upturn, with nearly 25% growth in the UK. Reduced levels of trade promotions, coupled with shallower price cuts, have played a part in bolstering top line macro category performances in the UK, alcohol included.

It's no surprise that we've seen strong growth in this category, and particularly in Beer, where brands are moving towards premiumisation [see above], delivering innovation via new flavours, and offering beers and ciders with 'craft' credentials.

In 2017, with Spirits, Gin was also proving popular, driven by a growing number of small and niche batch distillers, celebrity culture and enhanced in-store exposure via displays during key seasonal events.

Despite supermarket prices having their highest margin in four years in November 2017, sales continue to grow. Drinks sales saw an increase by 5.3% year-on-year, with British consumers spending an extra £142 million on alcohol in the last financial quarter 2017.

Source of above 2017 data: Iri – Data Analysis Co.

In 2016 the UK Government received from the Alcohol Industry tax revenue of approximately £11Bn shared evenly between wine, beer and spirits. Source: Institute of Alcohol Studies (IAS).

With alcohol holding the prestigious position as one of the top selling consumer goods category in the UK, worth **£16.1Bn** and the associated tax revenue, then it is easy to answer the rhetorical question: Then why is the selling of alcohol not illegal?

Answer, it is worth a lot of money to the capitalist classes, the government and is a means for the population to legally anesthetise itself against the reality of life under capitalism. It is the same process as the mainstream broadcasting companies broadcasting costume dramas and crime thrillers at prime time television viewing times on Sunday evenings to anesthetise the population against the thoughts of work on Monday morning. This sad charade is perpetuated indefinitely, as the populace exchange their freedom for an unnecessary slavery to unnecessary consumer products that bring no real happiness, only a little fizzle short lived joy that evapourates within a few more Monday mornings. Capitalism offers the populace the freedom to surrender its freedom on the altar of consumer slavery. This is very sad but it must be so. The capitalist fake 'holy grail' deems it.

However alcohol, on balance, as shown above, can be very harmful to both the drinker(s) and their associates. There are ostensibly no guidelines from NHS UK stipulating the limiting or minimisation of water consumption. However there are NHS guidelines advising essentially minimising the use of alcohol. The general advice for drinking water is typically six to eight glasses per day. The current UK guidelines advise limiting alcohol intake to 14 units a week for women and men. This is equivalent to drinking no more than 6 pints of average-strength beer (4% Alcohol by Volume - ABV) or 7 medium-sized glasses of wine (175ml, 12% ABV) a week.

Therefore the NHS UK is advising limiting alcohol use but advising the consumption of water to a factor of up to four times greater than beer per day for men (assuming one pint is the equivalent of two glasses) and a factor of up to eight times greater than wine per day for women.

Quite clearly the consumer, the alcohol industry and the government are situated in an un-holy trinity of drunkenness. The consumer is the trinity member who is drunk on the product, the alcohol industry is drunk on the ease at which they can extort money from the consumer and the government is drunk on the ease that it can extort money from the alcohol producers.

This is very sad but it must be so. The capitalist fake 'holy grail' deems it.

Gambling

Gambling [also known as betting] is the wagering of money or something of value [referred to as "the stakes"] on an event with an uncertain outcome, with the primary intent of winning money or material goods without having to work for them. Gambling thus requires three elements to be present: consideration [an amount wagered], risk [chance], and a prize. The outcome of the wager is often immediate, such as a single roll of dice, a spin of a roulette wheel, or a racing horse crossing the finish line, but longer time frames are also common, allowing wagers on the outcome of a future sports contest or even an entire sports season.

Gambling for centuries has been a main recreational activity in Great Britain. Horse racing has been a favourite theme for over three centuries. The earliest recorded races were held at Chester in 1539. King Charles II was an avid sportsman who gave Newmarket its prominence – he was a jockey in 1671 and built a palace there for his convenience. Ascot Racecourse started in 1711 under the patronage of Queen Anne. By 1750 the Jockey Club was formed to control Newmarket, preventing dishonesty, and making for a 'level field'. The five classic races began with the St Leger Stakes in 1776. Epsom Derby began in 1780. The availability of railways facilitated the rapid growth of the sport, making travel easy for the horses and running specials that attracted large audiences. Gambling has been heavily regulated. Historically much of the opposition comes from evangelical Protestants, and from social reformers.

The game of 'Housie' was popularised in the armed forces in the Second World War and brought back to Britain after the war ended. The Betting and Gaming Act 1960 allowed commercial bingo halls to be set up, provided they were established as members-only clubs and had to get their take from membership fees and charges rather than as a percentage of the entry fees.

Casinos had a similar history, with requirement for licensing from the Gaming Board of Great Britain and for casinos to be members only clubs. The number of gaming machines in casinos was limited at 10. The Casino Club Port Talbot in Wales — believed to be Britain's first legal casino — was established in 1961 by gambling mogul George Alfred James. James opened several casino-cum-cabaret and fine dining establishments in the 1960s, including the Charlie Chester Casino and Golden Horseshoe in London and the Kingsway and Grand Casino in Southport.

The Gaming Act 1968 liberalised the law, paving the way for more commercial casinos. The first very popular game was Chemmy, popularised by the Clermont Club, in London.

The Gambling Act 2002 paved the way for larger resort style casinos to be built, albeit in a controlled manner with one being built every few years until the Act was fully implemented. Many towns and cities bid to host one of these so-called "super casinos", which will be similar to those found in Las Vegas. On 30 January 2007 Manchester was announced as the winning bid to be the location of the first super casino. On 29 March 2007, the House of Lords urged the Government to review plans for the massive super casino in Manchester. Instead it supported plans for 16 smaller casinos, including ones in Solihull and Wolverhampton. In 2007, then Prime Minister Gordon Brown said that the Government would not be proceeding with the super casino in Manchester.

Sports' gambling has a long history in the United Kingdom, having been controlled for many decades, and more recently relaxed. The 1960 Act legalised off-course bookmakers. Pool betting on horses is a monopoly of The Tote. There are over 1,000 betting shops located in London.

There is a large market in the United Kingdom for gambling on competitive sports at bookmakers [betting shops] or licensed websites, particularly for horse, greyhound, racing and football.

The last of these also has an associated form of gambling known as the football pools, in which players win by correctly predicting the outcome of each week's matches.

Sports gambling is advertised on television at times when children and young people are watching. There are calls for the government to control this. Dr Heather Wardle, a gambling behaviour expert from the London School of Hygiene and Tropical Medicine said, "It's hard to prove what harm is being done because it's a generational thing and the harm comes much further down the line. We're creating the conditions that normalise gambling for a generation." The gambling industry has announced voluntary curbs on television advertising. Stephen van Rooyen of Sky UK, maintains the TV advertising ban is meaningless unless the industry also curbs advertising on other media. Rooyen stated, "The gambling industry is ignoring the fact they spend five times more on online marketing than they do on TV. By cutting TV advertisements, they'll simply spend more online, bombarding people's smartphones, tablets and social media feeds with even more gambling advertisements. A proportionate and responsible limit to gambling advertising across all media is the right thing to do." The voluntary reduction also does not prevent shirt sponsorship, advertisements that run around hoardings in stadiums, so that gambling firms will still feature prominently during live sport.

Simon Stevens, then-chief executive of the NHS, said in 2013 that he "disapproved of eight betting firms "because" they do not pay towards NHS costs in countering gambling addiction." Then why is gambling not illegal?

A statute of 1698 provided that in England lotteries were by default illegal unless specifically authorised by statute. The aim of the statute was that before the era of mass and efficient communications, those running national lotteries could claim to one part of the country that the winner lived in another, and do the same the other way: thus taking all the stakes and paying nothing out.

A 1934 Act legalised small lotteries, which was further liberalised in 1956 and 1976, but even then severely limited in the stakes, and the geographical scope that they could cover, so there could be no chance of the lottery organisers deceiving the bettors. There could be no big national lottery until the Government established one, however.

The United Kingdom's state-franchised lottery is known as the National Lottery, which was set up under government licence in 1993. Several games are run under this brand, including Lotto and Thunderball. As with other lotteries players choose a set of numbers, say 6 from 50, with six numbers then being drawn at random. Players win cash prizes depending on how many numbers they match.

The National Lottery launched a pan-European "super-lottery", called EuroMillions, in 2004. Currently this is available in nine countries.

The betting industry alone is reported to contribute £6 billion as of January 2010, 0.5% of GDP. Furthermore, it employs over 100,000 people and generates £700 Million in tax revenue.

According to the NHS Long Term Plan more than 400,000 people in England are problem gamblers and two million people are at risk. Health provision for problem gamblers is very limited, according to Bill Moyes, chair of the Gambling Commission. Simon Stevens, Chief Executive of NHS England, pointed out in 2019 that the industry spends £1.5 billion a year on marketing but under £10 million to picking up the health consequences.

Then why is gambling not illegal?

The answer:

The betting industry alone is reported to contribute £6 billion as of January 2010, 0.5% of GDP. Furthermore, it employs over 100,000 people and generates £700 Million in tax revenue.

To paraphrase the above answer: Industry and governmental cooperation in the perfect harmony of relentless capitalist greed.

The gambling industry refers to problem gamblers as VIP's [their best customers], according to, The Guardian, [or sometimes 'High Rollers'], the industry actively encourages VIP's to gamble more by providing them with free gifts. The industry recruits staff to target VIP's and get them to spend more, to contact VIP's who have not gambled for some time and get them to restart gambling, to identify less serious gamblers who could become VIP's and get them to gamble more. The gambling industry has now increased its strangle-hold on these poor people by introducing gambling on the internet. I am not being patronising when I use the term 'poor people'. Addicted gamblers, as do others under any form of addiction, often need social and possibly medical help to assist in releasing themselves from the life-draining grip of the gambling industry and its stupid, insincere messages on prime-time television by actors, who should hold a higher moral ground, to "gamble responsibly". That is the very last thing that the gambling industry wants.

Online gambling [or Internet gambling] is any kind of gambling conducted on the internet. This includes virtual poker, casinos, and sports betting. The first online gambling venue opened to the general public, was ticketing for the Liechtenstein International Lottery in October 1994. Today the market is worth around US $40 billion globally each year, according to various estimates.

So this sad threesome (ménage-a-trois) affliction continues in an ever increasing spiral of greed and stupidity: gambler – industry 'sales' – government revenue – gambler addiction[1] – industry 'sales' – government revenue – gambler addiction[2]......where will it end?

Summary

In summary the The Nicotine Delivery Business (Cigarettes and Tobacco), and the Alcohol and Gambling industries in UK are together achieving sales of around £43Bn or US $53Bn [US $ 53 @ £1 = $US1.23] with the Government receiving approximately £23.7Bn in tax revenue. Source: Wordometers.info

Interestingly the Gross Domestic Product of Tanzania in Africa is US $53.3Bn in 2018 with a population of 54M people producing this GDP which equates to 0.07% of the world's GDP!

So the UK Tobacco, alcohol and gambling consumer consumes approximately the equivalent of the wealth created by 54M people in Tanzania!!

Words fail me! Actually, I've recovered, words do not fail me [I am teetotal, non-smoking and never gamble].

What greater example can there be of the greed and stupidity of Mankind than the fact that the UK Tobacco, alcohol and gambling consumer consumes approximately the equivalent of the GDP (per annum 2018) wealth created by 54M people in Tanzania being GDP US $53.3Bn?

Answers please via the website: www.saveyourselfsaveusall.com

Chapter 5

The Internet's Silent Surreptitious Influencers

Yahoo Amazon Google Facebook

Only VIRTUE and TRUTH are of any importance in the Realm of Man

In the late 20th century the United States of America was the prime mover for global corporate capitalism. Its global corporations had the financial muscle and the resources to dominate the world markets. Corporations such as Exxon Mobil, IBM and General Electric (USA) dominated global markets. In 1985 the top ten corporations had revenues of up to US $90.8Bn with profits of US $5.5Bn to revenues of US $26.9Bn and profits of US $2.1Bn. See table below, source: Fortune 500.

Rank	Company	Revenues ($ millions)	Profits ($ millions)
1	Exxon Mobil	90,854.0	5,528.0
2	General Motors	83,889.9	4,516.5
3	Mobil	56,047.0	1,268.0
4	Ford Motor	52,366.4	2,906.8
5	Texaco	47,334.0	306.0
6	IBM	45,937.0	6,582.0
7	DuPont	35,915.0	1,431.0
8	AT&T	33,187.5	1,369.9
9	General Electric	27,947.0	2,280.0
10	Amoco	26,949.0	2,183.0

Interestingly four of the top ten: Exxon Mobil, Mobil, Texaco, and Amoco are oil producing and refining companies and DuPont, at that time, an oil derivative company producing plastics. Two are automobile manufacturers: General Motors and Ford, one is Information Technology: IBM another Telecommunications: AT&T, and finally a multifarious global conglomerate General Electric (USA). It is interesting, but not surprising to note that the market sectors of these top ten corporations accurately reflect the obsessions of capitalism and its consumers in the last quarter of the 20th century. Namely: the automobile, the means to propel the automobile – petroleum, a major component of the automobile industry – plastics [DuPont has more than one hundred products used throughout automobiles], corporate and consumer computing facilities, corporate and consumer telecommunications facilities, and finally General Electric GE (USA) a global multi-faceted conglomerate that covered 'everything': Plastics, Medical Systems, Housewares and Audio, Broadcasting, Jet Engines, Financial Services, Information Systems. This was around the time that GE could practically completely build and equip a consumer's entire home with all the consumer fixed and moving electro-mechanical products [fridges to radios etc.], the plastic window frames, the kitchen units, bathroom units, down to electrical sockets, plugs and light bulbs etc.

One immediately identifies that these corporations were primarily involved in the production of physical products and their support systems. The advent of the World-Wide-Web [WWW] or [The Web] changed the global business model from primarily manufacturing processes and products; to information, data processing and acquisition of the manufacturing products, and services and other information related services often using on-line transactions for purchase of these goods and services.

The World Wide Web, is an information system where documents and other web based resources identified by Uniform Resource Locators [URLs, such as *https://www.example.com*], which may be interlinked by hypertext, and are accessible over the Internet. The resources of the WWW are transferred via the Hypertext Transfer Protocol [HTTP] and may be accessed by users by a software application called a web browser and are published by a computer hardware and software application called a web server.

English scientist Tim Berners-Lee invented the World Wide Web in 1989. He wrote the first web browser in 1990 while employed at French Conseil Européen pour la Recherche Nucléaire CERN near Geneva, Switzerland. The browser was released outside CERN in 1991, first to other research institutions starting in January 1991 and then to the general public in August 1991. The World Wide Web has been central to the development of the Information age and is the primary tool billions of people use to interact on the Internet.

In its most basic form, the World Wide Web/Internet may be understood to be simply a number of computers [servers] located in various parts of the world, that are electronically connected to one another; and the stored data that these servers have access to, [possibly stored on another computer storage facility] may be retrieved, viewed and interacted with, by a user with a computer/ laptop/mobile phone connected to the WWW/Internet. In essence it is formed from the basis of corporate computing where terminals located anywhere in the world, within the corporation, could communicate with one another; but the WWW/Internet is far more sophisticated. In principle it is very simple; the implementation is far from simple.

The industry uses the term 'cloud computing' however there are no clouds used in computing and never likely to be, there is merely computer hardware, firmware, software and networks. The difference between cloud computing and corporate computing is that the computer hardware, firmware, and networks are owned by another corporation rather than the user. The software applications may be 'owned' by the user and the computing and network infrastructure is 'hired' from the 'cloud' provider.

With the advent of the World Wide Web/Internet causing the shift of the global business model from primarily manufacturing processes and products; to information, data processing and web based electronic communications, new players entered the market-place to seek the opportunities that this new and essentially unknown market offered. Some of the traditional manufacturing companies were founded over 100 years ago [GE 1892] and grew steadily over a long period of time.

These new players did not come from the previous long-term manufacturing base; they came from nowhere and grew to global significance in a very short time with structures based upon the WWW and the Internet.

Yahoo! - Founded 1994 (Twenty-six years old)

Yahoo! was founded in 1994 and was started at Stanford University, USA by Jerry Wang and David Filo, who were Electrical Engineering graduate students when they created a website named 'Jerry and David's Guide to the World Wide Web'. The Guide was a directory of other websites, organized in a hierarchy, as opposed to a searchable index of pages. In this way it was not a search engine as such. In April 1994, Jerry and David's Guide to the World Wide Web was renamed "Yahoo!". The word "YAHOO" is an acronym for 'Yet Another Hierarchically Organized Oracle' or 'Yet Another Hierarchical Officious Oracle'. Oracle is the database management company of California USA. The yahoo.com domain was created on January 18, 1995.

Yahoo! grew rapidly throughout the 1990s and diversified into a web portal, followed by numerous high-profile acquisitions.

A web portal is a specially designed website that brings information from diverse sources, like emails, online forums and search engines, together in a uniform way. Usually, each information source gets its dedicated area on the page for displaying information; often, the user can configure which ones to display.

The company's stock price skyrocketed during the dot-com bubble and closed at an all-time high of US $118.75 in 2000; however, after the dot-com bubble burst, it reached an all-time low of US$ 8.11 in 2001. Yahoo! formally rejected an acquisition bid from the Microsoft Corporation in 2008. In early 2012, the largest layoff in Yahoo!'s history was completed and 2,000 employees (14 percent of the workforce) lost their jobs.

While the yahoo.com domain was created in January 1995, by the end of 1995 Yahoo! had already received one million hits. Yang and Filo realized their website had massive business potential, and on March 2, 1995, Yahoo! was incorporated Yang and Filo sought out fund injection. In 1995, Yahoo! achieved two rounds of venture capital, raising approximately US $3 million. In 1996, Yahoo! had its initial public offering, raising US $33.8 million by selling 2.6 million shares at the opening bid of US $13 each.

The word "Yahoo" had previously been trademarked for barbecue sauce, knives and human propelled watercraft by Ebsco Industries. Therefore, in order to get control of the trademark, Yang and Filo added the exclamation mark to the name. However, the exclamation mark is often incorrectly omitted when referring to Yahoo!.

In the late 1990s, Yahoo!, MSN, Lycos, Excite, and other web portals were growing rapidly. Web portal providers rushed to acquire companies to expand their range of services, generally with the goal of increasing the time each user stays within the portal.

On March 8, 1997, Yahoo! acquired online communications company Four11. Four11's webmail service, Rocketmail, became Yahoo! Mail. Yahoo! also acquired ClassicGames.com and turned it into Yahoo! Games. Yahoo! then acquired direct marketing company Yoyodyne Entrtainment Inc. on October 12, 1998. In January 1999, Yahoo! acquired webhosting provider GeoCities. Another company Yahoo! took over was eGroups, which became Yahoo! Groups in June 2000. On March 8, 1998, Yahoo! launched

Yahoo! Pager, an instant messaging service that was renamed Yahoo! Messenger a year later.

When acquiring companies, Yahoo! often changed the relevant terms of service. For example, they claimed intellectual property rights for content on their servers, unlike the previous policies of the companies they acquired. As a result, many of the acquisitions were controversial and unpopular with users of the existing services.

Despite many 'ups and downs' in its twenty-six year history Yahoo! went from essentially US $0 (zero) to US $4.48Bn from start up in 1994 to its sale in 2017, a total of only 23 years of trading. It was also created by two graduates with little or no business experience. Jerry Yang was twenty-six years old at the time and still studying at Stanford University, USA and David Filo was twenty eight and only four years after completing his M.S. studies at Stanford University. Comparisons as this, may sometimes be misleading, but it is interesting to note the American conglomerate General Electric, founded in 1892, took almost ninety years to achieve a market value of US $12Bn in 1981 compared to Yahoo! purchase price of US$ 4.48Bn from start up in 1994 to its sale in 2017, a total of only 23 years of trading. This is an increase in US$ value, growth per unit time, of Yahoo! being circa 1.5 times faster than that of General Electric. I use General Electric in such comparisons because it was, in the last century before the World Wide Web and the Internet, the bastion of the global corporate world.

However, a most interesting statistic is the number of employees of both companies. General Electric in 1980 had 411,000 employees who generated the US $12Bn, whereas Yahoo! in 2016 had 8,500 employees who generated the US $4.48Bn sale price of the company.

In table form we have:

Employer	Year	Employees	Revenue (US$Bn)	Time to achieve Revenue (Years)
General Electric	1980	411,000	12	90
Yahoo!	2016	8,500	4.48	23

If the number of employees is brought into the equation, then the US$ value, growth per unit time, of Yahoo! being 1.5 times that of General Electric; becomes the US$ value, growth per unit time per employee becomes 72.5 times that of General Electric!

There are obviously many parameters that are not included in this simple analysis, however it is certainly indicative of the larger and more quickly attained business opportunities and growth, at less cost and less business experience, available to entrepreneurs and business people in the post-industrial global digital age of the world-wide-web and Internet.

The hypothesis being presented here, is that the World Wide Web and the Internet offered 'economies of scale', access to global markets, fast corporate growth, global information services and many other digital facilities, at lower business expertise and at a much lower 'unit' cost, that were total anathema and completely unheard of in the old 'smoke-stack' manufacturing and production industries committed to supplying physical products with complex design, manufacturing, supply-chains and distribution mechanisms and procedures.

In the Yahoo! case, even more alarming is that the CEO's of General Electric and other traditional manufacturing corporations are typically very mature men at the peak of the careers and life experiences typically 45 to 55 years of age; whereas the founders of Yahoo! was created by two graduates with little or no business experience. Jerry Yang was twenty-six years old at the time and still studying at Stanford University, USA and David Filo was twenty eight and only four years after completing his M.S. studies at Stanford. The potential danger of such relatively youthful and inexperienced young men having such a large global corporate business and its inherent responsibilities is clear. The second danger is the fact that such a large global corporate business as Yahoo! was founded on such a simple concept as an electronic global directory of websites. The acquisition of such wealth from such a simple concept in such a relatively short space of time with so small human resources may be said to be fast, easy money. Fast, easy money is, in itself, potentially dangerous. The third danger is what is done with the fast, easy money when developing the business into potentially more complex and more socially responsible enterprises. Do these young CEO's have the moral maturity for such decisions?

In this post-industrial, global, digital revolution entrepreneurs and business people saw a wealth of global business opportunities that outstripped perhaps to an order of magnitude or more greater than the opportunities seen in the Industrial Revolution that was in full flow in 1892 when General Electric USA was founded.

Amazon - Founded 1994 (Twenty-six years old)

Jeff Bezos, founder of Amazon was born in 1964 and attended Princeton University USA graduating in 1986 with a degree in electrical engineering and computer science. He worked on Wall Street in a variety of related fields from 1986 to early 1994.

In the same year as Yahoo! was founded Jeff Bezos, founded Amazon as a result of what Bezos called his "regret minimization framework", which described his efforts to fend off any regrets for not participating sooner in the Internet Business Boom during that time. In 1994, Bezos left his employment as vice-president of D. E. Shaw & Co., a Wall Street firm, and moved to Seattle, Washington, where he began to work on a business plan for what would become Amazon.com.

On July 5, 1994, Bezos initially incorporated the company in Washington State with the name Cadabra, Inc. perhaps from the term <u>Abra</u>Cadabra which is an incantation used as a magic word in stage magic tricks, and historically was believed to have healing powers when inscribed on an amulet. He later changed the name to Amazon.com, Inc. a few months later, after a lawyer misheard its original name as "cadaver". In its early days, the company was operated out of the garage of Bezos's house on Northeast 28th Street in Bellevue Washingtion. In September 1994, Bezos purchased the domain name relentless.com and briefly considered naming his online store Relentless, but friends told him the name sounded a bit sinister. The domain is still owned by Bezos and still redirects to the retailer Amazon.com.

Jeff Bezos was thirty years of age when he founded Amazon and only eight years out of his graduation from Princeton University. As the founder, CEO, and president of Amazon, he became the first centi-billionaire [a person who possesses a net worth of US $100 billion or higher] on the *Forbes* wealth index, Bezos has been the world's richest person since 2017 and was named the "richest man in modern history" after his net worth increased to US $150 billion in July 2018. In September 2018, *Forbes* described him as *"far richer than anyone else on the planet"* as he added US $1.8 billion to his net worth when Amazon became the second company in history to reach a market capitalization of US $1 trillion.

After reading a report about the future of the Internet that projected annual web commerce growth at 2,300%, Bezos created a list of 20 products that could be marketed online. He narrowed the list to what he felt were the five most promising products, which included: compact discs, computer hardware, computer software, videos, and books. Bezos finally decided that his new business would sell books online, because of the large worldwide demand for literature, the low unit price for books, and the huge number of titles available in print. Amazon was founded in the garage of Bezos' rented home in Bellevue, Washington. Bezos' parents invested almost US $250,000 in the start-up.

In July 1995, the company began service as an online bookstore. The first book sold on Amazon.com was Douglas Hofstadter's *'Fluid Concepts and Creative Analogies: Computer Models of the Fundamental Mechanisms of Thought'*. In the first few months of business, Amazon sold to all 50 states and over 45 countries. Within two months, Amazon's sales were up to US $20,000/week. In October 1995, the company announced itself to the public. In 1996, it was reincorporated in Delaware. Amazon issued its initial public offering of stock on May 15, 1997, at US $18 per share, raising US $54M trading under the NASDAQ stock exchange symbol AMZN.

Barnes & Noble booksellers sued Amazon on May 12, 1997, alleging that Amazon's claim to be "the world's largest bookstore" was false because it "...isn't a bookstore at all. It's a book broker." The suit was later settled out of court and Amazon continued to make the same claim. Walmart sued Amazon on October 16, 1998, alleging that Amazon had stolen Walmart's trade secrets by hiring former Walmart executives. Although this suit was also settled out of court, it caused Amazon to implement internal restrictions and the reassignment of the former Walmart executives.

In June 2017, Amazon announced that it would acquire Whole Foods, a high-end supermarket chain with over 400 stores, for US $13.4 billion. The acquisition was seen by media experts as a move to strengthen its physical holdings and challenge Walmart's supremacy as a brick and mortar retailer. This sentiment was heightened by the fact that the announcement coincided with Walmart's purchase of men's apparel company Bonobos. On August 23, 2017, Whole Foods shareholders, as well as the Federal Trade Commission, approved the deal.

In September 2017, Amazon announced plans to locate a second headquarters in a metropolitan area with at least a million residents. Cities needed to submit their presentations by October 19, 2017 for the project called HQ2. The US $5 billion second headquarters, starting with 500,000 square feet and eventually expanding to as much as 8 million square feet, may have as many as 50,000 employees. At the end of 2017, Amazon had over 566,000 employees worldwide.

Amazon expanded its portfolio from book sales to search and advertising technology, membership free two-day shopping, an application programming interface, cloud computing, data storage services, a grocery service, on-line music store, Amazon kindle [electronic books], physical delivery lockers and other services.

The situation at Amazon is comparable to that at Yahoo!. In the Amazon case it was a single person of only 30 years of age, only eight years out of University, again building a huge global corporation, initially on essentially a simple concept of purchasing on-line rather than purchasing by physically visiting retail premises. A concept that came about singularly from the World Wide Web and the Internet. In the Amazon case, the accumulation of wealth by Jeff Bezos in only twenty three years from founding Amazon in 1994 to 2017 when he became the richest person in the world at forty three years of age is truly staggering. Jeff Bezos net worth is estimated at US $131Bn in 2019. In comparison, a retailer born in 1936 in Europe started his in-store retail chain business in 1994 and now has a net worth of say US $65 Bn but was fifty-eight when he started his retail chain business and is now eighty four. It presumably took him twenty-six years of business experience to build up the expertise required to launch a global manufacturing and retail business.

In the case of Amazon's start-up model nothing is researched, designed, developed or manufactured; it is little more than a warehouse of somebody else's hard work and product.

These differences between the business global growth and personal wealth acquisition of the new World Wide Web and Internet based businesses compared to the traditional manufacturing and retail methodologies are almost beyond belief. As with Yahoo! the potential danger of such a relatively youthful and inexperienced young man as the Founder of Amazon having such a large global corporate business and its inherent responsibilities is clear.

The acquisition of such wealth from such a simple concept in such a relatively short space of time may be said to be fast, easy money. Fast, easy money is, in itself, potentially dangerous. Another danger is what is done with the fast, easy money when developing the business into potentially more complex and more socially responsible enterprises. Do these young CEO's and Presidents at Yahoo! and Amazon have the moral maturity for such decisions?

Google - Founded 1998 (Twenty-two years old)

Google LLC is an American multinational technology company that specializes in Internet-related services and products, which include online advertising technologies, a search engine, cloud computing, software and hardware.

Google was founded in September 1998 by Larry Page and Sergey Brin while they were Ph.D. students at Stanford University USA. They were both twenty five years of age at the time. Together they own about 14 percent of its shares and control 56 percent of the stockholder voting power through supervoting stock. They incorporated Google as a California privately held company on September 4, 1998, in California. Google was then reincorporated in Delaware on October 22, 2002. An initial public offering (IPO) took place on August 19, 2004, and Google moved to its headquarters in Mountain View, California, nicknamed the Googleplex. In August 2015, Google announced plans to reorganize its various interests as a conglomerate called Alphabet Inc. Google is Alphabet's leading subsidiary and will continue to be the umbrella company for Alphabet's Internet interests.

After enrolling on a computer science PhD program at Stanford University, Larry Page was in search of a dissertation theme and considered exploring the mathematical properties of the World Wide Web, understanding its link structure as a huge graph. Page focused on the problem of finding out which web pages linked to a given page, considering the number and nature of such backlinks as valuable information for that page. The role of citations in academic publishing would also become pertinent for the research. Sergey Brin, his fellow Stanford PhD student, would soon join Page's research project, nicknamed 'BackRub'. Together, the pair authored a research paper titled 'The Anatomy of a Large-Scale Hypertextual Web Search Engine', which became one of the most downloaded scientific documents in the history of the Internet at the time.

To convert the backlink data gathered by BackRub's web crawler into a measure of importance for a given web page, Brin and Page developed the PageRank algorithm, and realized that it could be used to build a search engine far superior to existing ones. The algorithm relied on a new technology that analyzed the relevance of the backlinks that connected one web page to another.

Combining their ideas, the pair began utilizing Page's dormitory room as a machine laboratory, and extracted spare parts from inexpensive computers to create a device that they used to connect the now nascent search engine with Stanford's broadband campus network. After filling Page's room with equipment, they then converted Brin's dorm room into an office and programming centre, where they tested their new search engine designs on the Web. The rapid growth of their project caused Stanford's computing infrastructure to experience problems.

The company's rapid growth since incorporation has triggered a chain of products, acquisitions, and partnerships beyond Google's core product the search engine (Google Search). It offers services designed for work and productivity (Google Docs, Google Sheets and Google Slides), email (Gmail), scheduling and time management (Google Calender), cloud storage (Google Drive), instant messaging and video chat (Duo, Hangouts), language translation (Google Translate), mapping and navigation (Google Maps, Waze, Google Earth, Street View), video sharing (YouTube), note-taking (Google Keep), and photo organizing and editing (Google Photos). The company leads the development of the Android mobile (telephone) operating system, the Google Chrome web browser, and Chrome OS, a lightweight operating system based on the Chrome browser. Google has moved increasingly into hardware; from 2010 to 2015, it partnered with major electronics manufacturers in the production of its Nexus devices.

Alphabet Inc. a multinational conglomerate was created through a restructuring of Google in 2015, and became the parent company of Google and several former Google subsidiaries. The two founders of Google assumed executive roles in the new company, with Larry Page serving as CEO and Sergey Brin as president. It released multiple hardware products in October 2016, including the Google Pixel smartphone, Google Home smart speaker, Google wifi mesh wireless router, and Google Daydream virtual reality headset. Google has also experimented with becoming an Internet carrier (Google Fiber, Google Fi, and Google Station).

Google.com is the most visited website in the world. Several other Google services also figure in the top 100 most visited websites, including YouTube and Blogger. Google was the most valuable brand in the world as of 2017, but has received significant criticism involving issues such as privacy concerns as tax avoidance, antitrust, censorship, and search neutrality.

Larry Page and Sergey Brin have net worth's of US $57Bn and US $55.5Bn respectively both at fifty six years of age. If we then include Jeff Bezos at fifty five years old with US $131Bn between three people we have a net worth of 243.5Bn US $ which compares to the Gross Domestic Product of Rumania being 243.698 US $ Bn, the 46th largest economy in the world [Source: International Monetary Fund estimates for 2019] with a population of almost 20 Million people [2019].

This financial fact above is almost beyond immediate comprehension.

Never, in the History of Human Endeavour, has so much wealth been owned by so few, in such a short space of time, by the creation of so little. Did Winston Churchill say that?

In reality Amazon started as little more than a book 'warehouse' and Google started as little more than a piece of software that searched the contents of server databases located throughout the world. An employee of Google, in 2015, estimated the lines of software code for the Google Search Engine software at a maximum of 300,000 lines depending on how well the code was written [Source: Quora.com]. In my estimate, perhaps a maximum of .5M lines of code.

The first major issue with Google is that for the most part it does not create anything of added value worth itself. At best it allows one to find information faster than looking the information up in text references in libraries and elsewhere. There are other Internet search engines available that do not litter one's life and consciousness with advertisements.

Its revenue is primarily created through advertising. The main way Google generates its revenue is through a pair of advertising services called Ads and AdSense. With Ads, advertisers submit ads to Google that include a list of keywords relating to a product, service or business. When a Google user searches the Web using one or more of those keywords, the advertisement appears on the Search Engine Results Page (SERP) in a sidebar. The advertiser pays Google every time a user clicks on the advertisement and is directed toward the advertiser's site.

AdSense is similar, except that instead of displaying advertisements on a Google SERP, a webmaster can choose to integrate advertisements onto a site. Google's spiders crawl the site and analyse the content. Then, Google selects advertisements that contain keywords relevant to the webmaster's site. Webmasters can customize the type and location of the advertisements that Google provides. Every time someone clicks on an advertisement on the site, the site receives a portion of the advertisement revenue [and Google receives the rest].

The second major issue with Google is that its revenue is created by advertising. In 2019 it was reported that Alphabet/Google's revenue was US $161Bn with advertising accounting for US $ 135Bn i.e. 84% of revenue. Google, in terms of its revenue generating business profile, is little more than a globalised, personal, on-screen advertising board. The advertising of products and services for which the demand is artificially created and continually stimulated and none of these products and services are manufactured or provided by Google itself. Refer to Chapter 4 – 'The Failure of Capitalism' section entitled 'The False Market and Two Myths of Capitalism'.

Google, YouTube, Facebook and Global Public Interest Information Control

The third major issue, and a very important one, is that of the disruption of global democratic information flow in terms of Freedom of Information Act 2000 UK, Freedom of Information Act 1967 USA etc. This also applies to Facebook below.

Google owns YouTube, Facebook owns Facebook and Facebook also own the following five companies: **Instagram**: Photo and video-sharing app acquired 2012, **WhatsApp**: Mobile messenger service acquired 2014, **Oculus**: Virtual reality technology company acquired 2014, **Onavo**: Mobile web analytics acquired 2013, **Beluga**: Messaging service 2011.

As explained earlier, capitalism follows its false, perpetual, ever-increasing growth paradigm to the Abyss, either by internal growth and the stifling wherever possible of the competition or by synergistic acquisition growth of other companies or by both methodologies. In the second methodology, the 'successful' capitalist buys up, typically smaller companies where their added value when integrated into the 'fat mama' mother company results in the sum total of the parts being greater than the separate none-integrated parts in terms of market share and market business efficiency.

This is bad enough with capitalist companies selling relatively harmless things such as bicycle repair outfits but when global capitalist companies are controlling global, essentially **'in the public interest' information** we have a very significant and very important problem.

This is best explained with a simple personal example:

Covid-19 Crisis and Internet/Social Media Global Information Control

Whilst writing this book, I have been observing the Covid-19 virus and its effect upon the world. It was difficult not to!

Because of my deep concern for the survival of our species and the importance of the minimising of unnecessary suffering [of which there is far too much!], hence the writing of this book, I took the opportunity of writing an open letter to Boris Johnson, Prime Minister UK, Members of his Cabinet and the major press organisations in the UK.

On 19th May 2020 I tried to hand deliver the letter(s) to 10 Downing Street, and also to the Cabinet Office on Whitehall but was instructed to use a post box and post the letters by Royal Mail. I was surprised by this because, in the past, I have posted letters by hand to Her Majesty Queen Elizabeth II. However, the posted letter(s) brought to the attention Mr Johnson and his senior cabinet, a Professor of Epidemiology's view of the Covid-19 crisis and how it should best be dealt with. This was done by way of an interview posted on the YouTube video channel (owned by Google). This interview had been available for a few weeks.

On my return to my office in the evening of 19th May 2020 I wanted to watch the interview again but much to my surprise I found that it was deleted! I was dumbstruck!

Consequently, I wrote another Royal Mail letter confidentially to Boris Johnson and his senior cabinet on 21st May 2020 – two days later, explaining that the interview had unfortunately been deleted and as an alternative, I provided the Professor of Epidemiology's website URL, his postal address and his 'Linkedin' account which contained the deleted interview and other interviews on the Covid-19 crisis. In the absence of Prof. Ferguson's expertise, having so abruptly resigned, I trust that he contacted him.

It is exceedingly morally repugnant to me, that in an interview with a world leading expert with circa 30 years of experience in a most important field of study relating to the biggest global human crisis since WWI providing Mission Critical Information, that a member of the public should be prevented from relaying the content of that interview to the highest elected person, Prime Minister UK, of the 6th largest GDP country in the world, a country with one of the most democratic institutions in the world and one of the finest judiciaries, and as consequence the UK Prime Minister should be prevented from viewing this important interview by a privately owned company run by a handful of people with its headquarters on the other side of the world!

I have since learnt that YouTube have deleted many such Covid-19 crisis interviews with professional specialists.

WHY?

THIS MUST CHANGE!

Facebook - Founded 2004 (Sixteen years old)

Facebook is an American online social media and social networking service based in California USA and a flagship service of the namesake company Facebook Inc. It was founded in 2004 by Mark Zuckerberg [born 1984] along with fellow Harvard College students and roommates Eduardo Saverin [born 1982], Andrew McCollum [born 1983], Dustin Moskovitz [born 1984] and Chris Hughes [born 1983].

The founders initially limited Facebook membership to Harvard students. Membership was expanded to Ivy League universities, MIT, and higher education institutions in the Boston area, then various other universities, and lastly high school students. Since 2006, anyone who claims to be at least 13 years old has been allowed to become a registered user of Facebook, though this may vary depending on local laws. The name comes from the face book directories often given to American university students.

The Facebook service can be accessed from devices with Internet connectivity, such as personal computers, tablets [this author knew on their introduction, that tablets were little more than a capitalist marketing gimmick now with a global unit sale reduction of 41% since a peak in 2014, – data source stastica.com] and smartphones. After registering, users can create profile revealing information about themselves. They can post text, photos and multimedia which are shared with any other users that have agreed to be their "friend", or, with a different privacy setting, with any reader. Users can also use various embedded apps, join common-interest groups, buy and sell items or services on Marketplace, and receive notifications of their Facebook friends' activities and activities of Facebook pages they follow. Facebook with almost 2.5 billion monthly active users as of the fourth quarter of 2019, it is the biggest social network worldwide. In the third quarter of 2012, the number of active Facebook users surpassed one billion, making it the first social network ever to do so.

Facebook with 2.5 billion active users per month represents 33% of the global population of 7.7 billion in 2019. One third of the world's population was busily cretinising itself.

Facebook has been subject to extensive media coverage and many controversies. Primarily perhaps because Facebook's business model does not require Facebook to have any liability whatsoever for its social media application content.

These media coverage controversies often involved user privacy (as with the Cambridge Analytica data scandal), political manipulation (as with the 2016 US Elections), psychological effects such as addiction and low self-esteem and content that some users find objectionable, including fake news, conspiracy theories, and copyright infringement. Commentators have accused Facebook of helping to spread false information and fake news. In 2017, Facebook partnered with fact checkers from the Poynter Institute's International Fact-Checking Network to identify and mark false content, though most advertisements from political candidates are exempt from this program. Critics of the program accuse Facebook of not doing enough to remove false information from its website. Facebook was the most downloaded mobile application [App] of the 2010s globally.

In October 2008, Facebook announced that its international headquarters would locate in Dublin, Ireland. In September 2009, Facebook said that it had achieved positive cash flow for the first time. A January 2009 Compete.com study ranked Facebook the most used social networking service by worldwide monthly active users.

The company announced 500 million users in July 2010. Half of the site's membership used Facebook daily, for an average of 34 minutes, while 150 million users accessed the site from mobile devices. A company representative called the milestone a "quiet revolution." In November 2010, based on SecondMarket Inc. [an exchange for privately held companies' shares], Facebook's value was US $41 billion. The company had slightly surpassed eBay to become the third largest American web company after Google and Amazon.com.

The company celebrated its 10th anniversary during the week of February 3, 2014. In January 2014, over one billion users connected via a mobile device. As of June, mobile accounted for 62% of advertising revenue, an increase of 21% from the previous year. By September 2014 Facebook's market capitalization had exceeded US $200 billion, in just ten years!

Tim Kendall former Facebook Executive, told US Congress that the company intentionally made its product as **addictive** as cigarettes. Source: CBS (USA) News 2020

"Tobacco companies initially just sought to make nicotine more potent. But eventually that wasn't enough to grow the business as fast as they wanted. And so they added sugar and menthol to cigarettes so you could hold the smoke in your lungs for longer periods, At Facebook, we added status updates, photo tagging, and likes." Kendall stated to Congress.

He continued, "So what's happened is you basically have an advertising business model [85% of business generated by advertisements] that's combined with just ever-growing, ever-more intelligent technology, and that combination is really potent."

He said further, "What it's leading to is a product that's just fundamentally addictive for people, and it's causing all kinds of mental health issues, and I think it's eroding aspects of society."

Silent, surreptitious capitalism at its worst?

In 2020 Facebook Inc had a market capitalization estimated at US $535Bn. The primary founders of Facebook, have personal net worth of approximately: Mark Zuckerberg US $ 70.3 Bn, Eduardo Saverin US $11.3Bn, Dustin Moskovitz US $12Bn; a total of US $93.6 Bn between three people all in their mid-late thirties.

In the Internet companies described above, Yahoo!, Amazon, Google, Facebook, we see vast corporate wealth, and enormous personal wealth both created by relatively young inexperienced people in a very short timeframe completely unprecedented in pre-Internet industrial capitalism. Again, as with Google, the primary revenue stream of Facebook is through advertising. In the case of Facebook, approximately 85% of the business revenue is from advertising, which is almost identical to the estimate for Google of 84%. The revenue for the advertising of products and services for which the demand is artificially created and sustained. The potential danger of such relatively youthful and inexperienced young men having such a large global corporate business and its inherent responsibilities is clear. The second danger is the fact that such a large global corporate businesses were all founded on relatively simple concepts, such as an electronic global directory of websites – Yahoo!, an on-line warehouse - Amazon, a search engine software package - Google, internet social networking - Facebook. These internet businesses are far simpler in their concept, structure and implementation than the industrial capitalist structures of say General Motors USA or General Electric USA. The design, production, supply chain of a new automotive every four to six years with the bulk of the product not manufactured by the primary producer but by a very complex, often international, supply chain or the management of such a huge multifarious con-glomerate as General Electric with products as diverse as aircraft engines, medical systems, engineering polymers, house and audio business products, broadcasting services etc. are far more complex businesses to run than the internet businesses whose framework and spine – the World Wide Web/Internet were already existent. Yahoo!, Amazon, Google, Facebook merely had to use the pre-existing computer hardware, operating systems and global network communications framework-spine expediently by developing the applications that ran on this framework-spine.

In the post-industrial, global World Wide Web-Internet world, entrepreneurs and business people saw a wealth of global business opportunities that outstripped perhaps to an order of magnitude or more greater than the opportunities seen in the Industrial Revolution that was in full flow in 1892 when General Electric was founded.

The combined personal net worth of the eight major founders of the Internet companies Yahoo!, Amazon, Google and Facebook is approximately US $342Bn. US $342Bn is larger than the Gross Domestic Product GDP of Egypt being US $331Bn, the forty second largest economy in the world and a country with a population of 102M. Source: International Monetary Fund estimates for 2019.

The US $342Bn wealth of the eight major founders listed above compares very interestingly to the wealth of the entire world's bottom 50% of households. The global bottom 50% household wealth is approximately US $1.67 trillion [as of Q3 2019]. Therefore Yahoo!, Amazon, Google and Facebook founders, **all eight of them,** have approximately one fifth of the wealth of the bottom 50% households of the entire world.

There is a danger with such vast corporate and personal wealth in the hands of so few people who are relatively young and inexperienced in terms of global multifarious business and ethical and moral judgment. Will these youngsters have the ethical and moral backbones to make the far-reaching and soul-searching judgments required for the simultaneous introduction of such dangerous, complex, multifarious and far-reaching products: 5G, Quantum Computing, Robotics and IA, Internet of Things, Big Data? So far, I see no sign of it. My advice to my readers – Duck!

The acquisition of such wealth from such essentially simple concepts in such a relatively short space of time with often relatively small human resources may be said to be fast, easy money. Fast, easy money is, in itself, potentially dangerous. The third danger is what is done with the fast, easy money and will its deployment be ethical and moral when developing the business into potentially more complex and more socially responsible enterprises such as: 5G, Quantum Computing, Robotics and IA, Internet of Things, Big Data?

The fourth danger, and this is the most important and far-reaching danger, is that these companies have such huge global reach with divisions posted in tax heavens all over the world that they in essence, operate in a realm of being, beyond the immediate legislative and taxation reach of countries, the European Union and even perhaps continents. Is it apparent that, more than any other societal group, entrepreneurs and their ilk are more reluctant than any other group to pay their lawfully required taxes? Avarice perhaps?

Do these young, get rich quick, CEO's have the moral maturity to take the business decisions that they are taking now and those that they will be taking in the very unknown future?

Chapter 6

Climate Change, Potential Tragedy of Emerging Technologies

The Forces of Implosion

To Live This Life without Bitterness is Success,
To Sleep at Night is Happiness.

The Forces of Implosion:

6.1 CLIMATE CHANGE, 6.2 5G, 6.3 INTERNET OF THINGS,
6.4 ROBOTICS AND ARTIFICIAL INTELLIGENCE 'AI',
6.5 QUANTUM COMPUTING, 6.6 BIO-TECHNOLOGY,
6.7 BLOCKCHAIN, 6.8 NANO-TECHNOLOGY, 6.9 BIG DATA

Chapter 6 Sections 6.2 – 6.8 primary data source – World Economic Forum 2020 – With Thanks to WEF

6.1 Climate Change (including Global Warming)

World hits record high for heat-trapping carbon dioxide in air.

Chief greenhouse gas averaged record levels in May [2020] *despite reduced emissions amid coronavirus* [Covid-19] *pandemic.*

The world has hit another record high for heat-trapping carbon dioxide in the atmosphere, despite reduced emissions because of the coronavirus pandemic.

Measurements of CO_2, the chief greenhouse gas, averaged 417.1 parts per million at Mauna Loa, Hawaii, for the month of May, when carbon levels in the air peak. That's 2.4 parts per million higher than a year ago.

Source: National Oceanic and Atmospheric Administration (NOAA) – 4th June 2020

Note: No change there then.

'Climate Change' is the term generally used to describe the phenomenon of global climate change which has been accelerated unnaturally because of mankind's enormous, disparate, all-encompassing global industrial activities and their derivatives. The most significant result of these global industrial activities and their derivatives within the context of 'climate change', is for the Earth's surface mean temperature to be continually changing and predominately rising at a rate higher than that that would occur by natural, non-human inflicted causes only. Hence the term 'Global Warming' has taken preference over the more generic term 'Climate Change'.

This phenomenon of 'Global Warming', the mean temperature rise of the Earth's climate system, has been demonstrated by direct temperature measurements and by measurements of various effects of the warming. It is a major aspect of climate change which, in addition to rising global surface temperatures, also includes its effects, such as changes in rainfall or precipitation. While, it is understood that there have been prehistoric periods of global warming, observed changes since the mid-20th century have been unprecedented in rate and scale. The increase in global surface temperature from 1880 to 2020 has been observed to be approximately 1.2 deg. Celsius, with natural 'drivers' contributing 0.1 deg. Celsius, with the 'human drivers' contributing approximately 0.9 deg. Celsius, with the remaining 0.2 deg. Celsius increase caused by other, unspecified factors. **The 'human drivers' therefore represent the great majority of the global warming causes at 75% of the total.**

The primary, root cause of global warming may therefore be laid at the door of industrial capitalism and the preposterous concept of continual, unrestrained perpetual global economic growth. The inherent dangers and foolishness of this concept have been explained in Chapter 4 above.

This data is from the observed temperature from NASA vs the 1850–1900 average used by the Intergovernmental Panel on Climate Change (IPCC) as a pre-industrial baseline. The primary driver for increased global temperatures in the industrial era is human activity, with natural forces adding variability.

The IPCC concluded that, *"human influence on climate has been the dominant cause of observed warming since the mid-20th century"*. These findings have been recognized by the national science academies of major nations and are not disputed by any scientific body today of national or international standing.

[My emboldening]

In a domestic garden 'greenhouse', heat and light from the sun passes through the glass roof and sides of the greenhouse to heat the plants and ground inside. Objects heated by sunlight heat emit infrared radiation. The heated objects' emitted infrared radiation is absorbed or reflected by the glass roof and sides, thus trapping the thermal energy in the greenhouse instead of letting it escape. This helps to keep the building warm and thus the plants are kept warm which encourages their growth. In the global context, the term 'greenhouse gases' has come into use because the 'greenhouse effect' of global temperature rise has come about primarily because of two gases, where these gases in the earth's upper atmosphere have the same effect as the glass of a greenhouse.

The largest human influence on global temperature rises has been the emission of these greenhouse gases, with over 90% of the impact from carbon monoxide and methane [natural gas].

Environmental carbon monoxide is produced by incomplete combustion process from any carbon containing fuel. A great amount of carbon monoxide [CO] is released into the atmosphere by burning fossil fuels, [petroleum, coal, natural gas] i.e. in particular the carbon monoxide of vehicle exhaust emission.

Fossil fuel burning is the principal source of these gases, with agricultural emissions and deforestation also playing significant roles. Climate sensitivity to these gases is impacted by additional, potentially environmentally detrimental phenomena such as loss of snow cover, increased water vapour, and melting permafrost. 'Permafrost' being a thick subsurface layer of soil that remains below freezing point throughout the year, occurring chiefly in Polar Regions.

Energy flows between space, the atmosphere, and Earth's surface. Current greenhouse gas levels are causing a radiation emission imbalance of about 0.9 W/m^2 [Watts/metre^2]

Land surfaces are heating faster than the ocean surface, leading to heat waves, wildfires, and the expansion of deserts. Increasing atmospheric energy and rates of evaporation are causing more intense storms and weather extremes, damaging infrastructure and agriculture. Surface temperature increases are greatest in the Arctic, which have contributed to the retreat of glaciers, permafrost and sea ice. Environmental impacts include the extinction or relocation of many species as their ecosystems change, most immediately in coral reefs, mountains and the Arctic. Surface temperatures would stabilize and decline a little if emissions were cut off, but other impacts will continue for centuries, including rising sea levels from melting ice sheets, rising ocean temperatures, and ocean acidification [increase in acid content/acidity] from elevated levels of carbon dioxide.

The seriousness of this capitalist induced global warming pandemic is so great, that global organisations have now been formed to fight the results of their own stupidity.

Mitigation efforts to address global warming include the development and deployment of low carbon energy technologies, policies to reduce fossil fuel emissions, reforestation, forest preservation, as well as the development of potential climate engineering technologies. This is not a 'linear' analogy but 'Climate engineering technologies' sounds very ominous, rather like if Victor Frankenstein (per Mary Shelley 1797-1851) were to commence a project of designing and creating a new Monster to kill off Mary Shelley's first Monster creation. How can we be certain that this second Monster, which must by definition be more aggressive than the first Monster; otherwise it could not kill it off, will not cause as great or a greater pandemic than the current global warming crisis that it will strive to correct? Answer; we will most probably not be certain of this.

Societies and governments are also working to adapt to current and future global warming impacts, including improved coastline protection, better disaster management, and the development of more resistant crops. All no doubt at significant cost to the taxpayer, but not directly to the capitalist who caused it.

Countries work together on climate change under the umbrella of the United Nations Framework Convention on Climate Change (UNFCCC) which has near-universal membership. The goal of the convention is to *"prevent dangerous anthropogenic interference with the climate system"*.

"Near-universal membership" is a novel concept for only one particular planet. However, the situation and intention is clear. After over one hundred years of the abuse of the planet by the advocates of the false goals and false beliefs of capitalism; the capitalist practitioners, belatedly recognising the errors of their ways, are setting about methods contradictory to the core beliefs in capitalism, in order to correct capitalism's and their, catastrophic errors.

Catastrophic errors so profound and far-reaching, that without urgent effective dramatic radical changes, brought about immediately on a concerted and globally coordinated program to correct these errors, that will, in themselves, cause a significant detriment and frustration on the western worlds need to satisfy its greed, that one dreads to think what life would be like, in the fourth quarter of this century for our grandchildren.

The Intergovernmental Panel on Climate Change IPCC has stressed the need to keep global warming below 1.5 °C (2.7 °F) compared to pre-industrial levels **in order to avoid some irreversible impacts.**

With current policies and pledges, global warming by the end of the century [2100 - Eighty years off!] is expected to reach about 2.8 °C (5.0 °F). At the current greenhouse gas (GHG) emission rate, the emissions budget for staying below 1.5 °C (2.7 °F) would be exhausted by 2028.

2028 is only eight years away! There are another 72 years to go to 2100 after 2028! That won't work! We will all be cremated maggots long before the end of the century.

Multiple independently produced instrumental datasets confirm that the 2009–2018 decade was 0.93 ± 0.07 °C (1.67 ± 0.13 °F) warmer than the pre-industrial baseline of 1850–1900.

Currently, surface temperatures are rising by about 0.2 °C (0.36 °F) per decade.

Note: If this continues then we hit the 1.5 °C limit increase in 75 years i.e. 2095. **Therefore irreversibility starts in 2095 and then it is only a matter of time before its lights out!** Why should I worry, why should I care? I won't be here! Well, for better or worse, I do care. That is the reason for writing this book.

Since 1950, the number of cold days and nights has decreased, and the number of warm days and nights has increased. Historical patterns of warming and cooling, like the Medieval Climate Anomaly and the Little Ice Age, were not as synchronous as current warming, but may have reached temperatures as high as those of the late-20th century in a limited set of regions. The observed recent rise in temperature and CO2 concentrations have been so rapid that even abrupt geophysical events that ostensibly took place in Earth's history do not approach current rates.

Climate proxy records show that natural variations offset the early effects of the Industrial Revolution so there was little net warming between the 18th century and the mid-19th century, when thermometer records began to provide global coverage. The Intergovernmental Panel on Climate Change (IPCC) has adopted the baseline reference period 1850–1900 as an approximation of pre-industrial global mean surface temperature.

The warming evident in the instrumental temperature record is consistent with a wide range of observations, documented by many independent scientific groups. Although the most common measure of global warming is the increase in the near-surface atmospheric temperature, over 90% of the additional energy in the climate system over the last 50 years has been stored in the ocean, warming it. The remainder of the additional energy has melted ice and warmed the continents and the atmosphere. The ocean heat uptake drives thermal expansion which has contributed to observed sea level rise. Further indicators of climate change include an increase in the frequency and intensity of heavy precipitation, melting of snow and land ice and increased atmospheric humidity. Flora, fauna and wildlife also portray behaviour consistent with warming, such as the earlier timing of spring events, such as the flowering of plants and the early nesting of birds.

By itself, the climate system experiences various cycles which can last for years [such as the El Nino-Southern Oscillation] or decades or centuries. Other changes are caused by an imbalance of energy at the top of the atmosphere: 'external forcings'. These 'forcings' are "external" to the climate system, but not always external to the Earth. Examples of external forcings include changes in the composition of the atmosphere [e.g. increased concentrations of greenhouse gases], solar luminosity, volcanic eruptions, and variations in the Earth's orbit around the Sun.

Attribution of climate change is the effort to scientifically show which mechanisms are responsible for observed changes in Earth's climate. First, known internal climate variability and natural external forcings need to be ruled out. Therefore, a key approach is to use computer modelling of the climate system to determine unique "fingerprints" for all potential causes. By comparing these fingerprints with observed patterns and evolution of climate change, and the observed history of the forcings, the causes of the observed changes can be determined. For example, solar forcing can be ruled out as major cause because its fingerprint is warming in the entire atmosphere, and only the lower atmosphere has warmed as expected for greenhouse gases. The major causes of current climate change are primarily greenhouse gases, and secondarily land use changes, and aerosols and soot.

It is no coincidence that the 1850–1900 average earth temperature was used by the Intergovernmental Panel on Climate Change (IPCC) as a pre-industrial global mean surface temperature. The largest human influence on global temperature rises has been the emission of the greenhouse gases, with over 90% of the impact from carbon monoxide and methane [natural gas]. The rapid increase in the release of these greenhouse gases commenced during the second industrial revolution 1880-1920 – see Chapter 4 'The Failure of Capitalism'.

On October 1, 1908, the first production Model T Ford motor car was completed at the company's Piquette Avenue plant in Detroit.

Between 1908 and 1927, Ford would build some 15 million Model T cars. It was the longest production run of any automobile model in history until the Volkswagen Beetle surpassed it in 1972.

It had a 22-horsepower, four-cylinder engine and was made of a new kind of heat-treated steel, pioneered by French race car makers, that made it lighter [it weighed just 1,200 pounds] and stronger than its predecessors had been. It could go as fast as 40 miles per hour and could run on gasoline or hemp-based fuel.

It would very clearly not be fair to suggest that the crisis in climate change rests solely on the shoulders of Henry Ford. However, Human activities are responsible for almost all of the increase in greenhouse gases in the atmosphere over the last 150 years. The largest source of greenhouse gas emissions from human activities in the United States is from burning fossil fuels for electricity, heat, and transportation. In 2018 the largest source of greenhouse gas emissions in USA was transportation at 28%. Source: United States Environmental Protection Agency EPA.

The USA is the second largest polluter of the planet at 15% contribution to greenhouse gas emissions. 15% of 28% is 4.2%, therefore it is not unreasonable, providing you have the appropriate sense of humour, to allow 4.2% responsibility for global warming to fall firmly and squarely upon the shoulders of Henry Ford. It is not fair to give all the glory to Henry. A lot of the glory is most certainly deserved by the marketers in the Automobile Industry.

In Chapter 4 – 'The Failure of Capitalism' section 'The False Market and Two Myths of Capitalism', in 2018 we can see how the marketers fanatically drew blood by ruthlessly exploiting the market at a cost to the global economy of approximately £616Bn in automobile depreciation over a three year period. As explained, the Gross Domestic Product for Belgium in 2018 was reported as £409,740M (US $532,131M) i.e. circa £410Bn.

Therefore from the statistics above [for 2018], we see that the global depreciation of new cars in the automobile industry for three years [when we all (except me) rush out and buy a new car] was approximately 1.5 times the GDP of Belgium for 2018! Belgium is ranked at the 28th highest GDP country in the world. This £616Bn global depreciation of new cars is wiped of these asset values forever. This £616Bn is lost for ever. £616Bn could feed a lot of the starving people of the world for quite a long time.

However the automobile marketer's wonderful achievement does not end there. They also take a Gold Award in their contribution to 'Greenhouse Gases and the Potential End of Humanity circa 2095'. I think that I now understand the logic of this. If we rid the planet of Human Beings because when they all die in the industrial cities of greenhouse gas fog poisoning, then Nature can go back to its peaceful and tranquil existence that it enjoyed before Mankind started on its relentless and stupid self-exterminating career of ever increasing mindless global consumption. Some years ago, in my misspent youth, I had the joy of working for a company in California. The company was started by an *'entrepreneur'* – the term typically I believe, used to describe a person whose prime purpose for existence is money. This man, as Founder and CEO of the company was the proud possessor of twelve cars much to the great fawning admiration of the huddled herd of doting 'wannabe' employees. This very sad man and most of his even sadder employees, were well entrenched and on their way along their Roads to Nowhere and their Slavery for Ever. See Chapter 4 – 'The Failure of Capitalism' section Perpetual Self-Inflicted Slavery.

A second example of the wonder of the *'entrepreneur'* was witnessed a few years ago on a popular UK television capitalist investment seeking programme, one of the capitalist panel judges aged in his fifties of net worth £0.5Bn, did not know who Bertrand Russell was. An astonishing achievement! Bertrand Russell and A N Whitehead's *'Principia Mathematica'* 1910 was generally considered the greatest intellectual achievement of the century.

The seeking of truth whether it be philosophical, scientific or spiritual or any other form, is ostensibly not of interest to the *'entrepreneur'*.

All that is of interest to the *'entrepreneur'* or the capitalist, is the perpetual, relentless global growth in markets and therefore the consequential mindless and soulless pursuit of the consumption of acquisitions that lead no further towards Mankind's genuine improvement nor genuine long-term self-realisation or happiness. This slavery to mindless consumption and therefore the required, ensuing, mindless production means that the populace is kept so busy that they do not realise what is really going on. Strapped with mortgages, families, school fees and other expenses they have no time to question whether this is the route to true happiness. They are all Hamsters in the Wheel, and so they will remain, unless we all do something about this dreadful business.

6.2 5G – Fifth Generation Wireless Communication Platform

Capitalism has not had a trustworthy record in a large number of its various money making ventures. The capitalist method seems to be; get the product out there, as cheaply as possible and as quickly as possible with the minimum testing required and worry about the consequences afterwards – if you have to. The History of Capitalism is riddled with many proven examples of this, often unlawful and/ or criminal behaviour. This must be so because the nature of capitalism necessitates it. It is an imperative inherent in the very core of the capitalist method. To corner the market one must be an innovator or at least an early adopter. Grab as much of the market as you can, as quickly as you can, corner the market, and buy off as many competitors or synergistic businesses as soon as possible. Obtain the maximum market share and kill your competitors. The Capitalist must be wary of monopoly laws, but I am sure that clever lawyers can assist the capitalist's need for global 'conquest' with appropriate designs to mitigate one's lawful obligations. Regarding ethical and moral considerations – forget that!

As I write this in May 2020, I am not aware of any independent scientific testing of 5G and/or of its related technologies that proves beyond all reasonable doubt, using approvals of the research results from peers, and standard scientific methodologies of using independent, 'un-contaminated', blind, nil effect placebo groups, [if required] that 5G and its related technologies are not in any way harmful to human beings. I understand that my borough in London is intending to erect 5G masts. I have written to them requesting the results from such research as outlined above. If the research results are not forthcoming, the residents of my borough will know who they should be suing.

Is it not true that, outside of China, Google has a global monopoly on search engine usage? The real danger now, with the World Wide Web, the Internet and the complete global reach of many internet based companies that these companies 'transcend' the legislative of individual countries, the EU block, and possibly entire continents. Therefore these Global companies: Google, Facebook, Amazon, Yahoo etc. may position their respective operations to minimise their tax revenues and therefore essentially operate above and beyond practically the entire global taxation schemes. It appears that Google has a global search engine monopoly, Facebook had a global social network monopoly, Amazon has a global internet based warehousing monopoly. These are global monopolies ostensibly beyond the reach of legislation designed to restrict monopolies.

Here briefly, are two examples of less than perfect moral records of two entirely different industry sectors. I could cite hundreds of documented examples but have no wish to bore the reader with the self-evident. Two examples should suffice:

Dentistry

Quote:

"Amalgam fillings are safe. A great deal of research has examined these fillings and found them to be an effective, long-lasting

*treatment for dental decay. Amalgam or silver fillings are made with mercury, silver, tin and copper. ... Amalgam is a **safe** and durable choice for fillings."* Source: American Dental Association ADA.

Quote from ADA: *"The American Dental Association (ADA) exists to power the profession of dentistry.."*

Ergo ADA is a front for capitalism. Dental expenses are so high in the USA that patients travel to Mexico for treatment. Source: BuzzFeed.News 2017.

Quote:

*"All dental amalgam restorations contain approximately 50% mercury, and reports and research are consistent that these fillings emit mercury, exposing dental patients, dental professionals, dental staff, and their foetuses to this **known neurotoxin**."*

"Additionally, in research published in 2011, Dr. G. Mark Richardson reported that more than 67 million Americans aged two years and older exceed the intake of mercury vapour considered "safe" by the United States Environmental Protection Agency - U.S. EPA due to the presence of dental mercury amalgam fillings, whereas over 122 million Americans exceed the intake of mercury vapour considered "safe" by the California EPA due to their dental mercury amalgam fillings."

Source: International Academy of Oral Medicine and Toxicology:

https://iaomt.org/resources/dental-mercury-facts/dental-amalgam-safety-myth-truth/

I know which version I would 'go with'. Dr G. Mark Richardson rather than The American Dental Association.

Cigarettes and Tobacco

"A demand for scientific proof is always a formula for inaction and delay and usually the first reaction of the guilty ... in fact scientific proof has never been, is not and should not be the basis for political and legal action" An example of (private) candour from a scientist at the tobacco company BAT 1 . (S J Green 1980)

Source for next three paragraphs:

'Tobacco Explained – the truth about the tobacco industry... in its own words'

'Tobacco Explained' was originally developed and written by Clive Bates and Andy Rowell for the London-based Action on Smoking and Health (ASH).

https://www.who.int/tobacco/media/en/TobaccoExplained.pdf

At the beginning of the fifties, research was published showing a statistical link between smoking and lung cancer. **At the same time the tobacco industry's own research** began to find **carcinogens**, a substance capable of causing cancer in living tissue, in smoke and began to confirm the relationship between smoking and cancer.

This posed a serious problem for the industry: whether to admit to the health problems and try and find marketable solutions, or whether to basically deny everything. In the face of mounting damning evidence against their product, the companies responded by creating doubt and controversy surrounding the health risks, whilst at the same time by responding to the growing public concern by putting filters on cigarettes and promising research into the health effects of smoking. They lulled the smoking public into a false sense of security, because, whilst this had the hallmarks of responsible companies acting in the public interest, it was actually a public relations strategy to buy time, at the expense of public health. Many of the internal documents reveal that the industry was trying to look responsible in public, but privately was out to convince the public that smoking was not harmful. Despite decades of evidence to the contrary, and millions of deaths caused by tobacco, the industry still largely maintains that the case against the cigarette is unproven.

By the late fifties industry scientists had privately accepted the association between smoking and lung cancer, believing it to be one of cause and effect. Thirty years later, the majority of the industry still publicly denies the causation theory – with one exception – the US manufacturer Liggett, who broke ranks in 1997, much to the dismay of the other tobacco majors.

Quod erat demonstrandum Q.E.D.

Back to **5G – Fifth Generation Wireless Communications Platform**:

Why should the public believe the 5G/mobile phone industry if there are so many examples of reasons to not believe the marketing drivel of capitalist companies and their governments out for the fastest and easiest buck. How many more examples would you like – children grovelling their way up chimneys in 1870 – children miners crawling around in coal seams in 1840, Global slave labour in 2020 – examples of modern slavery?

"We were only there to work. It felt like I was in jail." Laboni, Nepal 2020 – Anti Slavery.

Source: Anti-Slavery https://www.antislavery.org/slavery-today/ modern-slavery/

What is 5G?

Faster mobile phones? 5G is about a lot more than faster mobile phones.

The Geo-Economic and Trade Impacts of 5G

"The [5G] *technology is fuelling geo-economic one-upmanship.."*

Source: World Economic Forum - 2020

Did I not state: *"Modern capitalism is an anti-intellectual brutalism, an inward-looking nationalistic competitive avarice with little or no broad-seeing, long-term planning. Furthermore of course, modern capitalism today is now world-wide."* – Chapter 4 'The Failure of Capitalism' this volume. I wrote that sentence before I knew of the World Economic Forum's confirmation of my Genius. The sentence from the World Economic Forum substantiates a very significant core and its derivatives of this polemic.

Does your 2G, 3G, 4G mobile phone work OK? Have you returned it to the retailer because it does not work? You may have returned one particular product item that you had difficulties with, but you probably have a perfectly acceptable working device now. The figures support my profound hypothesis.

In 2020 reputedly the approximate number of smartphone users in the world is 3.5 Billion, which translates to approximately 45.04% of the world's population owning a smartphone. In total, the number of people who own a smart and feature phone ('dumb' phones that do not have the advanced functionality of the 'smart' phone) is 4.78 Billion, making up approximately 61.51% of the world's population.

Numerous controlled scientific studies of 2G, 3G and 4G technologies (mobile phone technologies) have shown that stress, sperm and testicular damage, neuropsychiatric effects, including changes to electrical activity in the brain, cellular DNA damage and calcium overload can all occur in humans as a result of exposure to Electro Magnetic Fields EMFs.

The United States Food and Drug Administration FDA state:

"Cell phones emit low levels of non-ionizing radiation when in use." The type of radiation emitted by cell phones is also referred to as radio frequency (RF) energy – [non-ionizing radiation].

Source: https://www.fda.gov/radiation-emitting-products/cell-phones/do-cell-phones-pose-health-hazard

Radio frequencies may be lower frequencies but one does not typically have a radio held next to one's ear for many, many hours every day. 4G mobile phone frequency is typically 2.5 Ghazi but 5G frequency is up to 39 Ghazi. 5G is therefore operating on a frequency sixteen times higher than 4G.

Cancer Research UK has stated that: Too much UV radiation from the sun or sunbeds **can** damage the genetic material (the DNA) in your skin cells. If enough DNA damage builds up over time, it can cause cells to start growing out of control, which can lead to skin cancer. Anyone can develop skin cancer, but some people can have a higher risk.

Source: https://www.cancerresearchuk.org/about-cancer/causes-of-cancer/sun-uv-and-cancer/how-does-the-sun-and-uv-cause-cancer

The majority of sun light emission is non-ionising and it is well know that too much sun light can cause skin ailments and skin cancer. Sun light is non–ionising radiation, mobile phones are non-ionising radiation. Different frequencies perhaps but the same type of radiation.

My recently acquired 4G mobile telephone handset product documentation states the following:

"CE certification information (SAR)

This device is tested for typical body-worn applications with the back of the handset 0.5cm away. To maintain compliance with RF [radio frequency] exposure requirements, use accessories that maintain 0.5cm separation distance between the user's body and the back of the handset. The use of belt clips, holsters and similar accessories **should not contain metallic components in its assembly.** The use of accessories that do not satisfy these requirements may not comply with RF exposure requirements, and should be avoided.

If you are using a pacemaker, hearing aid, cochlear or other device, please use the phone according to the doctor's advice."

Which "doctor"? Witch doctor?

I looked thoroughly throughout the product documentation and could find no contact details for "the doctor[s]" so that I might seek his or her advice on this important matter. In consideration of the fact that no such "doctor" appears to exist within the product supplier's organisation chart, I am compelled to wonder which "doctor" they were referring to. The most logical assumption is that "the doctor" is in fact many doctors; "the doctor" is presumably one's local General Practioner. However, in consideration that a 'General Practitioner' is exactly that, and perhaps is not an expert in the harmful effects of radio frequencies, then he/she may be obliged to refer the person to a specialist consultant.

I looked again throughout the product documentation and could find no details to explain answers to these two questions:

1. Who pays for the "doctor's advice" from the [General Practioner] and, if required, the advice from the specialist consultant – the phone manufacturer, the phone user through his/her health insurance, the taxpayer?
2. If the doctor or consultant proffers their advice, the phone user follows their advice but becomes ill – who is legally liable

– the doctor, the consultant or the mobile phone provider and who pays the fees for the treatment for a remedy?

Please send your answers to question 1 and 2 above to: *www. saveyourselfsaveusall.com*

From my studies, and the wording of the CE certification information (SAR) information note quoted above, I would surmise that for both questions 1 and 2 above, the mobile phone company would have **no legal liability whatsoever, nothing whatsoever, not even if your head fell off when using the mobile phone.**

Interestingly I have purchased over some recent years: a motor car, an electric toothbrush, a camera, a watch, matches, tooth-picks and at the height of the Covid-19 pandemic pandemonium even some toilet rolls but not one of these esteemed product providers stated on their product information details:

"If you are using a pacemaker, hearing aid, cochlear or other device, please use the [phone] [motor car, electric toothbrush, camera, watch, matches, tooth-picks or Covid-19 toilet rolls] according to the doctor's advice."

Strange old world, isn't it?

The above facts represent a simple example of the putrid moral worth of the capitalist classes. On a scale of 1 to 10 for this little example, where 1 is the poorest score and 10 is the best; what score does the mobile phone company deserve for its Moral Worth?

Answers please to: *www.saveyourselfsaveusall.com*

The Geo-Economic and Trade Impacts of 5G (contd.)

Source: World Economic Forum – 2020

"5G is designed to be a foundation connecting billions of devices and enabling better ways of doing things. The total number of 5G subscriptions has been projected to reach 2.6 billion by 2025". However, the World Economic Forum does not include its definition of "better".

Ultimately, those countries able to take a leading position in terms of deployment are expected to enjoy relatively greater economic growth.

> Note: There goes that old chestnut again - perpetual global unrestrained growth. See 'Chapter 4' - section 'Unrestrained Perpetual Growth' which explains the stupidity of this concept.

5G's promise is one of the reasons it is a factor in trade tensions and geo-economic positioning; in 2019, for example, China established a two-year action plan to promote the purchase of consumer goods including 5G handsets as a means to offset the impact of an escalating trade war with the USA.

5G Business Model Transformation

5G technology is a critical enabler of driverless cars, efficient factories and smarter power use.

5G is a potential game changer for a number of industries, though they will have to adapt their business models in order to harness its true potential. Some important services made possible by 5G will include "digital twin" technology that creates a digital mirror of a physical object in order to predict its performance, augmented and virtual reality (thanks to better download and upload speeds), and predictive maintenance in factories.

The fast, intelligent internet connectivity enabled by 5G technology is expected to create about US $12 trillion in global economic value within the next two decades. In order to make that happen, however, trillions will first have to be invested in the rollout of global 5G networks [which may be delayed in some cases due to Covid-19]. Greater cooperation is needed to foster deployment; when used to power the Internet of Things, artificial intelligence AI, and Big Data; 5G can deliver significant social value. While several countries have initiated roadmaps for 5G rollout, others are falling behind - partly due to the lack of alignment among policy-makers, regulators and the private sector.

Apart from 5G technology being a critical enabler of driverless cars, efficient factories and smarter power use, 5G is also expected to support high-density autonomous vehicle platooning (to improve aerodynamic performance and traffic flow), remote vehicle control, remote driver health monitoring, in-car infotainment, and smart traffic control. The energy sector could meanwhile use 5G for the real-time monitoring of utility networks with drones, sensing hazards and maintenance needs, and monitoring residential smart meters.

Ride-hailing platforms like Uber, Lyft, and Didi are expected transition within the next decade from human-driven, internal combustion engine cars to autonomous electric vehicles - potentially spawning millions of driverless cars on the roads, and potentially thousands of pilot-less vertical take-off and landing aircraft.

An aggressive transition to self-driving vehicles is not a given, however. For such a transition to occur, political and regulatory support will be required. This will in turn largely determine the investment available for necessary infrastructure like vehicle charging stations and 5G connectivity.

Intel has predicted the rise of a "passenger economy" worth US $800 billion by 2035, as people in cars have more time on their hands to shop and secure everything from entertainment to doctors' appointments [to buying more worthless junk they don't really need]. As related technologies like artificial intelligence and virtual reality come to the fore, software companies and other industry players are expected to play a major role in designing new 5G business models. Those models will in turn rely on having a set of standardized regulations for 5G data monetization, related to cross-border data and services-sharing.

> Note: The standardized regulations for this data transmission backbone may provide the required structure to allow governments to have cross-border data sharing that may assist in procuring the appropriate tax revenues from internet companies that currently appear to 'float' across the world ostensibly impervious to local country government laws and taxation regulations.

6.3 The Internet of Things – IoT

The Internet of Things is exactly that; "all 'Things' bright and beautiful" that may be wired up to one another **will be**! Do not try to deny it! 'All Things Bright and Beautiful' is an Anglican **hymn**, also sung in many other Christian denominations. The words are by Cecil Frances Alexander and were first published in her '*Hymns for Little Children*' 1848 based upon The Bible, Chronicles 16:23-29.

> Note: A most suitable metaphor for the technology that will be the connectivity backbone, along with 5G that should within a few years of its introduction reduce all adult sentient human life on the planet to "Little Children".

Ergo, any electrical, electro-mechanical or electronic device or similar that may be 'usefully' connected to other such devices such as every single item in the home, office, warehouse, factory, Government infrastructure, service suppliers [gas, electricity, water, [oxygen?]] retail outlet, restaurant, car, fridge, electric oven, mobile phone, garage doors, computer home-help assistant, electric toothbrush, electric cat-feeder, robot dog-walker, electric toilet flush, electric nail-pick, electric nose-hair-remover, electric ..., electric ... electric human brain...etc. etc. so that no one will have to think any more [not that many people do anyway] than the absolute minimum so that unfortunately the human brain atrophies and rots and exudes like puss from every human orifice that is not jammed with electrical probes or other electrical equipment. This is 'The Internet of Things'. In England we call this sort of writing an attempt at Satire or perhaps Irony. However, this description above of potential future events, is probably not that much of an exaggeration.

Architecture and Standards

The Internet of Things requires thoughtful architecture and standard selection.

[Understatement of the Century!]

The Internet of Things, which is rapidly connecting everything from **doorbells to dams** to the web, requires scalable, future-proof, and cost-effective architectural choices in order to thrive.

> Note: The very clever **d**oorbells to **d**ams consonantal alliteration that would presumably have gained the endorsement of Shakespeare – if he was still alive.

By building on already-established reference architectures, companies and governments can develop standards with robust interfaces, and ensure healthy environments capable of addressing performance and safety issues. There is no one-size-fits-all solution for IoT architecture - whether it is in relation to sensing, communication, analytics, or actuation [turning an electric signal into a physical action]. However, two specific models have become commonest; the first is the concept of digital mirroring [sometimes referred to as Digital Twins], where real-world physical objects are duplicated as purely digital objects. These digital objects are able to interact with the physical world, with other digital duplicates, and with computing services - often using the cloud as a platform. [Secondly the use of] Cloud services can in turn accommodate massive increases in computing power, which can be used to analyse large amounts of data or to create "Cognitive Firewalls" that protect physical systems against digital misdeeds.

Note : 'Firewalls' are software systems and programmes that check for computer viruses, malicious or otherwise, to prevent unnecessary computer malfunction or function interruption. In this case "Cognitive Firewalls" protect physical [i.e. mechanical] systems against computer viruses or 'misdeeds'.

Note : The clouds in the sky, referred to so eloquently by William Wordsworth 1770-1850 are not used in these services. 'Cloud Computing' is the on-demand availability of computer system resources, especially data storage and computing power, without direct active management by the user. The term is generally used to describe data centres available to many users over the Internet, or in this case the Internet of Things. In reality the 'Cloud Computers' are typically Service Provider Company's computer servers which serve the clients on the Internet/Internet of Things. The 'clients' are the laptops or whatever other computer they may be, that the Cloud Computing customer uses.

Making the Rules for a Beneficial IoT

The Internet of Things can truly benefit society **if the right kind of governance is in place**.

IF?

The rapid but relatively uncoordinated evolution of the Internet of Things, a technology that makes our essential machines and devices [washing machines and dish washers with husband 'to repair' them] smarter by connecting them to the web, has led to decentralized systems that lack proper governance. [That's normal]

In order for the IoT to realize its potential, these fragmented systems have to find a way to effectively interact with one another. This requires governance that takes stock of the broader context. While the IoT does benefit from a certain level of governance, it is not at a level that can foster sustained growth. There is technical governance in the form of standards, for example, yet over-standardization has led to as many problems as it has tried to solve by spawning infighting [that's normal] and incompatibility [again this is normal]. One of the IoT's biggest opportunities is therefore also one of its biggest challenges: diversity. One, single set of standards must be created that works equally well for dishwashers, autonomous cars, and smartwatches [and toothpicks]. The obstacles to this are considerable, however; every object, service, or network has its own design considerations, and within any given industry there may be several conflicting standards. [As always]

There is therefore a serious need for both corporate and international governance in the world of the Internet of Things. The real challenges are to determine how much governance is too much, [why not determine the correct amount] and to create the right incentives to bring all interested parties to the table. The IoT requires a significant amount of investment to be of real use, and as a result it is primarily being deployed in relatively wealthy, well-resourced places - even though it is the less well-to-do areas that truly stand to benefit from the efficiency improvement and cost savings the IoT can facilitate. [This sounds normal, has been happening for centuries - why change now?]

Anyone working to boost the adoption of the technology has to try to ensure that the IoT tide lifts all boats, rather than sending a tidal wave of disparity in the direction of the most vulnerable. [This is a very pretty metaphor, but History shows that modern capitalism has lifted no more than say four to half a dozen 'boats' on a tsunami of greed and left most of the remaining world to drown.]

Ultimately, the Internet of Things could create societal value that aids progress in achieving the United Nations Sustainable Development Goals, established in 2015 to guide **responsible** [there has never been such a thing in the past] global development until 2030. Mobility services powered by the IoT can reduce vehicle ownership, fuel consumption, and emissions, for example, while IoT-enabled monitoring of agriculture and supply chains can ensure that the food being produced is not wasted, and gets to the people who need it most. [That won't happen. "Nearly half the world lives off of less than US $5.5 per day." – Source: Worldbank 2018]

The Internet of Things, or "IoT," surrounds us with networks of smart, web-connected devices and services capable of sensing, interconnecting, inferring, and acting. It is enabling the development of new products and business models, while creating ways for governments to deliver more useful services and better engage with the public. Some of the most important issues related to IoT include technology architecture and standardization, safety and security risks, threats to privacy and trust, potentially missed opportunities for broad social benefits - and a need for responsible governance.

> Note: With regard to most of the above "…standardization, safety and security risks, threats to privacy and trust, potentially missed opportunities for broad social benefits - and a need for responsible governance" capitalism has singularly failed to achieve these in many past business sectors so why should we anticipate any change with a future technology such as IoT?

IoT Value Creation and Business Models

The Internet of Things can help a number of industries thrive.

The Internet of Things can improve efficiency and productivity as it connects everyday machines via the web - but it cannot create value out of nothing. It requires significant innovation, greater investment, and broader participation in every industry where it is poised to have an impact.

The IoT draws from multiple disciplines in order to build some-thing greater than would be possible through siloed innovation [innovation in isolation from related innovation in related technol-ogies]; as a result of its deployment, technology providers can see increased hardware and service sales, marketing firms can grow through improved analytics, and standardization, safety and security risks, threats to privacy and trust, potentially missed opportunities for broad social benefits - and a need for responsible governance, or by reducing monitored fuel consumption.

While there is a continual need to innovate via the IoT, and to capi-talize on its power to disrupt, ["disrupt" – what a boring cliché] its greatest potential is to create sustainable, shared value. For example, smart thermostat providers can turn a profit through an initial sale and subsequent offering of data analytics, while the homeowner buying the device can reap monthly savings from smart energy management and improved consumption data. Meanwhile so-called conversational commerce conducted with businesses by that homeowner via devices on his or her walls and shelves can drive retail sales and create ongoing customer relationships.

> Note: "can drive retail sales" of more things that you don't really need anyway.

Vehicles that are connected via the Internet of Things can collect data about themselves, help dealerships proactively schedule required maintenance, and improve efficiency while streamlining auto manufacturers' spare parts supply chains. Governments can meanwhile partner with technology companies to form public-private partnerships to draw capital investment needed to build infrastructure that utilizes the IoT to improve public services. An important part of drawing this investment is an ability to change conventional business models. For example, what was once a one-time sale can become a service model; for proof of this, look no further than to the IoT-fueled transition from selling individual vehicles, to car sharing, to shared mobility services, and eventually towards autonomous mobility services.

> Note: A potential danger of all-answering technological homogeneity is that human beings will think even less than they do now. The fall of the cretins, the rise of the Robots!

Subscription-based services can also pair seemingly dissimilar technologies together to create more value both for the companies selling them and for the people buying them - for example, by coupling an internet-enabled smoke detector with a home security webcam.

> Note: How profound!

Data analytics is another disruptive business model ingredient stemming from the IoT, where so-called "information exhaust" [the data footprints we leave online by using sites and services] can be turned into insights to develop better products or target ad campaigns. **To be sure, though, only a balanced and transparent approach to making use of this data is appropriate.**

> Note: Quote "another disruptive business model" – that is the second occurrence in this section of the cliché "disruptive". These people are fed batches of business-speak clichés by the thousand, without being aware of it and then thoughtlessly regurgitate them until they are fed the next batch of

stupid clichés. This author's many years of experience of 'Corporate-Speak' gave rise to expensive medical treatment for remedies for 'Intellectual Nausea', an illness never previously diagnosed in the History of Western Medicine.

Note: Quote: "target ad campaigns" – more junk you don't need. Google and Facebook business models may change from 85% advertising revenue to perhaps 99.9% advertising revenue. Advertising even more junk you don't need. When is this pointless, endless consumption going to end? [Pun intended]

Note: Quote: **"To be sure, though, only a balanced and transparent approach to making use of this data is appropriate."** - That will never happen, how can they be so naïve? We only have to look at current social media use of personal data to see the existent dangers.

Privacy and Trust on the IoT

Unsavoury services can expose digital identities and personal information via the Internet of Things. [Sounds Ominous!]

The current generation of heavy internet users are **digital denizens**, creating curated online personas out of heaps [mountains and mountains] of [personal, mostly totally irrelevant and worthless] information uploaded to social media sites. These people are also generating detailed "digital exhaust" [more pollution?] via the Internet of Things-connected devices with which they either knowingly or unknowingly engage [mostly unknowingly in terms of content]. Third parties with either good or bad intentions [often bad such as passing data to advertising people] can create rich identities out of these data deposits, to use and **abuse** as they see fit.

This issue actually stems from one of the biggest opportunities presented by the IoT: the sheer number of seamless connections proliferating among digital systems. Internet services promise wonderful things, yet users rarely take the time to think about the nature of the information required to accomplish their online goals. It is unusual for a user to actually read a website's terms of service, and then carefully set his or her privacy controls, for example. Worse yet, there are almost never repercussions for organizations that fail to abide by their terms of service, or that negligently leak information. Better user education could help to reduce the exposure to risk. [Wishful thinking]

The European Union's General Data Protection Regulation, which went into effect in 2018 and places disclosure requirements on companies aiming to unearth value in internet user information, has helped provide the public with some insight into online data collection and sharing. However, users still struggle to balance consent with utility when it comes to their interaction with the Internet of Things.

> Note: Why would there be a **"struggle to balance consent"** if the data collectors were trustworthy? Perhaps it is because in the entire history of capitalism there have been countless examples of the untrustworthiness of capitalists.

This is in part because **there are serious lingering questions about intent, policy, and procedures related to personally-identifiable information - and because platforms generally lack appropriate transparency on their data sharing and controls**. This can be a result of a lack of technologically and economically-aware governance, both in terms of creating adequate incentives for companies to implement consumer protections, and a result of ill-defined, or under-enforced repercussions for those who fail to design trustworthy systems.

> Note from above: *"This can be a result of a lack of technologically-and economically-aware governance, both in terms of creating adequate incentives for companies to*

implement consumer protections, and a result of ill-defined, or under-enforced repercussions for those who fail to design trustworthy systems."

Perhaps because there is no money to be made from *"implement consumer protections"* [sic] that the capitalist classes do not give a damn! There are plenty of examples of capitalist classes breaking local building regulations and simply paying the fine imposed, if one is imposed, because the fine is typically 'peanuts' compared to the money to be made from the project. Nothing must be allowed to get in the way of unrestrained perpetual global growth.

Individual internet users and businesses have taken note of this lack of transparency and protection, and have in the past resisted the implementation of the IoT due to a lack of confidence in existing privacy measures and to a fear that terms and conditions can suddenly change without notice.

Note: Hardly surprising when there are world-wide reports of people on the one side of the world using social media to surreptitiously influence democratic elections in a country on the other side of the world. If these reports are true, then we are living in very, very dangerous times.

In order for the Internet of Things to thrive, clear and user-centric policies regarding data collection, storage, and sharing must be developed. Appropriate governance could help ensure that maximum social and economic value is derived from this technology.

Note: Appropriate governance must assure that Human Rights are not violated by this technology the way that Human Rights have been violated by the capitalist classes in the past. This technology is very, very open to abuse by the very nature of it being capitalist proprietary. It appears that world governments are already having a lot of difficulty in holding to book global social media corporations.

Note: Potential Simple Solution:

All private companies involved in this technology and other technologies, that by their nature also inflict upon the world these very real dangers against the people's rights to privacy and freedom of information, would be obliged under law in all participating countries, that the source code of the software and firmware programmes be deposited with governments for their approval under Law. Obviously this would be done under the strictest of confidentialities and the software programme information would be accessible to a very few government officials for approval, officials whose confidentiality is held under the Official Secrets Act. This is no different in principle to the automobile industry being obliged, under recent laws, to provide evidence of their newly manufactured cars having reduced CO_2 emissions.

If the social media company or any other similar technology company wishes to trade in any particular country, it would be required to obtain an operating licence in that country or countries it wishes to release its product in and therefore trade in. The requirement of the license would ensure that the source code of the software and firmware programmes be deposited with governments for their approval under Law. The author is no advocate of unnecessary government intervention. In a 'democracy', perhaps the less government the better, providing that capitalist avarice does not run away with itself and cause global economic meltdowns as in the selling of precipitous junk in the sub-prime mortgage sector causing the 2008 global financial crash, resulting in the taxpayer bailing out those responsible for this greedy, vulgar and disgraceful irresponsibility. Another option that may come about through my recommendation is that governments, since they have the programme source code, should be able to assess the revenue statistics that the social media or other company is generating within their governmental border and its jurisdiction.

Therefore the taxable revenue that the social media company or similar is generating in the various countries would be available to the respective governments and they may then accurately apply their taxation regulations to that revenue stream. I should be charging a fee for this advice!

6.4 Robotics and Artificial Intelligence (AI)
The Robotics and AI Paradigm Shift

The enormous paradigm shift of robotics and artificial intelligence cannot be over-estimated.

In the Industrial Revolution in Chapter 3 of this volume we observe that in 1764 James Hargreaves of Lancashire invented the 'Spinning Jenny' a machine that weaved cotton with more than one spindle at a time. The device reduced the amount of work needed to produce cloth, with a worker able to work eight or more spools at once. This grew to 120 spools as technology advanced.

Furthermore, in 1776 James Watt, 1736-1819 a Scottish inventor, engineer and chemist improved upon Thomas Newcomen's 1712 steam engine and developed his own 'Watt Steam Engine'. Steam engines were used in all sorts of applications including factories, mines, locomotives, and steamboats. Steam engines use hot steam from boiling water to drive a piston (or pistons) back and forth. The movement of the pistons was then used to power a machine or turn a wheel.

So with these, and other similar technologies of the Industrial Revolution, the new methods adopted caused work patterns to change from one form to another; essentially from hand worked products to machine assisted manufactured products. Some employment 'fall out' from these changes was inevitable, as some workers had difficulty or reluctance in adapting to the new methods of working. The reason for the change however was primarily to increase productivity but the changes would still retain human labour albeit using this human labour in a different way.

Robotics and AI are inherently and distinctly different. With Robotics and AI it is not a simple change in manufacturing methods to increase productivity, but changes in methods that are deliberately designed to remove the necessity, or minimise the necessity, for human labour and replace it with robots and artificial intelligence technologies.

One could envisage a future where Robotics, Artificial Intelligence, 5G, Internet of Things - IoT and all other related technologies are permeated, integrated and communicable throughout practically every aspect of human life: at home, at the workplace, at leisure, driving the car, shopping etc. – all intelligently inter-connected together with all the intelligent interconnected real-time feed-back loops to ensure perpetual optimum efficiency.

Every single electro-mechanical device will be programmed into the Internet of Things at home: home heating, water heating, television, window blinds, refrigerator, electric oven, dish-washer, washing machine, washing dryer etc. Similarly in the car and at the place of work at places of leisure and at the places of shopping.

It may be possible, perhaps at some time in the very near future, for the refrigerator in every home to automatically order the next few days [weeks] of food, as it monitors stock depletion, the retail outlet or warehouse automatically receives the order from the control hub in the home, the retail outlet or warehouse stacks the products in pallets or boxes with robots which then wrap and distribute automatically by drone or driverless transport to the home where the home-help-robot takes the order and automatically restocks the fridge and automatically advices the human being [now reduced by technological overload and gross intellectual degeneration to a mere cretinous humanoid] that its fish-fingers, peas and potatoes have arrived. The home-help-robot then cooks the humanoid's fish-fingers, peas mashed potato and delivers to the mouth of the same, but not before checking the humanoid's pulse to ensure that it has not died from total, relentless, all-consuming boredom and intellectual atrophy.

In simultaneous real-time the retailer/warehouse IoT central system informs its stock control system of the reduction in fish-fingers, peas and potatoes and more are ordered from the producer or Bio-Engineering Global Food ConGlomerate Factory-Farming Robot Cooperative [no Human Access permitted] whose Robotics IoT system plants and grows more fish-fingers, peas and potatoes. Ad nauseam ad nauseam....

Welcome to the 'Brave New World' – Aldous Huxley 1894-1963

Please note that there will probably be the interaction of no more than 4 humans in the entire process. Homo Sapiens will have reduced itself to total irrelevance.

Brief History of Robotics

The very first robots of particular significance were those used primarily in the automotive industry were 'pick and place' robots that had jointed 'arms' and 'hand-like' mechanisms at the end of the 'arms' where the only significant control was of the i,j,k vectors of the arms and hands and their components and the x,y,z coordinate positioning of the hands and their components' fulcrum points. This was a most basic form of control. However, it was sufficient to efficiently automate large areas of automobile plant such as welding, painting, assembly, disassembly, pick and place for printed circuit boards and other such items, packaging and label-ling, palletizing, product inspection, and testing. The 'intelligence' placed upon these robots at that time was not 'artificial intelligence' in the manner of the technology and term used today. The robots were programmed to implement very simple tasks with little or no intelligent corrective real-time feedback loop in the design.

Robots have long been the focus of science fiction and literature, but it wasn't until recent decades that they became a viable part of our workforce. Science fiction lovers will recall Isaac Asimov and his Three Laws of Robotics. Whilst Asimov is fiction, these rules more or less define our robots today. Source: https://blog. robotics.com

We enjoy safe, collaborative robots that work right alongside us, but this wasn't always the case. The development of Numerically Controlled [NC] machines, and the rising popularity of the computer both helped bring about the first industrial robots. The earliest known industrial robot that fits into the ISO definition of the term was created by Griffith "Bill" P. Taylor in 1937 and appeared in Meccano Magazine the following year.

It was a crane-like design that used Meccano parts and was powered by a single electric motor. It had five axes of movement, including a grab and grab rotation. The robot was automated through the use of paper tape with punched holes in it to energize solenoids. This would create movement in the control levers.

This first robot could stack wooden blocks in patterns programmed by the paper tape. George Devol placed the first industrial robot patent in 1954. His robot was able to transfer objects from one point to another within a distance of 12 feet or less. He founded a company called Unimation in 1956 to build the robot and coined the term "Universal Automation."

Unimation manufactured UNIMATE in 1962, which was the first robot to be implemented by a major manufacturer. General Motors began using it in their New Jersey plant that same year. In 1969, Victor Scheinman invented the Stanford arm at Stanford University. This was an all-electric 6-axis articulated robot.

This new technology opened up the possibility for manufacturers to use robots in assembly and welding tasks. Scheinman later sold his designs to Unimation, which then developed them alongside General Motors.

Meanwhile, ASEA in Europe developed the ASEA IRB in 1975 that was the first fully electrically driven robot. It was also the first microprocessor-controller robot that used Intel's first chipset. In 1978, the PUMA robot arm was released by Vicarm and Unimation, with support from General Motors. This arm was originally used in assembly lines and is still used today by researchers in robotics. Finally, OTC Japan released the first generation of dedicated arc welding robots in 1979.

From 1980 on, the rate of new robotics started to climb exponentially. Takeo Kanade created the first robotic arm with motors installed directly in the joint in 1981. It was much faster and more accurate than its predecessors. Yaskawa America Inc. introduced the Motorman ERC control system in 1988. This has the power to control up to 12 axes, which was the highest number possible at the time. FANUC robotics also created the first prototype of an intelligent robot in 1992.

Two years later, in 1994, the Motorman ERC system was upgraded to support up to 21 axes. The controller increased this to 27 axes in 1998 and added the ability to synchronize up to four robots.

The first collaborative robot [cobot] was installed at Linetex in 2008. This Danish supplier of plastics and rubber decided to place the robot on the floor, as opposed to locking it behind a safety fence. Instead of hiring a programmer, they were able to program the robot through a touchscreen tool. Cobots, or collaborative robots, are robots intended for direct human to robot interaction within a shared space, or where humans and robots are in close proximity. Cobot applications contrast with traditional industrial robot applications in which robots are isolated from human contact.

It was clear from that point on, that this was the way of the future 'Road to Nowhere'.

Robotics and Artificial Intelligence (AI) Today

Source: World Economic Forum (where applied)

Robots and artificial intelligence were once used only for dull and difficult work on factory floors. Today, automation is everywhere - powering drones, cars, and surprisingly-realistic humanoids. [I dread to think of it.]

Robots are ready to get more social, and some of the latest models can even cross the "uncanny valley" by convincing us they are human. [Potentially very dangerous]

Meanwhile the increasingly sophisticated artificial intelligence powering popular entertainment and **social media platforms** is raising questions about whether it not only better engages audiences, but also helps spread harmful content like hate speech and conspiracy-mongering.

> Note: Are social media induced suicides following an exponential growth curve?

This World Economic Forum briefing is based on the views of a wide range of experts from the World Economic Forum's Expert Network and is curated in partnership with Charlotte Stix, Research Associate and Policy Officer for the Leverhulme Centre for the Future of Intelligence, University of Cambridge UK.

Robots at Work

Robot surrogates are increasingly being used for dangerous work and in extreme environments such as terrorist safe bomb explosion or deactivation.

Robots have long been used on factory floors for welding and painting. Now, they're making custom-ordered hamburgers, navigating through crowded hotel lobbies, hopping on elevators, and delivering room service. Amazon [see Chapter 5 above] has been at the forefront of introducing robots to our daily lives, with its clerk-free markets that enable automatic payment via credit card, Kiva merchandise handling systems, and drone delivery. Robots also enable exploration, by probing the depths of the ocean floor, deep space, the moon, and asteroids. The latest space-ready robots can work side-by-side with astronauts in the International Space Station, and US and Russian teams are working on robo-astronauts **that could explore other planets**.

Note:

"…Russian teams are working on robo-astronauts **that could explore other planets**. Whilst 80% of the global population of this planet live off of US $10 per day or less! No change there! *The priorities of these people will never cease to amaze me!* Please inform me what is the return on investment on global space research that has benefited this 80% of the global population. Please refer to 'Chapter 4 The Failure of Capitalism' section 'Maldistribution of Wealth'.

Robots are also being developed to perform crucial jobs during humanitarian crises. For example, the Defence Advanced Research Projects Agency (DARPA) Robotics Challenge is developing robots that would have been capable of saving lives during the 2011 Fukushima nuclear disaster in Japan.

Note:

Could this nuclear disaster not have been avoided by Government Health and Safety preventative measures? Please refer to' Chapter 4 The Failure of Capitalism' section 'The Unpreparedness of Capitalism and World Governments'.

The Defence Advanced Research Projects Agency (DARPA) is an agency of the United States Department of **Defence** responsible for the development of emerging technologies for use by the military. Carpet bombing, defoliation, napalm that type of thing.

Other robots in development may perform hazardous deep mining jobs, work with toxic substances, and clean sewers. Drones in particular have captured the popular imagination [this could be dangerous, they could be used to deliver bombs, as indeed they already are!]; they are a popular option for aerial photography, and Amazon and others are testing their use for delivery.

In less dramatic fashion, robots can use an electronic 'brain' located in the cloud [a proprietary computer server somewhere on the surface of the earth and certainly not in a cloud] to become trustworthy butlers, silently and faithfully [what a preposterous word] listening to queries about traffic, the weather, and turning on the air conditioning ["turning on the air conditioning" - very handy. Anyone who is sentient and fully fit and has difficulty flicking a switch might consider whether they are truly eligible for qualification for membership to the homo sapiens global gene pool.]

Next-generation robots will be performing tasks that require even more complex decision-making, aided by continuously increasing computing power. In January 2016 the company NVidia unveiled a supercomputer capable of up to 24 trillion operations per second, equal to the power of 150 MacBook Pro notebook computers. [See Quantum Computing – this chapter] This could enable a car to learn to drive by itself, through so-called reinforcement learning, rather than the conventional approach of finding a safe path by using real-time optimization. As related technologies mature, self-driving cars will become common, and will likely fundamentally change the job market by eliminating occupations like bus driver [and make the unemployment queues much longer at the expense of the tax payer – this will be dealt with later].

> Note: As Robotics and Artificial Intelligence sophistication advances then many occupations that are primarily mechanistic or primarily procedural and based on precedent such as doctor, surgeon, lawyer, high court judge, lorry driver, taxi driver, will or may, if so desired, be replaced by AI robots and or AI technology.

Researchers at Yale and Oxford Universities polled hundreds of attendees, some of whom are pioneers in the field of Artificial Intelligence, at two well-regarded AI conferences. The research provided the following data for the 50% probability for the year in which 'machines' would perform as well as humans for specific tasks:

Task	Year 'Machines' perform as well as humans (50% probability)
1.Maths Researcher	2063
2. Surgeon	2053
3. Write NY Times Best Seller	2051
4.Retail Salesperson	2030
5.Lorry Driver	2027
6.Write top-40 Pop song	2027
7.Telephone Banking Operator	2025
8.Fold Laundry	2022

Source: 'The Economist' December 2017

More than 5,000 surgical robots were used in more than 1 million procedures worldwide in the last year [2018]. These procedures spanned orthopaedics, urology, general surgery, gynaecology, neurology, thoracic, otolaryngology, bariatric, rectal and colon, multiple oncologies – even dental implants and hair transplants. Robotic surgery is no longer seen as a technology of the future – it's an active and effective technology of today.

Source: 'Robotics Business Review' February 2019.

These current techniques require human 'guidance' or 'collaboration' of the robot, presumably the date for Surgeon at 2053 in the table above is for fully un-aided Robot/AI surgery.

The number of jobs which AI and machines will displace in the future has been the subject of numerous studies and surveys and op-eds and policy papers since 2013, when a pair of Oxford academics, Carl Benedikt Frey and Michael Osborne, estimated that 47% of American jobs are at high risk of automation by the mid-2030s. Here are a few more recent examples:

McKinsey Global Institute: Between 40 million and 160 million women worldwide may need to transition between occupations by 2030, often into higher-skilled roles. Clerical work, done by secretaries, schedulers and bookkeepers, is an area especially susceptible to automation, and 72% of those jobs in advanced economies are held by women.

Oxford Economics: Up to 20 million manufacturing jobs worldwide will be lost to robots by 2030.

McKinsey Global Institute: At the high end of the displacement by automation spectrum are 512 US counties, home to 20.3 million people, where more than 25% of workers could be displaced. The vast majority (429 counties) are rural areas in the Americana and distressed Americana segments. In contrast, urban areas with more diversified economies and workers with higher educational attainment, such as Washington, DC, and Durham, NC, might feel somewhat less severe effects from automation; just over 20% of their workforces are likely to be displaced.

Source: Forbes Magazine June 2019

Critical tasks that go beyond physical labour, such as reading x-ray films and magnetic resonance imaging (MRI) scans, are already being performed by computers. Discovering new medicines might even be a possibility; after all, artificial intelligence is already helping to dispense financial advice to many people, with considerable accuracy and speed.

Autonomous Transportation

Source: World Economic Forum (contd.)

Self-driving vehicles are poised to become mainstream, but safety issues must first be addressed.

Large drones, originally invented for military missions, are almost ready for general transportation use. These drones are expected to be integrated into civil airspace after 2020, when the International Civil Aviation Organization releases rules for worldwide operation. Meanwhile smaller drones are already gaining popularity, thanks to their low operating costs and low risk. Agencies such as the National Aeronautics and Space Administration [NASA] in the US are developing a new drone traffic management system, and we may soon see crowds of drones in the sky that resemble scenes from a science fiction film. [Heaven forbid]

These machines are expected to create new job opportunities in some cases, and to take away jobs in others. [That socio/economic/ politico potential nightmare was easily dealt with – one sentence! The primary purpose of Robotics/AI is to remove human labour from existence and replace it with Robotic/AI labour. Perhaps the job creation to job removal ratio may be of the order of 1:100, or 1:1,000?]

Autonomous cars, unlike drones, are not yet ready for prime time. The latest self-driving cars, however, are equipped with sensors that can see in night time darkness and scan their surroundings more than 10 times per second, with extreme accuracy. Their 'brains' are state-of-the-art computers that can make trillions of calculations per second, and communicate both with other cars and with the cloud [propriety server computers] in order to receive the latest traffic updates.

Self-driving cars compute an optimal path by sensing their environment and predicting the movement of obstacles. During this process, artificial intelligence views human life as a cost in its calculations. But it is very difficult to represent the value of human lives as a cost function in a mathematical equation.

Note:

Quote: *"But it is very difficult to represent the value of human lives as a cost function in a mathematical equation."*

The arithmetic surely is quite simple:

Let X = the life-insurance policy payout for the age of the 'human' driver. Take X and multiply by a 'contingency' for the Insurance Company trying to get out of the deal say Z.

Ergo: For each dead human being that the robot has obliterated, the legal liability (whomever that may be!) has to pay the poor suffering human beings that remain i.e. Mum, Dad, Sister etc the following amount P (payout) (say in UK):

$$P = X * Z$$

So as an example case: If the human carcase that remains after robotic obliteration was previously ensured as a human being for Life Cover of say £1,000,000 then X = £1M and if say Z is 15% (seems reasonable) then

Payout P = £1M * 1.15

Therefore Payout P = £1,150,000

There, there, now that was not so difficult was it?

And no matter how sophisticated the on-board artificial intelligence, it is very difficult to assess how much collateral damage a potential collision will cause beyond impact. Only when autonomous cars' accident rate is proven to be significantly lower than that of human drivers will they be broadly welcomed and deemed safe enough to carry human passengers. In 2016, Airbus announced plans for an autonomous air taxi - and later that year Uber announced its own plans for an autonomous air taxi. In the meantime, however, Uber has had to deal with safety issues; in 2018, an Uber autonomous car struck and killed a pedestrian in Arizona. If and when autonomous drones and cars are granted equal right of way in civil airspace and on roads, it will prompt an interesting question: should robotic workers be granted similar privileges at work that protect them from discrimination?

Note:

Quote: *"If and when autonomous drones and cars are granted equal right of way in civil airspace and on roads, it will prompt an interesting question: should robotic workers* [what robotic workers? autonomous drones and cars presumably!] *be granted similar privileges at work that protect them from discrimination?"*

I cannot believe I am reading this!

So will an autonomous drone or car attend a Court of Law and defend itself if 'discriminated' against? The UK Courts use a system of trial by peer jury, so in the future, will we see a twelve drone jury or a twelve autonomous car jury presiding over the alleged crimes of drones or cars or their alleged crimes of discrimination?

The mind boggles!

Machine Cooperation and Coordination

Robots are increasingly being programmed to work with other robots and humans.

There are entire fields of research focused on enabling robots to cooperate. If robots are needed outside of controlled environments like factory floors, for example, they have to be able to quickly adapt to their surroundings in order to work both with other robots and with humans. Visual sensors help the machines to understand complex environments, while artificial intelligence aids their understanding of human gestures, facial expressions and even intentions.

One of the forerunners in this area is Baxter, an industrial robot developed in 2011 that can be easily taught new tasks, thanks to natural language processing and synthesis using so-called deep learning, or training computers to learn in a way that is similar to human brain absorbing information.

This variety of robot can be easily communicated with by using voice commands, and can be visually taught in a way that is much faster than the traditional method of entering commands into a handheld device. In addition to staffing an assembly line, **robots can be useful as companions**. Their powerful processors and advanced sensors allow them to recognize faces, understand voice commands, and do some **pretty neat tricks**.

[Quote: "do some pretty neat tricks"- this does not appear to be particularly mature writing.]

Amazon's Alexa and Google Home are examples of potentially helpful companion robots, as is Jibo, developed at the Massachusetts Institute of Technology, while Pepper, a humanoid robot from SoftBank, is designed to perceive human emotions. I dread to think if the SoftBank robot were to incorrectly perceive the emotional state of intention towards suicide and decided in its robotic wisdom to assist the sorrowful 'suicide'. Would the courts then have to charge the robot with the crime of manslaughter or in the worst case murder?

In recent years, robots have begun to compete against each other in soccer games, by autonomously adapting offensive and defensive strategies. One of the greatest advantages that robots have is a capability for high-speed communications. Whereas a typical human can speak 130 to 200 words per minute, which would translate into tens of bytes per second, robots can communicate as fast as one gigabyte (1 billion bytes) per second. [See Quantum Computing – this chapter, which is capable of trillions of floating-point operations per second]

Groups of robots can wirelessly work together even when separated by great distances, and can be synchronized by GPS technology with a great degree of accuracy. Extreme computation speed (more than one trillion operations per second) can enable these machines to cooperate regardless of the size of their grouping, or the distance between them, making humans far less competitive when it comes to many jobs. Just as data servers have made some aspects of traditional archives and libraries obsolete, robots - like data servers that can move around and behave autonomously - promise to impact our daily lives beyond anyone's imagination.

Note:

Quote: *"...robots - like data servers that can move around and behave autonomously - promise **to impact our daily lives beyond anyone's imagination.**"*

Presumably the World Economic Forum has included its own staff, its committee, its members and its authors under the term *"beyond anyone's imagination"*. If it is beyond their imagination then heaven help us. Again, the mind boggles!

This does not appear as though the noble and erudite World Economic Forum has instigated much forward planning in this regard! See Chapters 8 to 11 of this volume.

Machine Learning and Predictive Systems

It's becoming easier for machine learning systems to recognize patterns in large, evolving data sets.

Machine learning involves creating algorithms that can **recognize patterns in large, evolving data sets**, and drawing conclusions from past experience by using that data - in order to make machines smarter. [The larger the data set and the more rapidly the data set evolves, the more accurate and faster the conclusions may be arrived at – see below and Quantum Computing and Big Data in this Chapter]

When people refer to "artificial intelligence," they often really mean **machine learning**. Examples of technologies that make use of it include internet search engines, spam filters, and self-driving cars. Recently, an aspect of machine learning dubbed **"deep learning algorithms"** has received a lot of attention. That is because advances in computing power and masses of large-scale data, referred to as Big Data, have led to deep learning-based algorithms that are faster and more accurate than the human eye.

Note: Big Data is used by companies such as Facebook when 'harvesting' data that their users freely provide to the company most probably without being aware that they are doing so and also without being aware of the potential dangers of doing so.

In 2015, DeepMind, a UK-based firm that shares a parent company with Google, put the power of such algorithms on display when it pitted its AlphaGo computer program against a top human player of the board game 'Go'. The computer program won. More recently, in 2018, a company called Preferred Networks became the most valuable start-up in Japan, as investors including Toyota bet [predict] that the company's deep learning algorithms can eventually be applied to a number of manufacturing uses.

Machine learning is expected to have a profound impact on the job market. [More mass redundancies which Governments will perhaps have no idea how to handle].

Experts predict that both menial **and professional jobs** will be taken over by computers and robots equipped with learning algorithms. According to a study published by researchers from Carnegie Mellon University and MIT in the journal Science in 2017, evidence suggests that machine learning can do a better job of detecting skin cancer than a dermatologist, for example - though it would do a significantly poorer job of explaining to a patient why a lesion is cancerous or not. [At least at the moment.]

The potential advantages of the technology are clear, however, once machines learn, they never forget; a learning pattern can be efficiently copied from one machine to another; and, learning can be done in a parallel manner in order to improve and share. For example, if one unit masters the art of driving, that learning pattern can be copied into millions of other cars within a very short time. Cars connected through a network can therefore continuously share experiences to improve overall performance. Humans, on the other hand, take a long time to learn. Their experiences cannot be shared in the same way, and the value of their individual knowledge and experience can perish at death.

Intelligence Augmentation

Source: World Economic Forum

Robotic enhancement is helping humans exceed their natural limitations.

[Natural limitations regarding a propensity for War? Heaven forbid!]

Recent breakthroughs in wearable robotic systems may enable humans to perform physical feats that would have once been impossible, like walking extreme distances or carrying heavy loads. [Heavy weapons perhaps?]

In addition, research is underway that could result in better prosthetic limbs that are equipped with sensors and sophisticated algorithms, and are capable of receiving commands **from the human nervous system. [This sounds ominous].** These technologies could one day mean the end of physical disability - or the enhancement of existing brain functions. In addition to systems that are worn on the body, smart robotics systems have been developed to assist humans in tasks that require dedicated precision and repetition, such as surgery. Meanwhile so-called **telepresence robotics** enables people to be "present" for meetings or activities via a mobile video screen. Other forms of human enhancement include augmented reality devices that help people perceive their environment with richer relevant information. Google's Glass eyewear drew attention as one of the first such devices that could be worn in everyday situations, though the technology was widely panned [criticised] due to privacy issues and aesthetic appeal. Microsoft's Hololens wearable device can similarly map a user's environment and display data, though it is seen as bulky and uncomfortable.

These types of devices will generally become suitable for daily use, however. Google and other companies have also developed automatic, real-time [language] translators; once mocked, they can now provide accurate translation at lightning-fast speeds thanks to recent advances in deep learning, which mimics the functions of a human brain to help computers absorb information. When combined with mobile phones or augmented reality devices, these tools could potentially eliminate the need for human translators [there may even be less of a need for people to continue trying to learn foreign languages entirely].

Note: Perhaps in the future Robotics/AI will remove the need for human beings entirely – probably no bad thing. Peace and quiet at last!

Some have **envisioned neural implants** that **directly connect such technology to a human brain** in order to aid not only in translation, but also computation and memory.

Note: Here we enter a very, very dangerous field of endeavour. Once robotic devices and or artificial intelligence are 'hard-wired' into the human brain and consciousness, there is a real danger of 'Robotic-AI-Eugenics' – 'RAIE'. As far as I am aware, the term *'Robotic-AI-Eugenics' or 'RAIE'* was coined by this author.

There is a real danger of a Robotics-AI equivalent of the *Nationalsozialistische Rassenhygiene, 'National Socialist Racial hygiene'* a favourite concept with Adolf Hitler and his Nazis in Germany.

'Nationalsozialistische Rassenhygiene' Source: Too many to mention. Many fully authenticated references on the world-wide-web.

Those humans targeted for destruction under Nazi eugenics policies were largely living in private and state-operated institutions, identified as "life unworthy of life" (German: *Lebensunwertes Leben*), including prisoners, "degenerates", [that's where I fit in] dissidents, people with congenital cognitive and physical disabilities (including people who were "feeble-minded", epileptic, schizophrenic, manic-depressive, had cerebral palsy, had muscular dystrophy, were deaf, blind,) (German: *erbkranken*), homosexual, idle, [another of my strong points] insane, and the weak, for elimination from the chain of heredity.

More than 400,000 people were sterilized against their will, while up to 300,000 were killed under Action T4, a mass murder program. In June 1935, Hitler and his cabinet made a list of seven new decrees; number 5 was to speed up the investigations of sterilization.

You heard it here first [perhaps]. You have been warned. You have been reminded of History. If it happened once, it can happen again.

Back to World Economic Forum - Source

Some prosthetics are already controlled directly by a human nervous system - cameras can be linked to human brains in order to provide visual information to blind people, for example. [Excellent – anything that relieves suffering is a good thing]

While artificial intelligence systems will greatly increase our ability to interact with our environment, many jobs will be affected. That includes those that have generally been considered safe from **the invasion of robotic workers**, like travel guides and news 'journalists' i.e. auto-cue readers?

["Invasion of robotic workers" sounds like a science fiction horror film: *'Invasion of The Job Snatchers'* ['Invasion of The Body Snatchers' – 1956] - More mass redundancies].

AI Education and Awareness

Everyone must be empowered to master artificial intelligence. [Everyone! Even the criminally insane?]

Technological innovation in the realm of robotics and artificial intelligence is fundamentally transforming education, and updating the skills required to succeed in workplaces and classrooms. Building future-ready education systems requires curricula fit for the 21st century, and the consistent delivery of freely-available education for everyone.

In Finland, for example, a free online course, "Elements of AI," designed by the consulting firm Reaktor and the University of Helsinki, has garnered more than 130,000 registered students - and is intended to gradually educate larger swathes of the population about artificial intelligence in a bid to repurpose the economy for a new era. While specialized education should provide in-demand skills for new and existing workers, and address the disconnect [misunderstanding] between employer needs and existing instruction, public awareness must also be built regarding the impact of AI and robotics on the lives of ordinary people - and regarding its proper usage. Regardless of their age or socio-economic background, people must be empowered to engage with artificial intelligence and robotics and harness them to their advantage. This will require huge swathes of legislation to protect the human populace against the enormous possibilities for corruption in the use of AI.

When it comes to jobs that are dangerous and take a heavy toll on physical well-being, artificial intelligence and robotics can play a helpful role. However, there is a danger of increasing job loss due to automation. In England alone, about 1.5 million jobs are at high risk of being at least partially-automated, according to a report published by the Office for National Statistics in 2019.

Note: The current number of people employed in UK in 2019 is 33M. 1.5 million jobs vapourising equals circa 4.5% of the working population.

The Office for National Statistics further stated that in the three months to May 2017 the headline unemployment rate stood at 4.5%, or 1.49 million people. On this basis we may anticipate that the unemployment rate may indeed double to

9% owing to robotics and artificial intelligence if the unemployment rate at the time of robotics and artificial intelligence implementation, excluding the effect of robotics and artificial intelligence, is at 4.5%

The three occupations with the highest risk of automation are waiters, shelf fillers and elementary sales roles, according to the 2019 report. This threat calls for a rethinking of social security nets, as well as an effort to re-skill workers. Meanwhile young people must be inspired to master technology and to pursue work in related fields [and adjacent areas], while people in general need to become able to trust the technology that surrounds them - by better understanding its implications and practical uses. They must also be educated about those parts of AI systems where humans are still involved [the so-called hidden economy of AI], in order to blunt undue fear and hype.

Note:

I reiterate the information given earlier in this chapter in order that the gravity of this situation is not missed by the reader, even if it may have been missed by the World Economic Forum.

Researchers at Yale and Oxford Universities polled hundreds of attendees at two well-regarded AI conferences. The research provided the following data for the 50% probability for the year in which 'machines' would perform as well as humans for specific tasks:

Task	Year 'Machines' perform as well as humans (50% probability)
1.Maths Researcher	2063
2. Surgeon	2053
3. Write NY Times Best Seller	2051

Task	Year 'Machines' perform as well as humans (50% probability)
4.Retail Salesperson	2030
5.Lorry Driver	2027
6.Write top-40 Pop song	2027
7.Telephone Banking Operator	2025
8.Fold Laundry	2022

Source: 'The Economist' December 2017

The number of jobs which AI and machines will displace in the future has been the subject of numerous studies, surveys and policy papers since 2013, when a pair of Oxford academics, Carl Benedikt Frey and Michael Osborne, estimated that 47% of American jobs are at high risk of automation by the mid-2030s. Here are a few more recent examples:

McKinsey Global Institute: Between 40 million and 160 million women worldwide may need to transition between occupations by 2030, often into higher-skilled roles. Clerical work, done by secretaries, schedulers and bookkeepers, is an area especially susceptible to automation, and 72% of those jobs in advanced economies are held by women.

Oxford Economics: Up to 20 million manufacturing jobs worldwide will be lost to robots by 2030.

'Robots have already taken 66,000 jobs'. Each robot working in Britain's factories has cost the equivalent of 3.6 jobs, according to the first study of the impact of modern automation on employment. The research implies that the 18,500 robots deployed in vehicle manufacturing and other industries have already displaced about 66,000 posts. Carl Frey co-author of the research, and Oxford

Martin Citi Fellow at Oxford University, said *"Robots, just like technologies of the past, serve to boost productivity growth, but they do not create jobs, so far."*

Source 'Sunday Times' 29 April 2018

> Note: Quote: *" ... but they do not create jobs, so far."* Indeed, the very purpose of Robotics-AI is to remove the need for human employment and replace it entirely with more efficient and cheaper machines. It is not a displacement of one form of human labour to another, as has happened in the past. Robotics-AI implementation has the intention of the eradication of human labour, to be replaced by machines.

McKinsey Global Institute: At the high end of the displacement by automation spectrum are 512 US counties, home to 20.3 million people, where more than 25% of workers could be displaced. The vast majority (429 counties) are rural areas in the Americana and distressed Americana segments. In contrast, urban areas with more diversified economies and workers with higher educational attainment, such as Washington, DC, and Durham, NC, might feel somewhat less severe effects from automation; just over 20% of their workforces are likely to be displaced.

Source: Forbes Magazine June 2019

AI Safety, Security and Standards

The list of **potential malicious misuses of artificial intelligence is long and daunting[!!!!!]** Source: World Economic Forum

[My emboldening and exclamation marks]

Artificial intelligence systems may pursue goals that are different from what their designers intended, and cause unintended harm. For example, social media algorithms intended to increase engagement, and digital news algorithms intended to increase readership, may contribute to political polarization, misinformation, and internet addiction. The algorithms powering YouTube have come under related scrutiny, amid growing realization that the site's artificial intelligence tends to channel viewers to videos that have proven to be both highly-engaging and **filled with erroneous claims and outrage peddling** related to everything from how the Titanic "really" sank to anti-vaccination conspiracy theories, according to a report published in Scientific American in 2019.

Note: A similar criticism may be directed towards Google, Facebook, Yahoo and other digital services that direct unsuspecting and unaware mop-heads to related advertising that appears to 'prostitute' itself over every available square millimetre of one's internet communication device screen.

In relation to "anti-vaccination" reports it may be observed that in consideration that the US Government has made the US Pharmaceutical industry effectively immune from prosecution, then these "anti-vaccination conspiracy theories" may in fact be very true, very true indeed.

Note: **Before 2013, a US pharmaceutical company or a drug manufacturer could be sued.** Any serious side effects, injuries, illnesses, or deaths would mean a lawsuit. Countless millions of dollars were paid in drug lawsuit settlements. However, in 2013 the United States Supreme Court made a historic ruling that once a drug has been approved by the [Food and Drug Administration, USA] FDA, individuals are no longer permitted to sue the drug manufacturers, even though it has been confirmed or proven that the drug did cause harm. So, primarily after the FDA has approved a drug, people are prohibited from filing a lawsuit against a drug manufacturer. In such cases the lawsuit defendant is the US Government.

Source: MG Law USA

Other potential AI-related dangers come in the form of military drones operating without human control, which can cause unintentional harm to non-combatants. Clearly, artificial intelligence should be created and deployed with caution - and specialists and experts in the field should be educated in ethics.

> Note: "..specialists and experts in the field [of military drones operating without human control] should be educated in ethics." From the early conquests of the Greeks and the Romans to today, I have no recollection of any interaction between military forces and any concern for ethics.

Meanwhile clearer standards for the industry that emphasize accountability should be considered [in terms of killer drones, or Lethal Autonomous Weapon Systems, many have advocated for the development and deployment of clear restrictions on government and military use].

> Note: "Meanwhile clearer standards for the industry that emphasize accountability should be considered..." Sure, 'they' have considered it, and the motion was rejected.

Given that many artificial intelligence-related threats are unprecedented in scope, it will be necessary to update and amend both national and international regulation. In the US, the White House issued an executive order in 2019, "Maintaining American Leadership in Artificial Intelligence," that focuses on developing related technical standards, and California has adopted legislation supporting the Asilomar AI Principles including those related to safety - while several European countries are pushing for certification requirements for AI applications. AI can be used maliciously to target individuals, automate spear phishing attacks in a way that increases yield and decreases costs, and create realistic [but fake] online videos in a bid to incite public scandal and chaos. The list of other potential misuses is long: modifying traffic signs [turn red to green]; using drones to spy, make assassination attempts [as occurred in Venezuela in 2018] or ground flights; and using 'bots' to influence elections etc. As AI systems become more capable, related problems will have a larger impact. In the most extreme scenario, systems will entirely rid themselves of their human operators; in general, experts believe there is a 50% chance that artificial intelligence will outperform humans at everything in about 45 years. [i.e. 2065 A.D. – perhaps the beginning of the end but certainly not the end of the beginning]

AI Ethics and Values

Source: World Economic Forum

A shared value system is required for governing the data and decision-making behind artificial intelligence.

It is **increasingly evident** that **artificial intelligence systems can perpetuate historic biases, discriminate, and be used in ways that threaten human rights and democratic values [for example, image recognition technologies mis-categorize black faces, [or white faces] sentencing algorithms discriminate against black defendants, [or white defendants] and chatbots** [communicative robots] **can easily adopt racist and misogynistic language, according to a report published by the research institute 'AI Now' in 2019.** [my emboldening]

> Note: A chatbot is a software application used to conduct an on-line chat conversation via text or text-to-speech, in lieu of providing direct contact with a live human agent.

There are currently more than **40 sets of ethical guidelines** and principles for artificial intelligence in use in the world, which attempt to distil what values we can agree on - and advise on how best to implement them into institutional frameworks, technical research and applications, and regulations. The European Union, for example, published its "Ethics Guidelines for Trustworthy AI" in 2019, which includes requirements such as the transparency of related business models and the fostering of diversity. Ultimately, artificial intelligence is a multi-use technology that could drastically improve and prolong healthy lives, as [sic] and help us tackle some of our most difficult global challenges - and it is unlikely to be contained by national borders.

> Note: "...and it is unlikely to be contained by national borders." Very unlikely in consideration of the fact that drones are already used in cross-border, and indeed, cross-continent military applications.

That means that we must ensure that global use of artificial intelligence adheres to a shared value system [while being mindful of the potential for tensions and trade-offs stemming from the overlap of competing systems].

> Note: A "shared value system" does not necessarily exclude a shared value system where the sharers are in open competition, and potentially in open conflict, with one another. Indeed such a system is much more likely to be competitive amongst its sharers than not competitive amongst its sharers. The sustained situation between USA and China is of shared business trade deals but at the moment of writing they are in severe competition with one another and in conflict with one another. Indeed, under the modus operandi of modern capitalism, it cannot be otherwise.

Values inform our collective judgments about what is important, factor into our decision-making, and provide a crucial anchor amidst the technology-fuelled upheaval of the 'Fourth Industrial Revolution'. [Fourth Industrial Revolution as defined by the World Economic Forum not by this author.]

One of the key areas of artificial intelligence where values must be applied is data governance; the data used as fuel for AI systems should be acquired in a way that does not come at the expense of consumer privacy, and the type of data being used to make predictions should be transparent, according to an article published by McKinsey & Company in 2019. [Unlike, perhaps the current use of personal data by Google, Facebook and other social media platforms.]

An example cited in the article is a healthcare provider buying data about its patients from a broker, including information about which restaurants they frequent and how much TV they watch, in order to assess health risk. While the healthcare provider might believe this is in the best interest of patients, those patients might see it as an invasion of privacy.

> Note: Any practice as described in the above paragraph should be only permitted with the patient's approval in hand-written and dated signature. An interesting example of the quality of healthcare in the NHS UK is the case where a person was asked if he/she wanted his elderly parent to be resuscitated in the case of his/her conditions possibly requiring it. The person's answer was "I am not a qualified Doctor, I believe that you should follow your professional practice and do what is best for your patient which is ostensibly your sworn charter". A few days/weeks later the person who gave that answer above happened to read his mother's ward notes. On one page was written "Son agrees do not resuscitate". This was not only a lie, it was a damned lie, and possibly made the NHS UK liable for court action of criminal fraud.

6.5 Quantum Computing

Source: World Economic Forum

Quantum computing could eventually transform medicine, break formerly reliable encryption, [that sounds illegal!] and revolutionize communications and artificial intelligence. While the current Industrial Revolution has been built on technologies at a molecular level by integrating the physical, biological, and digital worlds, the advent of quantum computing means the next wave of technology may largely take place at an 'atomic' level [and a scale of computations being 10,000 times or more faster than current supercomputing]. However, despite recent advances, only a handful of quantum algorithms exist - and it remains an open question whether quantum computers will truly outshine their classical peers.

This briefing is based on a systematic review of academic articles on the topic and is curated in partnership with Frontiers, an open access publisher and open science platform.

Quantum Computing Theory

Pioneers have been laying the groundwork for quantum computing for nearly a century.

Since the dawn of modern computers, their design and implementation has been underpinned by the theory of information being processed as a series of classical "bits." In the case of Quantum Computing, researchers are working to develop the equivalent [quantum] theoretical foundation - one where information is encoded as a series of "quantum bits" or "qubits." The first appearance of the phrase "quantum information theory" could be traced to the physicists Charles Bennett and Stephen Wiesner, who met as undergraduate students in the 1960s and published important related ideas. Prior to that, in the 1930s, Alan Turing designed the Turing machine - providing the foundation for future theories about computing and computers - while Konrad Zuse designed and built what is considered to be the first electromagnetic binary computer: the Z1. In 1981 Richard Feynman, a winner of the Nobel Prize in Physics, challenged a group of computer scientists to develop a new breed of computer based on quantum physics. That helped lay the groundwork for a new paradigm, by introducing the idea that quantum computing could solve problems that classical [analogue or binary] computing cannot.

In 1994 Peter Shor, now a Professor of Applied Mathematics at Massachusetts Institute of Technology MIT, triggered excitement by showing that it is possible to factor a number into its primes efficiently on a quantum computer - and speed up classical computation exponentially. **For example, in order to break widely used RSA [Rivest–Shamir–Adleman] 2048-bit encryption, a classical computer running one trillion operations per second would require 300 trillion years; a quantum computer, as Shor demonstrated, could achieve the same feat in just 10 seconds.** The first working, 3-qubit Nuclear Magnetic Resonance (NMR) computer was built in 1997. Roughly a decade later, the Canadian start-up D-Wave revealed a 28-qubit quantum computer, and in 2017 IBM launched an industry initiative to build commercially-available quantum computing systems; in 2019 the company presented the world's first integrated quantum computing system for commercial use. Also in 2019, researchers from Google claimed to have created the first quantum computer able to perform a calculation impossible for a standard computer, and in 2020 the American conglomerate Honeywell said it would offer cloud-based [proprietary servers] access to the world's most powerful quantum computer, as measured by quantum volume.

> Note: Google just took a quantum leap in computer science. Using the company's state-of-the-art quantum computer, called Sycamore, Google has claimed "quantum supremacy" over the most powerful supercomputers in the world by solving a problem considered virtually impossible for normal machines.

> The quantum computer completed the complex computation in 200 seconds. That same calculation would take even the most powerful supercomputers approximately 10,000 years

to finish, the team of researchers, led by John Martinis, an experimental physicist at the University of California, Santa Barbara, wrote in their study published 23rd October 2019 in the journal 'Nature':

"It is likely that the classical simulation time, currently estimated at 10,000 years, will be reduced by improved classical hardware and algorithms." Brooks Foxen, a graduate student researcher in Martinis' lab, said in a statement, "But since we are currently 1.5 trillion times faster, we feel comfortable laying claim to this achievement," he added, referring to the supremacy of quantum computers.

Source: www.livescience.com October 2019.

Quantum Computer Design

Chips are being developed and programming is being done, but these computers require particular conditions.

Even if a quantum computer can be shown to work theoretically at this point, there are enormous technical challenges to overcome before it can actually work physically. These include a need to work at super-low temperatures, and in ultra-low electronic noise environments. Researchers are working to overcome these hurdles. Similar to classical digital computers, quantum computers have three main components: inputs/outputs (I/O), memory, and a processor. The quantum computer's I/O, however, involves a physical process of manipulating the states of quantum bits (qubits) to store a '1', '0', or '0-1' quanta state. While in classical, "binary" computing a bit is a single piece of information that can exist in two states - a '1' or a '0' - qubits can store much more information because they can exist in any superposition of these quantum states. One way to picture the process: while a classical bit can be at either of two poles on a sphere, a qubit can be any point on that sphere. This means a computer using these bits can store significantly more information, using less energy.

Multiple qubits can be grouped together, in order to make registers that help store and move large amounts of quanta data through the quantum system. The processor for these machines is created by using qubit logic gates - which are constructed to perform complex operations. In an effort to create a quantum computer that can out-compete conventional computers, technology giants such as Google and IBM are racing to achieve so-called "quantum supremacy" (IBM developed the first quantum computer programmable via the cloud in 2016). There is a great amount of difficulty involved in designing a stable quantum computer that can hold its quantum state long enough to be practically viable. A number of start-ups are focusing on achieving this kind of stability [rather than just increasing numbers of qubits]. Some companies have already created what they deem to be quantum computers, though there is some debate about what qualifies as a "true" quantum computer. Still, progress continues; Intel, for example, has said it is producing quantum processors, and is doing engineering targeting "production-level" quantum computing in the coming decade.

Quantum Computer Memory

Using 'qubits' instead of the traditional method involving 'bits'.

Quantum memory could be the key to dramatically increasing the amount of information that can be stored on a computer - and making computers much faster at solving certain types of problems. The field of quantum memory, or simply how to store information on a quantum computer, covers everything from the best-suited physical systems to abstract methods that can be used to increase the computer's performance. Quite simply, quantum memory is the quantum-mechanical version of ordinary computer memory because it takes advantage of the strange ability of sub-atomic particles to exist in more than one state at any given time.

Due to the way these tiny particles behave, certain computer operations can be done much more quickly and use less energy than classical computers - where information is traditionally stored as a series of '0's and '1's known as "bits." By way of contrast, quantum memory involves storing data within basic units of quantum information known as "qubits," or "quantum bits." The relative advantage of qubits is that they can have more than two states to process or store information, due to something known as the "quantum superposition" phenomenon.

A quantum computer has a third state, [whereas the traditional binary super-computer has two states, '0' and '1'] where the qubit can be a mixture of '0' and '1' - relative to the contribution of each of these two states. As a result, greater storage capacity as well as the utilization of sophisticated algorithms to process information may dramatically increase the efficiency of solving particular kinds of computational problems - and could revolutionize modern computing in the process.

Several ways to build a quantum computer based on qubits have already been proposed, and researchers are evaluating these proposals experimentally to find out which may be the most promising methods around which to build a fully-functional computer. The use of photons seems, as of now, to be the most promising solution. One recent advancement has been the successful secure storage and retrieval of qubits; while the efficiency rate of optical qubit storage was previously 30%, researchers at Laboratoire Kastler Brossel (LKB) in Paris managed to increase this to 70%. Because quantum memory will be essential to construct a quantum communication network, this development has been viewed as a significant step forward.

> Note: Quantum memory storage and quantum computing will revolutionise data storage and certain computing techniques and it may have a huge effect on Data Harvesting – the sort of personal data collecting mechanisms used by

social media for direct targeted marketing and advertising. So we may all be even more bombarded by advertising and marketing for junk that we don't need, and never have really actually needed. With the use of 3-Dimensional holograms and other forms of virtual reality, at some time in the future it may be possible to bombard the poor slave-consumer with not only 3-Dimensionality of marketing and advertising but with 4-Dimensionality+ of virtual texture and virtual smell. The use of smell is already widely used in retail outlets to induce a sense of well-being in the slave-consumer to heighten the possibility of over consumption.

Practical Applications for Quantum Computing

From financial markets to fertilizer, the technology could prove immensely useful.

Quantum Computing has the potential to revolutionize many aspects of our daily lives. While the topic is often over-hyped, quantum computers may prove to be particularly good at solving certain types of problems. Not those related to complex calculations, necessarily, or those related to search engine functionality, or image processing. But quantum computing can drastically improve optimization and artificial intelligence, potentially disrupting [significantly influencing] a number of industries.

AI is the perfect candidate for quantum computation, because it is based on the principle of learning from experience - which in turn is based on calculating the probabilities for many possible choices. Another primary application is the modelling of molecular interactions that can result in innovative products, **including pharmaceutical drugs** [Huge warning signs here, See 'Chapter 4' section: **'The Pharmaceutical Industry – The Pharmaceutical Paradox'**] and solar cells. It can also be applied to producing the fertilizer necessary to feed the planet; while current processes for creating fertilizer are incredibly energy-intensive, research suggests quantum simulations could help chemists [what are Chemists doing in the food-related industries?] develop more efficient methods. Cryptography is another area where quantum computers can outperform digital computers, **potentially rendering current online security methods obsolete.**

> Note: There is a very, very real danger here in a Quantum Computing technology race in Military, Security and related industries. First past the post countries could 'tear' into laggards' outdated super-computing security systems and with the speed of quantum computing probably infiltrate, extract and store on their quantum computer, every single security detail available within a matter of minutes. Google as stated above, claim that their quantum computer completed a complex computation in 200 seconds. That same calculation would take even the most powerful supercomputers approximately 10,000 years to finish. Quantum Computing, installed in a host country ahead of other countries, is a military and industrial spy's dream come true. Perhaps there is no greater, emerging capitalist induced nightmare.

Modern financial markets run on some of the most complicated systems in existence, and investors and analysts may turn to quantum computing to help make them more efficient. [Hopefully there will be 'quantum leap' improved Financial Market Regulations ensuring that there will be no more banking crashes]. Weather forecasting is another potential application that could benefit both the public and private sectors. Just about any country's economic health is directly or indirectly affected by the weather; [and the consequential health of the soil, plants and foodstuffs] improved forecasting would benefit food production, transportation, and many other facets of GDP. In addition, better climate models could give us more insight into future climate scenarios.

> Note: Weather pattern forecasting could be particularly crucial if the models can incorporate 'global warming' or

'global climate change' data. Also the ability to predict droughts, storms, tsunamis etc. so that preparation and provision for these potential weather crises may be put in place well in advance and the crises obviated. However, capitalists and governments have historically shown great reluctance to invest in 'preparedness'- see 'Chapter 4 The Failure of Capitalism' section 'The Unpreparedness of Capitalism and World Governments'.

In light of all of these potentially impactful applications, governments and businesses have scaled up research and development efforts. In 2018, the European Commission kicked off the ramp-up phase of its Quantum Technologies Flagship initiative, aimed at using a €1 billion budget to bring together research institutions, companies and public funding. Meanwhile the US is spending about US \$1.2 billion between 2019 and 2028 to make its mark on the technology, and China is building a US \$10 billion national laboratory for related research. However, while the development of quantum technologies is moving fast, it is still at a relatively preliminary phase.

Note: Interestingly the budget for quantum computing in China appears to be approximately ten times that of each of USA and the European Commission. You heard it here first!

Post-Quantum Computing Security

Quantum computers could crack current cryptography with relative ease.

The dawn of the quantum computing age brings with it many potential new risks - including those related to security. The privacy of online communication is currently protected by cryptography, which shields information as it travels around the internet. It secures everything from making online purchases to accessing work email remotely. Confidential and sensitive government and business information is highly valuable to hackers and corporate rivals, whether it relates to the R&D in a pharmaceutical business, geological surveys in the energy industry, trading data in financial services, or budgeting plans and employees' personal data. And while blockchain and cryptocurrencies have been hailed as revolutionary means to securely store data and financial information, they were built on existing public key encryption - which may not be a match for quantum computers. [It won't be.] In general, many of the security algorithms used to keep our information safe could be cracked relatively quickly by a quantum computer, which is able to factor large numbers more efficiently than the sort of classical [super] computer used to build current encryption standards.

Broad adoption of quantum computing might still be far in the future, but significant progress has been made. In 2019, IBM and Google each published studies claiming their quantum computers performed a task not possible with even the strongest [most powerful] traditional computers [though they differed on the value of their respective results].

As stated above: Google claim that their quantum computer completed a complex computation in 200 seconds. That same calculation would take even the most powerful supercomputers approximately 10,000 years to finish.

Meanwhile government agencies and industry groups have expressed a growing sense of urgency when it comes to transitioning to a quantum-safe future. It is expected to take a considerable amount of time to develop, standardize, and deploy post-quantum cryptographic techniques. Researchers are working on new algorithms resistant to the strength of a quantum computer but also able to meet business objectives. In order to ensure that everyone's data is safe in a quantum future, and to secure international support, it is crucial that the development of quantum-resistant cryptosystems is transparent - carried out in full view of cryptographers, governments, organizations, and the public. While it might not be an immediate threat, everyone should start considering potential implications of this impending reality.

> Note: One might reasonably question the possibility in "creating [truly] quantum-resistant cryptosystems" using traditional super-computing binary systems. As seen above 200 seconds versus 10,000 years to solve a complex computation is most certainly a 'quantum leap' forward [pun intended]. In terms of security of data and the threat of cyber spying, then with regard to quantum computing "He Who Has Wins" would be the slogan of choice perhaps, as opposed to "He Who Dares Wins" – "Who Dares Wins" 'Special Air Service' UK motto.

'Are We Ready for Quantum Computers'

'Hardware hasn't caught up with theory, but we're already lining up many previously intractable problems for when it does.'

Source: Scientific American – March 2020

A recent paper by Google claiming that a quantum computer performed a specific calculation that would choke even the world's fastest classical supercomputer has raised many more questions than it answered. Chief among them is this: When full-fledged quantum computers arrive, will we be ready?

Google achieved this milestone against the backdrop of a more sobering reality: Even the best gate-based quantum computers today can only muster around 50 qubits. A qubit, or quantum bit, is the basic piece of information in quantum computing, analogous to a 'bit' in classical computing but so much more.

Gate-based quantum computers operate using logic gates but, in contrast with classical computers, they exploit inherent properties of quantum mechanics such as superposition, interference and entanglement. Current quantum computers are so noisy and error-prone that the information in its quantum state is lost within tens of microseconds through a mechanism called decoherence and through faulty gates.

Still, researchers are making demonstrable, if slow, progress toward more usable qubits. Perhaps in 10 years, or 20, we'll reach the goal of reliable, large-scale, error-tolerant quantum computers that can solve a wide range of useful problems. When that day comes, what should we do with them?

We've had decades to prepare. In the early 1980s, the American physicist Paul Benioff published a paper demonstrating that a quantum-mechanical model of a Turing machine—a computer—was theoretically possible. Around the same time, Richard Feynman argued that simulating quantum systems at any useful scale on classical computers would always be impossible because the problem would get far, far too big: the required memory and time would increase exponentially with the volume of the quantum system. On a quantum computer, the required resources would scale up far less radically.

On a big enough quantum computer, we could simulate quantum field theories to study the most fundamental nature of the universe. In chemistry and nanoscale research, where quantum effects dominate, we could investigate the basic properties of materials and design new ones to understand mechanisms such as unconventional superconductivity. We could simulate and understand new chemical reactions and new compounds, which could aid in drug discovery.

However, simulating quantum physics is *the* **app** [application] for quantum computers. They're not going to be helping you stream video on your smartphone. If large, fault-tolerant quantum computers can be built, they will enable us to probe the strange world of quantum mechanics to unprecedented depths. It follows different rules than the world we observe in our everyday lives and yet underpins everything.

Note: Until such time that quantum computers and quantum algorithms are working and reliable, then our laptop passwords are relatively safe. So are, hopefully the passwords and systems that control financial markets, hold the country's secrets, hold company private and confidential data, hold personal confidential data and not least hold the security codes for Presidents around the world to release upon us all the might of global thermo-nuclear weapons.

6.6 Bio Technology

Source: World Economic Forum

Bio Technology is the exploitation of biological processes for industrial and other purposes, especially the genetic manipulation of microorganisms for the production of antibiotics, hormones, etc.

Medical biotechnology is personalizing medicine by keying in on our individual biology, industrial biotechnology is being used to develop more eco-friendly ways of building things, agricultural biotechnology [organic?] can help feed an expanding global population, and synthetic biology is helping to sustainably produce essential chemicals and materials. Meanwhile environmental biotechnology may yet solve the vexing problem of plastic pollution. However, while recent biotechnology-related advances have opened up incredible new possibilities, they have also created significant ethical issues - as society grapples with concepts like gene-edited babies. [gene-edited babies - heaven forbid!]

This briefing is based on the views of a wide range of experts from the World Economic Forum's Expert Network and is curated in partnership with Dr. Sang Yup Lee, Distinguished Professor, Department of Chemical and Biomolecular Engineering, Korea Advanced Institute of Science and Technology (KAIST), and colleagues.

Medical Biotechnology

Ageing populations and people with genetically-inherited diseases can benefit from gene editing, but there are ethical concerns.

Medical biotechnology is a rapidly developing means to rejuvenate the elderly and regenerate ageing or diseased organs - a potentially helpful development for the many countries with greying [ageing] populations [nearly 8.7% of the global population was aged 65 or older by 2017, up from 6.7% in 1997, according to World Bank data]. The use of "induced pluripotent" stem cells, which do not have to be derived from human embryos, has shown promise for regenerating an injured heart [while avoiding the ethical issues tied to the use of human embryonic stem cells], for example.

Biotechnology tools are also being used for the diagnosis and treatment of human disease in a personalized way. We are currently able to modulate each layer of biology, from genes to proteins and cells. When it comes to the immunological treatment of cancer, the clinical development of protein or antibody-based therapeutics is advancing, and the range of biological targets is expanding. In addition, genetically modified immune cells are being developed as immuno-oncology drugs, including chimeric antigen receptor (CAR)-T cells and T-cell receptor (TCR)-transduced T cells.

Regenerative medicine will be accelerated by gene-editing technology. CRISPR-Cas9, for example, enables the direct modification of genes in the interest of preventing and treating disease - though there are significant ethical issues related to altering the human genome in ways that will be passed from one generation to the next [a Chinese scientist stunned the world in 2018 when it was revealed that he had engineered the world's first gene-edited babies in a bid to make them resistant to their father's HIV infection].

Note: If one studies the human evolution, or lack of it, regarding Ethics and systems of Morality, then one may draw the conclusion that very, very little significant progress has been made since the birth of Plato. If this is the case, then one might further draw the conclusion that Humankind has not made the required progress in terms of Ethics and systems of Morality to engage in the very serious matter of engineering human baby's genes or similar enterprises. Humankind, it appears, does not have the maturity of Ethics and Morality to successfully cope with such precipitous and dangerous notions. Perhaps, it may be wise; to put such endeavours on hold, until such time that Humankind considers that it is of sufficient Ethical and Moral maturity to be able to undertake such enormous responsibilities. Natural Law is Natural Law and Humankind 'plays' with it at its peril. Mention has already been made of the preposterous and horrendous follies of that very misguided man, Adolf Hitler and his Nazis made in their enthusiasm for eugenics.

Tissue engineering has also evolved, thanks to organoid [a minia-turized organ produced in vitro] technology, novel biomaterials, and 3D printing. In general, a more personalized application of medical biotechnology is necessary, to enhance therapeutic efficacy and minimize unwanted side effects. The most important personal factor is the genome - in terms of genetic and acquired diseases. Integrating genome information into medical data is an important component of precision medicine, and is being aided by artificial intelligence. Personalized cancer vaccines, and drug tests using surrogates, are also major elements of precision medicine.

Environmental Biotechnology

Plastic pervades our lives while spoiling the environment and biotechnology may provide a sustainable solution.

Note: The significant reduction, or preferably the complete eradication, of unnecessary over-consumption may also help.

Metabolic and bioprocess engineering can be used to treat waste water and tackle serious environmental problems - including plastic pollution. The production and incineration of plastic will add more than 850 million metric tons of greenhouse gases to the atmosphere during 2019, equivalent to the pollution caused by 189 coal-fired power plants, according to a report published by the Center for International and Environmental Law. Plastics like polyethylene terephthalate (PET) pervade our daily lives because they are cheap to manufacture and highly durable. This durability causes serious damage; as much as 8.8 million metric tons of plastic waste is estimated to enter the ocean every year, **where it will remain indefinitely**.

> Note: This data is confirmed elsewhere. We are producing over 300 million tons of plastic every year, **50% of which is for single-use purposes** – utilized for just a few moments, but on the planet for at least several hundred years. More than 8 million tons of plastic are dumped into our oceans every year. Courtesy of the packaging industry's thirst for over-designed, plastic; 'sanitized' packaging that appears to require a pick-axe to open and typically results in a plethora of broken finger-nails.
>
> Source: Plasticoceans.org

> This data suggests that multi-use plastic is an absolute imperative and that it must be of a structure that will permit degradation to granular, liquid or semi-liquid matter that may readily be recycled to perpetuity. An alternative for single-use products might be paper-based or metal-based materials that are more readily recyclable.

Microorganisms, which have mostly been used for the production of chemicals and materials, can also be applied to the biodegradation of plastics in a way that enables a highly-sustainable recycling system. In 2016, a Japanese research team from the Kyoto Institute of Technology and Keio University published a report in the journal 'Science' about a bacterium called Ideonella sakaiensis, which contains an enzyme, PETase, that was found to be able to degrade Polyethylene Terephthalate - PET.

A Korean research team from the Korea Advanced Institute of Science & Technology - KAIST and Kyungpook National University further delved into this PET-degrading enzyme and determined its 3D crystal structure, while predicting a molecular mechanism of the PET degradation. They published their research in the journal 'Nature Communications' in 2018 - and the approaches behind it can now be applied to the study of enzymes that could degrade other types of plastics. Recent research on the biodegradation of plastics has created potential for synergy with the sort of microbial production of biodegradable polymers that have long been studied by microbial engineers. Microorganisms can now be engineered to produce polyhydroxyalkanoates [polyesters that can store carbon], polylactic acid [a biodegradable polyester], and, as of recently, aromatic polyesters that use renewable biomass feedstock as raw material. One lingering challenge has been to find a way to improve microbial production performance at an economically viable scale - which will need to be overcome in order to significantly mitigate plastic pollution and establish sustainable plastic recycling.

> **Note:** Quote: "...establish sustainable plastic recycling." Establishing sustainable, global non overconsumption would be much more profitable.

Agricultural Biotechnology

"Green" biotechnology can help generate more nutritious food for an expanding global population.

Note: As discussed in 'Chapter 4 The Failure of Capitalism' section 'Unrestrained Perpetual Population Growth' the need for very extensive and expensive Agricultural Biotechnology was inevitable. Here is another example of the potential for human beings to interfere with Natural Law. The disturbance to wildlife by the use of 'factory farming' techniques causing the decimation and sometimes extinction of many species of mammal, bird, butterfly, moth etc. is widely reported and well known.

Furthermore, also as shown in section 'Unrestrained Perpetual Population Growth', the global population is anticipated to be 9.7Bn in 2050 and 10.9Bn in 2100. This represents an increase by 2050 of 24% on the 2020 figure of 7.8Bn, and an increase of 39% by 2100. In 1928 the global population was estimated at 2Bn which means that with the population in 2020 being 7.8Bn then the increase in population in just the last 92 years was 290% or almost three times population increase. Here we see the challenge to feed the world with an unrestrained growth in global population.

Data Source: Our World in Data United Nations – 2019

Soon the world will have to start to consider synchronised population control on a pan-global scale. The only alternative is failure.

Agricultural, or "green" biotechnology can be used to help improve crop yields and quality, nutrient usage, disease resistance, environmental stress resistance, and flowering time. Technology has been used to modify the genetic content of plants throughout the history of human civilization - long before the discovery of DNA, Neolithic-era farmers developed domesticated crops by selecting those with desirable traits derived from naturally-occurring mutation. Later, the selection of the most desirable plants from the general population was crystalized into the concept of breeding - which spawned a plethora of modern crops. The pinnacle of breeding technology has been the development of "semi-dwarf" wheat, which is sturdier and higher-yielding, and now accounts for most of the wheat acreage in the world after appearing around the middle of the 20th century. Advances in DNA technology, coupled with the identification of genes essential for desired traits, raised green biotechnology to a new level; scientists became able to not only pinpoint a gene regulating a specific trait, but also to introduce the gene into plant genomes by using methods such as particle bombardment.

> Note: Here the inherent catastrophic dangers in this technology are obvious. Man may be able to get away with skirting around the edges of Natural Law, but to impinge upon it unduly without due regard for the potential consequences may well cause catastrophic repercussions. Climate change may be an example of impinging upon Natural Law without due regard for the potential consequences.

> "For every action there is an equal and opposite reaction."
> Isaac Newton 1643-1727

This ability to introduce a specific gene as a DNA fragment removed the biggest hurdle for conventional crop breeding: reproductive isolation separating different species. The successful generation of the blue rose using a blue gene from another plant species, for example, is testament to this. The removal of this species barrier has opened up new ways to mass produce valuable products, like edible vaccines and medicinal compounds.

> Note: Providing that "edible vaccines and medicinal compounds" are ethically produced and sold. 'Chapter 4 The Failure of Capitalism' section 'The Pharmaceutical Industry – The Pharmaceutical Paradox' lays to ruin any possibility of that happening.

Meanwhile genome editing technology enabled by ZFN, TALEN, and more recently CRISPR/Cas9, promises even more precise plant engineering. **This technology can knock out a specific gene, change the sequence of a specific gene, and replace one DNA fragment with another. This can occur without leaving a trace of foreign DNA or resulting in antibiotic-resistant genes** [a flaw often associated with genetically-modified organisms or GMO]. The recent development of a soybean variety that can produce high levels of heart-healthy oils and the engineering of wild ground cherries in a way that can make them as domesticated as strawberries, underline the ways green biotechnology may be able to help sustain a rapidly-expanding global population.

> Note: Quote "may be able to help sustain rapidly-expanding global population" see 'Chapter 4 The Failure of Capitalism' section 'Unrestrained Perpetual Population Growth'. "..a rapidly-expanding global population" is not what we want, if we are to obviate global starvation. An ever-expanding spiral, asymptoting at Armageddon.

Industrial Biotechnology

"White" biotechnology can help feed the undernourished and better protect the environment.

Industrial Biotechnology, also known as "white" biotechnology, involves the sustainable production of chemicals, pharmaceuticals, food, fibres, textiles, and energy. White biotechnology is often referred to as the third wave of biotechnology, following "red" biotechnology [medical-related] and "green" biotechnology [agriculture-related], and it has become a powerful means to address climate change, mounting energy demand, the depletion of fossil-fuel resources, and environmental issues including petroleum-based plastics and micro-plastics pollution. The field's underpinning technologies are mainly based on the engineering of microbial hosts, and it has been boosted over the course of the past decade by scientific breakthroughs in metabolic engineering, synthetic and systems biology, and advanced cultivation techniques. In particular, the recent establishment of systems metabolic engineering [combining metabolic engineering with systems biology, synthetic biology, and evolutionary engineering] has led to dramatic advances. Through the comprehensive optimization of existing methods, and the creation of new methods, the spectrum of possible commercial products has been expanded dramatically - including healthy food products that can be used to combat malnutrition in impoverished parts of the world.

> Note: Quote: "..including healthy food products that can be used to combat malnutrition in impoverished parts of the world." Hasn't happened yet in the last 2,000 years, why should it happen now?

Compared with traditional, fossil fuel-based chemical processes, an industrial biotechnology process completed via a single fermentation can be a way to make relatively affordable products that help protect the environment. As a result, the total industrial biotechnology market is expected to grow at a rate of nearly 9% annually, and reach a total size of US $472.3 billion by the end of 2025. According to a study published by the Organisation for Economic Co-operation and Development, OECD 'The Bioeconomy to 2030: Designing a Policy Agenda', industrial biotechnology will account for 39% of all economic value generated by biotechnology by the year 2030.

Bioethylene, for example, is expected to account for as much as 40% of all plastic polyethylene production by 2035 - and production of biodegradable polylactic acid, usable for everything from decomposable packaging material to medical implants, is expected to reach 800,000 tonnes by 2020, according to the International Energy Agency and International Renewable Energy Agency. Ultimately, industrial biotechnology can make a major contribution to achieving United Nations Sustainable Development Goals related to fostering affordable and clean energy, sustainable cities and communities, and responsible consumption and production.

Note: The development of biodegradable plastics of any form is to be welcomed. It has been a long time coming. However, in terms of the bigger picture, the problem of plastics is no more than a plastic pin-prick on the back of a mammoth.

Bio Big Data and Machine Learning

The automated analysis of increasingly large sets of genetic data promises to transform health care.

Biomedical science is transforming into big-data science. Thanks to next-generation genomic sequencing technology, there has been a dramatic data explosion; as of 2016, more than 100,000 human genomes had been sequenced from normal and diseased tissue, and petabytes of raw sequence data are now being produced and deposited in public genome data repositories such as International Cancer Genome Consortium data portal. This is transforming the scientific landscape, and entire healthcare systems. Currently-archived datasets represent only a small fraction of the genome-related big data yet to be produced, as sequencing capacity will continue to grow. If the current growth rate continues, doubling capacity about every seven months, exabytes-worth of genome data [one exabyte is equivalent to about 250 million DVDs worth of video] will be yielded in the next 5 years. As the global population pushes toward 8 billion within the next decade, it is possible that 15% or more of it will have their genome sequenced. In addition to genomics, high-resolution imaging, medical records, and lifestyle-related datasets will add new dimensions to bio big-data, and provide a foundation for next-generation healthcare.

Note: Quote "If the current growth rate continues, doubling capacity about every seven months, exabytes-worth of genome data [one exabyte is equivalent to about 250 million DVDs worth of video] will be yielded in the next 5 years." This program will perhaps require quantum computing and storage to be truly effective. There is a real danger that this is simply more of the same and will only accelerate and exacerbate the problems outlined in the previous chapters. The ethics shown to date in the pharmaceutical industry indicate that it may be unwise for this industry to be inadequately regulated in this field and others relating to this technology. Indeed, global pan-country regulations are imperative. Otherwise, we are all Dead Men Walking by 2040.

However, there is a long road ahead before big data can help deliver precision medicine - based on a patient's genetic makeup and environmental circumstances - to the masses. There are immense challenges when it comes to data storage, distribution, and proper interpretation in biomedical contexts. Large-scale machine learning systems need to be integrated with vast computing infrastructure in order for deep learning, one of the most promising branches of artificial intelligence, to help better enable the navigation of big data and detect things that are impossible to catch manually. Machine learning could facilitate the mining of gene-to-gene interaction, the classification of cellular images, and finding links between datasets. Yet, machine-learning algorithms require large-scale, high-quality "ground truth" data for algorithm training - which is difficult to acquire. In addition, machine learning can be biased, and understanding exactly how machine learning algorithms are classifying the features in datasets can [will] be challenging. Still, the analysis of big data will eventually have an enormous impact on disease prevention, on the ability to cure and care, and on the global healthcare system.

Note: Quote: "Still, the analysis of big data will eventually have an enormous impact on disease prevention." The best impact on disease prevention is food and diet, adequate clothing and shelter and excercise. The immune system is strengthened by good food, clothing, shelter, good work and good rest. Particularly nutritious food that is balanced so as to 'feed' the immune system; perhaps the most important components in the body that require strength of immunity are the heart, brain and gut. Good food, clean water and healthy exercise are the true sources, not analysis of analysis of analysis.

Synthetic Biology

Microbial cell factories can sustainably produce the chemicals needed to fuel an economy.

Civilization has largely committed itself to forging a more resource-efficient and sustainable global economy.

> Note: 'Civilisation' has largely committed itself to the consumption of more than its needs for the few to the detriment of the many. I perceive no change in capitalism over many, many years that would make me believe that capitalism really cares about "...a more resource-efficient and sustainable global economy." This is the domain of 'Think Tanks' and similar other 'talkers' not 'doers', capitalism is driven by quarterly sales figures and net profit margins, nothing more and nothing less, excepting perhaps shareholder value and shareholders are driven by nothing other than greed. The eternal greed-wheel turns – the trapped mouse/hamster responds, the wheel turns and the mouse/hamster helps to keep it turning. To mix metaphors; a pawn in a Game. However, the Game is also a pawn in its own game. A Non-Nietzschean 'Eternal Cycle of Recurrence'.

One of the ultimate goals is to reconcile demand for chemical materials needed to treat human disease, develop sustainable agriculture and fisheries, bolster food security, and power industrial applications with the need to ensure biodiversity and environmental protection. In order to help achieve this, many countries have leveraged advances in synthetic biology and metabolic engineering by using natural biological processes to produce important chemicals - and by making use of standardized, intelligent "cell factories" [collections of microbial cells, often built from bacteria or yeast, that can function like a chemical production facility]. The consequences of this could be as significant as the impact of alchemy on chemistry millennia ago, with enormous and **perhaps unimaginable implications for medicine and materials science**. The range of potential applications is vast, encompassing, and not limited to: diagnostics, therapeutics, sensors, environmental remediation, energy production, and biomolecular and chemical manufacturing. Studies have shown, for example, the potential to deploy bacteria-based cell factories to sustainably produce ethanol and butanol - which could in turn be used to de-carbonize transportation.

> Note: Quote: "…with enormous and perhaps **unimaginable implications for medicine and materials science**." If the World Economic Forum [the authors of this] cannot imagine the implications; then who the hell on earth can [pun intended]?

Following the emergence of recombinant DNA technology, which mashes up DNA from different species to produce combinations that have value for medicine or industry, biological systems have become widely used in industries such as chemicals and pharmaceuticals. However, the cell factories underpinning these processes often encounter systemic failure and suffer from instability. Synthetic biology and metabolic engineering can be applied to these problems by developing cells specifically designed for predictable, efficient, and streamlined production. Synthetic biology and metabolic engineering also enable the development of new biological systems capable of efficiently producing industrial chemicals and materials while consuming relatively less time, labour, and money. Some examples of this trend include reported advances in the microbial production of gasoline, terephthalic acid [an organic compound used to make clothing and plastic bottles], 1,4-butanediol [used to make fibres such as Spandex], and aromatic polyesters. In 2016, systems metabolic engineering was selected as one of the Top 10 emerging technologies by the World Economic Forum, for the ways that it can be used to more sustainably and affordably produce chemicals by using plants instead of fossil fuels.

> Note: Quote: "...affordably produce chemicals by **using plants instead of fossil fuels.** These geniuses realise that we are completely depleting fossil fuels to non-existence, so now let's start on plants and do the same with plants!

Gene and Genome Engineering

DNA can now be picked apart and rearranged like a bouquet of flowers.

[More genius from The World Economic Forum.]

> Note: Or alternatively, DNA can now be picked apart and rearranged like a nightmare of tangled, irrepressible and ugly weeds.

> Note: DNA deoxyribonucleic acid, a self-replicating material which is present in nearly all living organisms as the main constituent of chromosomes. It is the carrier of genetic information.

As the 20th century drew to a close, biotechnology's equivalent of Promethean [recourse to the demigod Promethean is perhaps singularly inappropriate] fire appeared: the first detailed sequence of the human genome. Now, the ability to decrypt genetic sequences has empowered us - albeit while creating significant risks.

Note: Quote ".. while creating significant risks" - must be the understatement of the century.

The DNA structure discovered by Watson and Crick in 1953 begat a restriction enzyme that can cleave DNA within seconds which begat the discovery of biochemical enzymes that process DNA, which begat gene-editing technology that could be used to directly control the expression of intracellular genes within a nucleus. However, it was neither cost-effective nor efficient to manipulate gene expression within the nucleus - a problem solved by the breakthrough discovery of the CRISPR-Cas9 system in the early 21st century. Researchers found that by attaching a specific sequence of guide RNA joined up with a protein called Cas9 to a genome, they could cut and delete (or add) DNA. Soon after its discovery, CRISPR-Cas9 became a global sensation due to its relative ease and compatibility with just about any type of organism.

Genome manipulation techniques were eventually discovered that can eradicate or correct erroneous genes, to create recombinant embryos, treat cancer, or prevent infectious diseases. In the near future, gene therapy drugs could be injected, potentially eliminating the need for surgery to avoid genetic defects - such as the procedure the actress Angelina Jolie underwent to address her predisposition to breast and ovarian cancer.

Note: Herein again is the danger of transgressing Natural Law. Nature is not perfect and is unlikely to ever be so. For mere human beings, creatures that ostensibly have a very low average IQ of approximately IQ 100, tampering with things infinitely beyond their comprehension in terms of Universal Natural Law, is potentially a path to disaster. However, such a proposition is completely immaterial if the capitalist classes can see a money making opportunity out of it.

Epigenetics, or the study of genetic expression that doesn't involve changing a DNA sequence, promises future innovation for genome engineering. Epigenetics could eventually enable humans to adapt to, and evolve in, environments such as the atmosphere of Mars.

> Note: Why go to Mars? We haven't finished the job of ruining this planet yet.

However, genome engineering comes with ethical issues. [See example below:]

> Note: The second 'understatement of the century'! In only three paragraphs, this must be a first in the History of Western Literature.

A Chinese scientist's successful effort in 2018 to create genetically-engineered babies in order to endow them with a resistance to their father's HIV infection shocked the scientific community and points to a need for greater global awareness of the perils of genetic engineering technology as a means of artificial reproduction [Chinese officials have since declared that the scientist's conduct was illegal]. Prometheus's gift, after all, had serious repercussions for civilization.

> Note: Quote "Prometheus's gift, after all, had serious repercussions for civilization."

> This is a rather glib throwaway line, is it not? When you consider that the business of gene and genome engineering could bring about dangerous and irreversible effects at the very core of the human condition. Secondly, why more Greek pretension?

6.7 Blockchain

Source: World Economic Forum

A blockchain provides an immutable record of transactions performed across a network without the need to rely on an intermediary, such as a central bank. It is a concept that brings together economics and digital technologies in a way never before conceived. Blockchain enables not just new means by which to deliver financial services and support cryptocurrencies, but can also reshape and redefine government, legal services, accounting, insurance, supply chains, and energy distribution.

> Note: Cryptocurrency[ies] is a digital currency in which encryption techniques are used to regulate the generation of units of currency and verify the transfer of funds, operating independently of a central bank.

This briefing is based on the views of a wide range of experts from the World Economic Forum's Expert Network and is curated in partnership with Professor William Knottenbelt and Dr Catherine Mulligan, Director and Associate Director of the Centre for Cryptocurrency Research and Engineering, Imperial College London.

Financial Products and Services

Blockchain can potentially facilitate everything from cross-border payments to insurance claims.

> Note: A blockchain is a database that is shared across a network of computers. Once a record has been added to the chain it is very difficult to change it. The records that the network accepted are added to a block. Each block contains a unique code called a hash. It also contains the hash of the previous block in the chain.

Blockchain technology may be best known as the underpinning of virtual currencies such as **Bitcoin,** which have touched off a speculative fury as investors place bets on new, decentralized means of payment.

Note : Quote "...**Bitcoin,** which have [sic] touched off a speculative fury as investors place bets on new, decentralized means of payment."

"Investors" is this not a rather grand term? "place bets" sounds rather more like the coinage [pun intended] of some cheap east-end London casino venue complete with sad, addicted, dysfunctional people in need of medical help rather than even more capitalist exploitation. "Bet responsibly" the Gambling Industry falsely cries. More capitalist avarice – will it ever end? Refer to 'Chapter 4 – The Failure of Capitalism' section 'Maldistribution of Wealth'.

But blockchains can help to efficiently address the need for multiple, cost-effective financial products and services that can comply with relatively exacting financial regulation. For example, transparency and auditability requirements can potentially be more easily met by using blockchain. Theoretically, instead of having to send requests for information to a bank or other type of organization, an auditor could simply verify transactions on a publicly-available blockchain ledger thanks to its fixed permanence, according to an article published by the consultancy Deloitte in 2017.

Note: Perhaps such a blockchain ledger(s) could be assigned to Social Media companies and others regarding their user transactions and made accessible to Governments to ensure appropriate tax payments.

In addition, because a high value financial transaction on blockchain can potentially require only about one hour to be cleared, whereas a traditional transaction of the same value might require as much as a month or more to be cleared, the technology could make more frequent audits possible, according to the article.

More broadly, blockchain can be viewed as moving the financial services industry away from process-oriented approaches, and towards data-based workstreams.

Insurance is another example of a service where blockchain could dramatically improve processes. In 2016, a group of insurance and reinsurance companies including Allianz, Swiss Re and Munich Re launched an initiative to explore ways to use blockchain technology to provide faster and more secure services. The following year, the group presented a prototype smart contract management system, designed to cover everything from setup to settling claims. When it comes to cross-border financial transactions, blockchain could also theoretically play a helpful role. In March 2018, the Society for Worldwide Interbank Financial Telecommunication, or SWIFT, tested the use of blockchain technology to reconcile payments among accounts spread across 34 banks; the test showed that the technology has made significant progress in terms of security and governance, though it was not yet ready to support large-scale, mission-critical global infrastructures, according to SWIFT. Compliance with international trade regulations could also be improved through the use of blockchain, by creating immutable audit trails. In 2017, Deloitte and the Hong Kong Monetary Authority announced they had developed a blockchain technology proof of concept for trade finance, which included participants such as the Bank of China [Hong Kong], Hang Seng Bank and Standard Chartered Bank.

Decentralized Asset Management

Blockchain may spur greater innovation in the ways that assets are managed.

The growth of the sharing economy, which provides everything from vacation rentals to car service, can be better enabled through the use of blockchain. Thanks to its transactional capabilities, the technology is able to help co-ordinate loosely coupled assets, companies, and individuals, and can help dramatically reduce the transaction costs associated with both sharing business models and so-called "as a service" models. It also allows for radically new forms of ownership to emerge.

In 2017, for example, the non-profit Crypto Valley Association in Switzerland introduced the concept of a Blockchain Crypto Property, or purely digital property rights registered on a blockchain that can be transferred around and carry out functions. Blockchain can also play a fundamental role in re-configuring how utility services are provided. For example, it can redefine how telecom network services are constructed and delivered, by changing how spectrum, or the radio waves needed for mobile phones and wireless networks to function, and physical infrastructure are delivered, managed and paid for. In addition, energy and water systems can utilize blockchain to create peer-to-peer energy markets that provide greater flexibility to users and infrastructure owners.

A key challenge is presented by the need to measure the economic output of digital systems with large numbers of decentralized assets. Blockchain can assist in this task, through its ability to capture a record of transactions and bolster the data collection used to measure the digital economy. An increasingly digitalized world, however, means that the number and variety of cyberattacks are growing. In addition, data breaches are becoming more common [commoner], as reduced storage costs mean more data is being held for longer periods. The sensors that are increasingly a part of our daily lives also multiply the possibility of an attack. A clear understanding of the privacy policies and regulation associated with blockchains and similar digital technologies is required. Security concerns specifically tied to blockchain include the potential to take control of enough participating nodes in a ledger to tamper with the validation of transactions [a so-called "51% attack," in the case of Bitcoin], and distributed denial of service attacks that increase processing time, according to a report published in 2017 by the European Union Agency for Network and Information Security.

> Note: There are inherent strengths and weakness with the database structure of Blockchain. Its lack of ability to edit data is a strength in terms of preventing fraudulent activity but a weakness when requiring authorised and proper editing of data. Cyber-attacks against such a rigid database structure may cause problems when trying to rectify the harm of the attack.

Bitcoin had a global estimate of 7.1 million active users. These were split by 2.3 million using Bitcoin to make payments regularly, and 4.8 million using it to facilitate the speculative trade of cryptocurrency, i.e. by converting to other currencies and back again, or simply trading back and forth during volatile periods.

Source: The 'Chainalysis' Report 2018

> Note: From this we see that the speculative currency traders [raiders] outweigh the genuine users by 209%. Here we see as above capitalist avarice – will it ever end? Refer to 'Chapter 4 – The Failure of Capitalism' section 'Maldistribution of Wealth'.

> "How About Doubling Your Money in 12 months?"

> "Imagine being able to take advantage of crypto's volatility, up and down, to make high profits without any particular risk or knowledge. That's what we have been doing for over 4 years now (with impressive records). Find out how right away…"

Source: Crypto Daily Advertisement:

https://cryptodaily.co.uk/2020/06/jason-morgan-creek-btc

Note: The unstoppable avarice goes on and on and on and on!

Environmental Sustainability

The environmental credentials of blockchain technology are under review.

The environmental impact of some blockchain technologies - especially those that rely on "mining," or confirming transactions by using computing power to solve difficult math problems - is a source of controversy.

Note: 'Mining': To add a block [of data] to the chain, computer nodes must demonstrate that they have done 'work' by solving an increasingly difficult computation. This process is called 'mining'.

The mining employed to support the Bitcoin cryptocurrency, for example, sucks up enough electricity to power about 6.4 million US households, a consumption level roughly equivalent to that of the Czech Republic, according to the Bitcoin Energy Consumption Index published by the website Digiconomist; a single Bitcoin transaction could power nearly 33 US households for an entire day, according to the index.

Note: Quote "..a single Bitcoin transaction could power nearly 33 US households for an entire day, according to the index."

What a joke! When the entire world of global government is extoling the virtue of energy consumption reduction! Capitalism, as currently practiced, will invoke an involuntary mass suicide. This must be stopped.

As the price of a single Bitcoin rose from about US $2,300 in May 2017 to more than US $7,000 roughly one year later, [304% per annum 'growth' – the capitalist's avarice dream come true] demand for cryptocurrency mining surged. Despite projected advances in the energy efficiency of mining hardware, cryptocurrency miners have sought out cheaper, more abundant energy sources in places such as the Nordic countries in Europe and rural areas of the USA. [A long way to travel for an electricity socket] Some utilities have expressed reservations about providing energy for mining [Hardly surprising]. Still, utilities have found their own internal uses for blockchain; in early 2018, European utilities disclosed plans to directly trade energy with each other using the technology.

So-called peer-to-peer energy markets are just one way in which blockchain technology can actually play a key role in better protecting the environment. The so-called circular economy, which involves re-using materials and resources in order to prevent waste, can benefit from the use of blockchain to better track materials like wood or fabric throughout their stages of use, according to a report published in 2016 by the Ellen MacArthur Foundation.

In addition, someone buying a bicycle, for example, could benefit from blockchain technology by automatically receiving an unaltered chain [pun not intended] of details about materials used to build the bicycle, where it was built, and who built it, according to the report.

> Note: This is a great idea. Use the annual power production of say half a dozen nuclear power stations to find out where my bike puncture repair outfit was made!

Blockchain can also be used to facilitate carbon trading, or the practice of businesses buying credits that offset the greenhouse gas emissions caused by their operations through funding environmentally-friendly initiatives. Ice cream maker Ben & Jerry's launched a pilot program in 2018 that uses blockchain to directly connect the sale of individual scoops sold over the counter to carbon credits that fund a forest conservation project in Peru.

Note: This is getting better. However, perhaps the GDP of Czech Republic is required to pay for the electrical power for the computing of the sales numbers of the ice cream scoops. No wonder I cannot afford a Ben & Jerry's ice cream in St James's Park, London.

Economic and Social Structures

Blockchain can make supply chains more efficient and environmentally friendly.

Blockchain is the first truly digital economy technology - one that brings economics and technology together in a genuinely novel way. It enables the redefinition of trust not just within industries, but also across societies.

Note: Quote: "It enables the redefinition of trust not just within industries, but also across societies."

Surely, it does no such thing. Surely there is little need for trust because it is very; very difficult to 'hack into' the blockchain system. Computer data security is blockchain's raison d'etre. In a greed driven method such as capitalism, genuine 'trust' is very thin on the ground, if it actually exists at all. Any corporation or individual involved in blockchain may be the biggest corporate criminal in the world, but it/he/she will have little success when trying to circumnavigate blockchain. Blockchain, in this regard, obviates the need for 'trust'.

Many aspects of current interaction on the internet could be improved by blockchain, for example, thanks to its ability to handle verification and transactions in a peer-to-peer, secure way that does not rely on large intermediaries. Supply chains, the essential circulatory system that ensures that global commerce can carry on uninterrupted, may receive a healthy re-balancing between local and global due to the use of blockchain; as a mechanism for exchanging value and creating an immutable record of transactions, even small companies could use blockchain to better collaborate and in some cases even compete with global players. The technology could also help to reduce environmental damage, by cutting down on the unnecessary transport of goods around the world. The so-called "greening" of global supply chains will require greater traceability and transparency, according to a report published in 2017 by the International Finance Corporation (IFC). Blockchain, as a system that effectively cannot be tampered with, can provide more reliable information on where food originated and how it was produced, according to the IFC report.

Blockchain can also create new insights for regulators, who may in some circumstances and at certain times need to see the provenance of different elements within a supply chain. For example, within a food supply chain, the technology can provide greater transparency when it comes to food scandals or contamination, enabling regulators to see exactly what areas have been affected and to better direct their efforts at solving problems. A number of start-ups are working on related issues, including a United Kingdom based company that launched a pilot program in Indonesia that uses blockchain-enabled tagging to track tuna fishing, according to the IFC's 2017 report. A key challenge with blockchain is ensuring that industrialized systems based on the technology are robust and secure enough to handle the volume of transactions that occur in large supply chains. For example, transactions on blockchain in the Bitcoin cryptocurrency currently require an average of 10 minutes to be confirmed, and the system is limited to a throughput of around seven transactions per second - due to a trade-off between scalability and resilience against malicious actors.

Note: Quote "..can provide greater transparency when it comes to food scandals or contamination..". Perhaps China might research the advantages of this capability regarding virus limitation viz Covid-19 and others?

Identity and Persona Management

Effective identity management is indispensable, and could be aided by blockchain.

Identity and the management of identity are critical foundations for our everyday interaction with the world as taxpayers, consumers and employees. Increasingly digitalized societies and economies mean that the manner in which identity is managed is essential for realizing related benefits. For industries ranging from banking to healthcare, blockchain can be used to respond to the need for digital identity and persona management by providing a system more in tune with changing needs. As the use of internet services grows, for example, people may have an increasing desire to be able to actively manage their digital identities independent of the control of a public entity or private company, like a bank or a social network. So-called self-sovereign identity systems provide a way to do that, by enabling single online identities to form independent, online relationships with each other and with other services. In a report updated in 2017, the non-profit Sovrin Foundation suggested that such systems, underpinned by blockchain, could turn organizations that are now identity providers into "identity proofers," as users securely take their own identity from place to place.

Note: All good stuff, providing that the organisations storing the data and those having access to this data are known to the taxpayers, consumers and employees about whom the data is being stored. Furthermore, the taxpayers, consumers and employees should be up-dated on the data being stored on them in real-time and have the legal right to challenge the data for errors. The challenges should be implemented in an uncostly and timely manner. The corrections, if any, should also be implemented in a timely manner.

Personally, I would not be very happy, if my data was confused with someone who invaded say, a Middle East country and I ended up in The Hague in a splendidly impressive oak-panelled court room full of large plaques with Latin inscriptions and some very serious men opposite me as I reside behind large bullet-proof screens protecting me from I dare to think what.

Note: It is interesting that the reference is to storing the data of taxpayers, consumers and employees. It may be a good idea to have data stored on capitalist corporations and their CEO and Board of Directors together with that of Parliamentarians. At least those Parliamentarians found guilty of expense fraud. Just a thought.

Identity management is also critical for enabling the achievement of the United Nations Sustainable Development Goals established in 2015. Goal 16 specifically calls for the provision of a legal identity for everyone in the world by 2030 - in order to ensure access to basic services and rights. According to the UN, as of 2017 the regional average for populations that had been assigned a birth registration was just 71%, while less than half of children under five years of age in sub-Saharan Africa had had their births registered. Effective identity management systems, utilizing a shared blockchain infrastructure, could ultimately help bolster social protection, assist in dealing with disasters, create more resilient economies, reduce corruption, and empower women. ConsenSys, a company that has been recognized by the UN for its efforts, has developed a blockchain-based identification system designed to help end child trafficking in Moldova, for example. In any country, resilient digital identity systems can potentially help citizens to better understand all the data being stored about them, and to know when others have accessed that data. Key challenges, however, include both the scalability of the blockchain, and the need to maintain individual privacy while using the technology.

Note: Quote: "..to know when others have accessed that data."

Also to know who or what organisation it was who accessed their data and for what purpose.

Note: Quote: "Key challenges, however, include both the scalability of the blockchain, and the need to maintain individual privacy while using the technology."

Maintaining individual privacy should, hopefully not be a problem, providing access is limited to the known authorised on a need-to-know basis and access approval is secure.

Governance and Law

Industries, standards groups, developers and users want guidance on the legal ramifications of adopting blockchain.

Note: This is always a problem with governments being required to legislate for new technologies, the future ramifications of which are often not readily identifiable at the time that legislation is needed. Further, the trans-country global reach of many of these technologies and their companies becomes a significant problem when the legislation of a particular country or region is applicable to the particular country or region only. Perhaps blockchain may be used to 'hoover-up' all the spurious un-paid taxes held in off-shore accounts beyond the immediate reach of the economy that the capitalists are making so much money out of. Global blockchain connectivity between tax authorities may help to obviate much capitalist banditry and add perfectly acceptable tax revenue to help pay for infrastructure, schools, hospitals etc. rather than a particular individual purchasing a desert island that they will probably only visit once every full, blue moon.

Digital technologies have often outpaced the development of related regulation and legal standards, but blockchain has pushed this dynamic to a new extreme by fundamentally challenging the ways that governments manage economies and make policy, and by potentially altering the underlying framework for providing legal services. Blockchain challenges the very meaning of citizenship, [Really? How?] and the ways that public goods have traditionally been delivered. It can enable central governments to devolve power to regions, while retaining stewardship over an overall system. The Dubai Land Department, for example, has developed a blockchain project intended to better share property data among multiple parties, including government entities, and secure related transactions, while Sweden's land mapping and registration authority has tested using blockchain in order to make recording and transferring land titles more efficient. The effort in Sweden could theoretically eliminate fraud, and reduce the time required to complete transactions from several months to several hours.

6.8 Nano Technology

Source: World Economic Forum

Nanotechnology [or "nanotech"] is the manipulation of matter on an atomic, molecular, and supramolecular scale. The earliest, widespread description of nanotechnology referred to the particular technological goal of precisely manipulating atoms and molecules for fabrication of macroscale products, also now referred to as molecular nanotechnology. A more generalized description of nanotechnology was subsequently established by the National Nanotechnology Initiative, which defines nanotechnology as the manipulation of matter with at least one dimension sized from 1 to 100 nanometers. This definition reflects the fact that quantum mechanical effects are important at this quantum-realm scale, and so the definition shifted from a particular technological goal to a research category inclusive of all types of research and technologies that deal with the special properties of matter which occur below the given size threshold. It is therefore common to see the plural form "nanotechnologies" as well as "nanoscale technologies" to refer to the broad range of research and applications whose common trait is size.

Nanotechnology as defined by size is naturally very broad, including fields of science as diverse as surface science, organic chemistry, molecular biology, semiconductor physics, energy storage, microfabrication, molecular engineering, etc. The associated research and applications are equally diverse, ranging from extensions of conventional device physics to completely new approaches based upon molecular self-assembly, from developing new materials with dimensions on the nanoscale to direct control of matter on an atomic scale.

Scientists currently debate the future implications of nanotechnology. Nanotechnology may be able to create many new materials and devices with a vast range of applications such as in nanomedicine, nanoelectronics biomaterials energy production, and consumer products. On the other hand, nanotechnology raises many of the same issues as any new technology, including concerns about the toxicity and environmental impact of nanomaterials, and their potential effects on global economics, as well as speculation about various doomsday scenarios. These concerns have led to a debate among advocacy groups and governments on whether special regulation of nanotechnology is warranted.

> Note: Quote"… whether special regulation of nanotechnology is warranted." This author would consider the special regulation of nanotechnology to be imperative.

Fundamental Concepts

Nanotechnology is the engineering of functional systems at the molecular scale. This covers both current work and concepts that are more advanced. In its original sense, nanotechnology refers to the projected ability to construct items from the bottom up, using techniques and tools being developed today to make complete, high performance products.

One nanometer (nm) is one billionth, or 10^{-9}, of a meter. By comparison, typical carbon-carbon bond lengths, or the spacing between these atoms in a molecule, are in the range 0.12–0.15 nm, and a DNA double-helix has a diameter around 2 nm. On the other hand, the smallest cellular life-forms, the bacteria of the genus Mycoplasma, are around 200 nm in length. By convention, nanotechnology is taken as the scale range 1 to 100 nm following the definition used by the National Nanotechnology Initiative in the US. The lower limit is set by the size of atoms [hydrogen has the smallest atoms, which are approximately a quarter of a nm kinetic diameter] since nanotechnology must build its devices from atoms and molecules. The upper limit is more or less arbitrary but is around the size below which phenomena not observed in larger structures start to become apparent and can be made use of in the nano device. These new phenomena make nanotechnology distinct from devices which are merely miniaturised versions of an equivalent macroscopic device; such devices are on a larger scale and come under the description of microtechnology.

To put that scale in another context, the comparative size of a nanometer to a meter is the same as that of a marble to the size of the earth. Or another way of putting it: a nanometer is the amount an average man's beard grows in the time it takes him to raise the razor to his face.

Two main approaches are used in nanotechnology. In the "bottom-up" approach, materials and devices are built from molecular components which assemble themselves chemically by principles of molecular recognition. In the "top-down" approach, nano-objects are constructed from larger entities without atomic-level control.

Areas of physics such as nanoelectronics, nanomechanics, nanophotonics and nanoionics have evolved during the last few decades to provide a basic scientific foundation of nanotechnology.

Materials reduced to the nanoscale can show different properties compared to what they exhibit on a macroscale, enabling unique applications. For instance, opaque substances can become transparent [copper]; stable materials can turn combustible [aluminium]; insoluble materials may become soluble [gold]. A material such as gold, which is chemically inert at normal scales, can serve as a potent chemical catalyst at nanoscales. Much of the fascination with nanotechnology stems from these quantum and surface phenomena that matter exhibits at the nanoscale.

Bottom-up approaches should be capable of producing devices in parallel and be much cheaper than top-down methods, but could potentially be overwhelmed as the size and complexity of the desired assembly increases. Most useful structures require complex and thermodynamically unlikely arrangements of atoms. Nevertheless, there are many examples of self-assembly based on molecular recognition in biology, most notably Watson–Crick basepairing and enzyme-substrate interactions. The challenge for nanotechnology is whether these principles can be used to engineer new constructs in addition to natural ones.

Molecular Nanotechnology: a long-term view

Molecular nanotechnology, sometimes called molecular manufacturing, describes engineered nanosystems (nanoscale machines) operating on the molecular scale. Molecular nanotechnology is especially associated with the molecular assembler, a machine that can produce a desired structure or device atom-by-atom using the principles of mechanosynthesis. Manufacturing in the context of productive nanosystems is not related to, and should be clearly distinguished from, the conventional technologies used to manufacture nanomaterials such as carbon nanotubes and nanoparticles.

When the term "nanotechnology" was independently coined and popularized by Eric Drexler [who at the time was unaware of an earlier usage by Norio Taniguchi] it referred to a future manufacturing technology based on molecular machine systems. The premise was that molecular scale biological analogies of traditional machine components demonstrated molecular machines were possible: by the countless examples found in biology, it is known that sophisticated, stochastically [a process involving a 'randomly' determined sequence of events] optimised biological machines can be produced.

It is hoped that developments in nanotechnology will make possible their construction by some other means, perhaps using biomimetic principles. However, Drexler and other researchers have proposed that advanced nanotechnology, although perhaps initially implemented by biomimetic means, ultimately could be based on mechanical engineering principles, namely, a manufacturing technology based on the mechanical functionality of these components (such as gears, bearings, motors, and structural members) that would enable programmable, positional assembly to atomic specification. The physics and engineering performance of exemplar designs were analysed in Drexler's book *'Nanosystem's'*.

In general it is very difficult to assemble devices on the atomic scale, as one has to position atoms on other atoms of comparable size and stickiness. Another view, put forth by Carlo Montemagno, is that future nanosystems will be hybrids of silicon technology and biological molecular machines. Richard Smalley argued that mechanosynthesis are impossible due to the difficulties in mechanically manipulating individual molecules.

Research and Development

Because of the variety of potential applications [including industrial and **military**], governments have invested billions of dollars in nanotechnology research. Prior to 2012, the USA invested US $3.7

billion using its National Nanotechnology Initiative, the European Union invested US $1.2 billion, and Japan invested US $750 million. Over sixty countries created nanotechnology research and development [R&D] programs between 2001 and 2004. In 2012, the US and EU each invested US $2.1 billion on nanotechnology research, followed by Japan with US $1.2 billion. Global investment reached US $7.9 billion in 2012. Government funding was exceeded by corporate R&D spending on nanotechnology research, which was US $10 billion in 2012. The largest corporate R&D spenders were from the US, Japan and Germany which accounted for a combined US $7.1 billion.

Nanotechnology Applications

As of August 21, 2008, the Project on Emerging Nanotechnologies estimates that over 800 manufacturer-identified nanotech products are publicly available, with new ones hitting the market at a pace of 3–4 per week. The project lists all of the products in a publicly accessible online database. Most applications are limited to the use of "first generation" passive nanomaterials which includes titanium dioxide in sunscreen, cosmetics, surface coatings, and some food products; Carbon allotropes used to produce gecko tape; silver in food packaging, clothing, disinfectants and household appliances; zinc oxide in sunscreens and cosmetics, surface coatings, paints and outdoor furniture varnishes; and cerium oxide as a fuel catalyst.

Further applications include nanoscale additives in polymer composite materials are being used in baseball bats, tennis rackets, bicycles, motorcycle helmets, automobile parts, luggage, and power tool housings. Source: https://www.nano.gov/

Note: From above: sunscreen, cosmetics, surface coatings, gecko tape, food packaging, clothing, disinfectants, household appliances, paints and varnishes, baseball bats, tennis rackets, bicycles, motorcycle helmets, automobile parts, luggage, and power tool housings. None of these appear to be particularly mission critical to the survival of our species.

Further applications allow tennis balls to last longer, golf balls to fly straighter, and even bowling bowls to become more durable and have a harder surface.

> Note: Tennis balls, golf balls and bowling bowls as above; none of these appear to be mission critical to the survival of our species. Here we see the capitalist justification for new technology; mostly in reality, technology for technologies sake. Technology was rarely a solution to any real problem i.e. starvation; it has usually been simply a means of generating capitalist sales revenue.

Trousers and socks have been infused with nanotechnology so that they will last longer and keep people cool in the summer. Bandages are being infused with silver nanoparticles to heal cuts faster. Video games consoles and personal computers may become cheaper, faster, and contain more memory thanks to nanotechnology. Also, to build structures for on-chip computing with light, for example on chip optical quantum information processing, and picosecond transmission of information.

> Note: Trousers, socks, video games – critique as tennis balls etc. above.

Nanotechnology may have the ability to make existing medical applications cheaper and easier to use in places like the general practitioners' office and at home. Cars are being manufactured with nanomaterials so they may need fewer metals and less fuel to operate in the future.

In the field of medicine and medical research, here are three examples below:

Source: https://www.nano.gov/

A. Research in the use of nanotechnology for regenerative medicine spans several application areas, including bone and neural tissue engineering. For instance, novel materials can be engineered to mimic the crystal mineral structure of human bone or used as a restorative resin for dental applications. Researchers are looking for ways to grow complex tissues with the goal of one day **growing human organs for transplant**. [my emboldening]

> Note: "growing human organs for transplant." This has alarm bells ringing all over it. It sounds like a career advancement strategy for would be Nobel Prize winner enthusiasts. We have spoken of Alfred Nobel in a previous chapter.

B. The design and engineering of advanced solid-state nanopore materials could allow for the development of **novel gene sequencing** technologies that enable single-molecule detection at low cost and high speed with minimal sample preparation and instrumentation.

> Note: "novel":- Limitations can be expected in any technology, especially in a novel one. The limitations of genome sequencing include: analytical validity, structural variants, interpretation, clinical validity and utility, test failure, psychological impact, privacy, discrimination and others.

Source:https://merogenomics.ca/en/advantages-and-limitations-of-genome-sequencing/

C. Nanotechnology is being studied for both the diagnosis and treatment of atherosclerosis, or the build-up of plaque in arteries. In one technique, researchers **created a nanoparticle that mimics the body's "good" cholesterol,** known as HDL (high-density lipoprotein), which helps to shrink plaque.

Note: More invasive medico-technology it seems, with all the dangers that that implies.

Nanotechnology also has a prominent role in the fast developing field of Tissue Engineering. When designing scaffolds, researchers attempt to mimic the nanoscale features of a cell's microenvironment to direct its differentiation down a suitable lineage. For example, when creating scaffolds to support the growth of bone, researchers may mimic osteoclast resorption pits.

Note: More invasive medico-technology it seems, with all the dangers that that implies.

Energy applications are also prevalent and hopefully less dangerous than medical applications.

Researchers are developing wires containing carbon nanotubes that will have much lower resistance than the high-tension wires currently used in the electric grid, thus reducing transmission power loss.

Nanotechnology can be incorporated into solar panels to convert sunlight to electricity more efficiently, promising inexpensive solar power in the future. Nanostructured solar cells could be cheaper to manufacture and easier to install, since they can use print-like manufacturing processes and can be made in flexible rolls rather than discrete panels. Newer research suggests that future solar converters might even be "paintable."

Nanotechnology is already being used to develop many new kinds of batteries that are quicker-charging, more efficient, lighter weight, have a higher power density, and hold electrical charge longer.

In the area of energy harvesting, researchers are developing thin-film solar electric panels that can be fitted onto computer cases and flexible piezoelectric nanowires woven into clothing to generate usable energy on the go from light, friction, and/or body heat to power mobile electronic devices. Similarly, various nanoscience-based options are being pursued to convert waste heat in computers, automobiles, homes, power plants, etc., to usable electrical power.

Source: https://www.nano.gov/you/nanotechnology-benefits

Although most of the press coverage has been on the dangers of 'nano-goo' such as self-replicating particles that get out of control, or 'nano-robots', the real risks are much more simple, and real. *The miniature size of nanomaterials and the way their surfaces are modified to increase the ease with which they can interact with biological systems - the very characteristics that make them attractive for applications in medicine and industry - makes nanomaterials potentially damaging for humans and the environment.* [My emboldening]

Nanoparticles are likely to be dangerous for three main reasons:

1. **Nanoparticles may damage the lungs. We know that 'ultra-fine' particles from diesel machines, power plants and incinerators <u>can cause considerable damage to human lungs</u>. This is both because of their size [as they can get deep into the lungs] and also because they carry other chemicals including metals and hydrocarbons in with them.**
2. **Nanoparticles can get into the body through the skin, lungs and digestive system. This may help create 'free radicals' which can cause cell damage and damage to the DNA. There is also concern that once nanoparticles are in the bloodstream they will be able to cross the blood-brain barrier.**
3. **The human body has developed a tolerance to most naturally occurring elements and molecules that it has contact with. It has no natural immunity to new substances and is more likely to find them toxic.**

The danger of contact with nanoparticles is not just speculation. As more research is undertaken, concerns increase. Here are some of the recent findings:

- **Some nanoparticles cause lung damage in rats. Several studies have shown that carbon nanotubes, which are similar in shape to asbestos fibres, cause mesothelioma in the lungs of rats [see below]**
- **Other nanoparticles have been shown to lead to brain damage in fish and dogs**
- **A German study found clear evidence that if discrete nanometer diameter particles were deposited in the nasal region [in rodents in this case], they completely circumvented the blood/brain barrier, and travelled up the olfactory nerves straight into the brain**
- **Inhaled carbon nanotubes can suppress the immune system by affecting the function of T cells, a type of white blood cell that organises the immune system to fight infections.** Source: https://www.ohsrep.org.au/

It is clear that the inherent miniscule size of nanotechnology particles is a barrier to the general public's understanding and therefore acceptance of the technology and its benefits. A very rigorous system of scientific study, independently peer reviewed, with fully blind 'nil' effect placebo groups (if required) will be imperative. This research will have to be supported by the appropriate legislation, regulation and control. If we look at past examples of capitalism's genius in this regard: tobacco, alcohol, asbestos, the mining industry, then I strongly advise that my readers do not hold their breathe.

6.9 Big Data

Big data is a field that treats ways to analyse, systematically extract information from, or otherwise deal with data sets that are too large or complex to be dealt with by traditional data-processing application software. Data with many cases [rows] offer greater statistical power, while data with higher complexity [more attributes or columns] may lead to a higher false discovery rate. Big data challenges include capturing data, data storage, data analysis search, sharing, transfer, visualisation, querying, updating, information privacy and data source. Big data was originally associated with three key concepts: *volume*, *variety*, and *velocity*. When we handle big data, we may not sample but simply observe and track what happens. Therefore, big data often includes data with sizes that exceed the capacity of traditional software to process within an acceptable time and *value*.

Current usage of the term *big data* tends to refer to the use of predictive analytics, user behaviour analytics, or certain other advanced data analytics methods that extract value from data, and seldom to a particular size of data set. "There is little doubt that the quantities of data now available are indeed large, but that's not the most relevant characteristic of this new data ecosystem." Analysis of data sets can find new correlations to "spot business trends, prevent diseases, combat crime and so on." Scientists, business executives, practitioners of medicine, advertising and governments alike regularly meet difficulties with large data-sets in areas including Internet searches, fintech, urban informatics, and business informatics. Scientists encounter limitations in e-Science work, including meteorology, genomics, connectomics, complex physics simulations, biology and environmental research.

Data sets grow rapidly, to a certain extent because they are increasingly gathered by cheap and numerous information-sensing Internet of Things devices such as mobile devices, aerial [remote sensing], software logs, cameras, microphones, radio-frequency identification [RFID] readers and wireless sensor networks. The world's technological per-capita capacity to store information has roughly doubled every 40 months since the 1980s; as of 2012, every day 2.5 exabytes (2.5×2^{60} bytes) of data are generated. Based on an IDC report prediction, the global data volume was predicted to grow exponentially from 4.4 zettabytes to 44 zettabytes between 2013 and 2020. By 2025, IDC predicts there will be 163 zettabytes of data. One question for large enterprises is determining who should own big-data initiatives that affect the entire organization.

Relational database management systems, desktop statistics and software packages used to visualize data often have difficulty handling big data. The work may require "massively parallel software running on tens, hundreds, or even thousands of servers". What qualifies as being "big data" varies depending on the capabilities of the users and their tools, and expanding capabilities make big data a moving target. "For some organizations, facing hundreds of gigabytes of data for the first time may trigger a need to reconsider data management options. For others, it may take tens or hundreds of terabytes before data size becomes a significant consideration."

Architecture and Structures

Big data repositories have existed in many forms, often built by corporations with a special need. Commercial vendors historically offered parallel database management systems for big data beginning in the 1990s.

Teradata Corporation in 1984 marketed the parallel processing DCB 1012 system. Teradata systems were the first to store and analyse 1 terabyte of data in 1992. Hard disk drives were 2.5 GB in 1991 so the definition of big data continuously evolves according to Kryder's Law.

[Kryder's 'Law' is the assumption that disk drive densities, also known as areal density, will double every thirteen months.]

Teradata installed the first petabyte [a unit of information equal to one thousand million million (10^{15}) or, strictly, 2^{50} bytes] class

RDBMS [Relational Database Management System] based system in 2007. As of 2017, there are a few dozen petabyte class Teradata relational databases installed, the largest of which exceeds 50 PB. Systems up until 2008 were 100% structured relational data. Since then, Teradata has added unstructured data types including XML, JSON, and Avro.

In 2000, Seisint Inc. (now LexisNexis Risk Solutions) developed a C++ based distributed platform for data processing and querying known as the HPCC Systems platform. This system automatically partitions, distributes, stores and delivers structured, semi-structured, and unstructured data across multiple commodity servers. Users can write data processing pipelines and queries in a declarative dataflow programming language called ECL. Data analysts working in ECL are not required to define data schemas upfront and can rather focus on the particular problem at hand, reshaping data in the best possible manner as they develop the solution. In 2004, LexisNexis acquired Seisint Inc. and their high-speed parallel processing platform and successfully utilized this platform to integrate the data systems of Choicepoint Inc. when they acquired that company in 2008. In 2011, the HPCC systems platform was open-sourced under the Apache v2.0 License.

CERN [French Conseil Européen pour la Recherche Nucléaire or European Organization for Nuclear Research] and other physics experiments have collected big data sets for many decades, usually analysed via high-throughput computing rather than the map-reduce architectures usually meant by the current "big data" movement.

In 2004, Google published a paper on a process called MapReduce that uses a similar architecture. The MapReduce concept provides a parallel processing model, and an associated implementation was released to process huge amounts of data.

With MapReduce, queries are split and distributed across parallel nodes and processed in parallel [the Map step]. The results are then gathered and delivered [the Reduce step]. The framework was very successful, so others wanted to replicate the algorithm. Therefore, an implementation of the MapReduce framework was adopted by an Apache open-source project named Hadoop. Apache Spark was developed in 2012 in response to limitations in the MapReduce paradigm, as it adds the ability to set up many operations [not just map followed by reducing].

MIKE2.0 is an open approach to information management that acknowledges the need for revisions due to big data implications identified in an article titled "Big Data Solution Offering". The methodology addresses handling big data in terms of useful permutations of data sources, complexity in interrelationships, and difficulty in deleting [or modifying] individual records.

2012 studies showed that a multiple-layer architecture is one option to address the issues that big data presents. A distributed parallel architecture distributes data across multiple servers; these parallel execution environments can dramatically improve data processing speeds. This type of architecture inserts data into a parallel DBMS [Database Management System], which implements the use of MapReduce and Hadoop frameworks. This type of framework looks to make the processing power transparent to the end-user by using a front-end application server.

The data 'lake' allows an organization to shift its focus from centralized control to a shared model to respond to the changing dynamics of information management. This enables quick segregation of data into the data lake, thereby reducing the overhead time.

Technologies

A 2011 McKinsey Global Institute report characterizes the main components and ecosystem of big data as follows:

- Techniques for analysing data, such as A/B testing, machine learning and natural language processing
- Big data technologies, like business intelligence, cloud computing [proprietary server computing] and databases
- Visualization, such as charts, graphs and other displays of the data

Multidimensional big data can also be represented as OLAP [Online Analytical Processing] data cubes or, mathematically, tensors.

[A tensor is an algebraic object that describes a [multilinear] relationship between sets of algebraic objects related to a vector space. Objects that tensors may map between include vectors and scalars, and, recursively, even other tensors.]

Array Database Systems have set out to provide storage and high-level query support on this data type. Additional technologies being applied to big data include efficient tensor-based computation, such as multilinear subspace learning, massively parallel-processing [MPP] databases, search based applications, data mining, distributed file systems, distributed cache (e.g., burstbuffer and Memcached), [memory cached] distributed databases, cloud and HPC-based infrastructure [High Performance Computing] applications, storage and computing resources and the Internet. Although, many approaches and technologies have been developed, it still remains difficult to carry out machine learning with big data.

Some MPP relational databases have the ability to store and manage petabytes of data. Implicit is the ability to load, monitor, back up, and optimize the use of the large data tables in the RDBMS.

DARPA's Topological Data Analysis program seeks the fundamental structure of massive data sets and in 2008 the technology went public with the launch of a company called Ayasdi.

The practitioners of big data analytics processes are generally hostile to slower shared storage, preferring direct-attached storage

[DAS] in its various forms from solid state drive [SSD] to high capacity SATA disk [Serial Advanced Technology Attachment] buried inside parallel processing nodes. The perception of shared storage architectures—Storage area network [SAN] and Network-attached storage [NAS] —is that they are relatively slow, complex, and expensive. These qualities are not consistent with big data analytics systems that thrive on system performance, commodity infrastructure, and low cost.

Real or near-real time information delivery is one of the defining characteristics of big data analytics. Latency is therefore avoided whenever and wherever possible. Data in direct-attached memory or disk is good—data on memory or disk at the other end of a FC SAN [Fibre connector storage area network] connection is not. The cost of a SAN [storage area connector] at the scale needed for analytics applications is very much higher than other storage techniques.

There are advantages as well as disadvantages to shared storage in big data analytics, but big data analytics practitioners as of 2011 do not favour it.

Applications

Big data has increased the demand of information management specialists so much so that Software AG, Oracle Corporation, IBM, Microsoft, SAP, EMC, HP and Dell have spent more than US $15 billion on software firms specializing in data management and analytics. In 2010, this industry was worth more than US $100 billion and was growing at almost 10 percent a year: about twice as fast as the software business as a whole.

Developed economies increasingly use data-intensive technologies. There are 4.6 billion mobile-phone subscriptions worldwide, and between 1 billion and 2 billion people accessing the internet. Between 1990 and 2005, more than 1 billion people worldwide entered the middle class, which means more people became more literate, which in turn led to information growth. The world's effective capacity to exchange information through telecommunication networks was 281 petabytes in 1986, 471 petabytes in 1993, 2.2 exabytes in 2000, 65 exabytes in 2007 and estimates put the amount of internet traffic at 667 exabytes annually in 2014. According to one estimate, one-third of the globally stored information is in the form of alphanumeric text and still image data,which is the format most useful for most big data applications. This also shows the potential of yet unused data (i.e. in the form of video and audio content).

While many vendors offer off-the-shelf solutions for big data, experts recommend the development of in-house solutions custom-tailored to solve the company's problem at hand if the company has sufficient technical capabilities.

The use and adoption of big data within governmental processes allows efficiencies in terms of cost, productivity, and innovation, but does not come without its flaws. Data analysis often requires multiple parts of government (central and local) to work in collaboration and create new and innovative processes to deliver the desired outcome.

There are many limitations with Big Data, here are seven of them:

1. User Data is Fundamentally Biased

The user-level data that marketers have access to is only of individuals who have visited your owned digital properties or viewed your online ads, which is typically not representative of the total target consumer base.

2. User-Level Execution only exists in Select Channels

Certain marketing channels are well suited for applying user-level data: website personalization, email automation, dynamic creatives, and RTB [Real-time bidding is a **means** by which advertising inventory is bought and sold on a per-impression basis, via programmatic instantaneous auction, similar to financial markets.] spring to mind.

In many channels however, it is difficult or impossible to apply user data directly to execution except via segment-level aggregation and whatever other targeting information is provided by the platform or publisher. Social channels, paid search, and even most programmatic display is based on segment-level or attribute-level targeting at best. For offline channels and premium display, user-level data cannot be applied to execution at all.

3. User-Level Results cannot be Presented Directly

More accurately, it can be presented via a few visualizations such as a flow diagram but these tend to be incomprehensible to all but domain experts. This means that user-level data needs to be aggregated up to a daily segment-level or property-level at the very least in order for the results to be consumable at large.

4. User-Level Algorithms have Difficulty Answering "Why"

Largely speaking, there are only two ways to analyse user-level data: one is to aggregate it into a "smaller" data set in some way and then apply statistical or heuristic [learn for oneself] analysis; the other is to analyse the data set directly using algorithmic methods.

Both can result in predictions and recommendations (e.g. move spend from campaign A to B), but algorithmic analyses tend to have difficulty answering "why" questions (e.g. why should we move spend) in a manner comprehensible to the average marketer. Certain types of algorithms such as neural networks are black boxes even to the data scientists who designed it. Which leads to the next limitation:

5. User Data is not suited for Producing Learnings

This will probably strike the reader as counter-intuitive. Big data = big insights = big learnings, right?

Wrong! For example, let's say you apply big data to personalize your website, increasing overall conversion rates by 20%. While certainly a fantastic result, the only learning you get from the exercise is that you should indeed personalize your website. While this result certainly raises the bar on marketing, it does nothing to raise the bar for *marketers*.

Actionable learnings that require user-level data – for instance, applying a look-alike model to discover previously untapped customer segments – are relatively few and far between, and require enormous amounts of effort to uncover. Boring, 'old' small data remains far more efficient at producing practical real-world learnings that you can apply to execution today.

6. User-Level Data is subject to More Noise

If you have analysed regular daily time series data, you know that a single outlier [a person or thing differing from all other members of a particular group or set] can completely throw off analysis results. The situation is similar with user-level data, but worse.

In analysing touchpoint data, one will run into situations where, for example, a particular cookie received – for whatever reason – a hundred display impressions in a row from the same website within an hour [happens much more often than one might think]. Should this be treated as a hundred impressions or just one, and how will it affect your analysis results?

Even more so than "smaller" data, user-level data tends to be filled with so much noise and potentially misleading artefacts, that it can take an inordinate amount of time and effort just to clean up the data set in order to get reasonably accurate results.

7. User Data is not easily Accessible or Transferable

Because of security concerns, user data cannot be made accessible to just anyone, and requires care in transferring from machine to machine, server to server.

The issue with scale concerns, is that not everyone has the technical know-how to query big data in an efficient manner, which causes database administrators to limit the number of people who have access in the first place.

Big data requires a huge amount of effort, therefore whatever insights that are mined from big data tend to remain a one-off exercise, making it difficult for team members to conduct follow-up analyses and validation.

All of these factors limit agility of analysis and ability to collaborate.

Source:https://marketingland.com/7-limitations-big-data-marketing-analytics-117998

One of the gravest dangers of Big Data is data harvesting giving rise to surveillance capitalism.

Big Data and Surveillance Capitalism

Source: Wikipedia with citations including Zuboff and Fuchs

Surveillance capitalism is a new term addressing the process of commodifying **personal data** with the core purpose of profit making and increasing market share. Since personal data can be **commodified** it has become one of the most valuable resources on earth. The concept arose after advertising companies saw the possibilities of using personal data to target consumers more specifically.

Increased data collection may have various advantages for individuals and society such as self-optimisation [Quantified Self], [self-tracking with technology] societal optimizations [such as by smart cities] and optimized services [including various web applications].

However, collecting and processing data in the context of capitalism's core profit-making motive might [will without doubt] present an inherent danger. Capitalism has become focused on expanding the proportion of social life that is open to data collection and data processing. This may [will] come with significant implications for vulnerability and control of society as well as for privacy.

Economic pressures of capitalism are driving the intensification of connection and monitoring online with spaces of social life becoming open to **[over] saturation by corporate actors**, directed at the making of profit and/or the regulation of action. Therefore, personal data points increased in value after the possibilities of targeted advertising were known. Due to the capitalist **[false]** market mechanism the increasing price of data has caused limited accessibility to the richest in society of buying personal data points.

> Note: From above: "Due to the capitalist **[false]** market mechanism" - See 'Chapter 4 - The Failure of Capitalism' section 'The False Market and Two Myths of Capitalism'

> Note: 'Click bait' – the process of enticement attention grabbing of the on-line user may be a form of subliminal, or semi-subliminal consumer manipulation.

Shoshana Zuboff writes that "analysing massive data sets began as a way to reduce uncertainty by discovering the probabilities of future patterns in the behaviour of people and systems". In 2014

Vincent Mosco referred to the marketing of information about customers and subscribers to advertisers as *surveillance capitalism* and makes note of the surveillance state alongside it.

> Note: This fusion of capitalism and government is perhaps the most significant fusion of this type since mercantilism in 16th and 17th centuries – see 'Chapter 2 – The Rise of Mercantilism – The Second Form of Capitalism'.

Christian Fuchs found that the surveillance state fuses with surveillance capitalism. Similarly, Zuboff informs that the issue is **further complicated by highly invisible collaborative arrangements with state security apparatuses**. According to Trebor Scholz, companies recruit people as informants for this type of capitalism. Zuboff contrasts mass production of industrial capitalism with surveillance capitalism with the former being interdependent with its populations who were its consumers and employees and the latter **preying on dependent populations** who are neither its consumers nor its employees and largely [**entirely** in terms of the vast majority of the global population] ignorant of its procedures.

Their research is demonstrating that the capitalist addition [and addiction] to analysing massive data sets has given its original purpose an unexpected turn.

> Note: I would argue that "..analysing massive data sets has given its original purpose an unexpected turn." Should read *"..analysing massive data sets has given its beginning purpose **an enormous and very fortunate exponential boost*** [for the capitalists].

Surveillance has been changing power structures in the information economy. This might present a further power shift beyond the nation-state and towards a form of coporatocracy/technocracy.

Zuboff notes that surveillance capitalism reaches beyond the conventional institutional terrain of the private firm and accumulates not only surveillance assets and capital, but also [has] rights and **operates without meaningful mechanisms of consent**.

> Note : "..without meaningful mechanisms of consent" **perhaps should read;** *"without any consent whatsoever, and barely any knowledge of, by the subject being almost subliminally manipulated, to buy products and services they probably do not in any sincere way need or want."*

In other words, analysing massive data sets was at some point not only executed by The State apparatuses but also companies. In Zuboff's research she claims that the two companies; Google and Facebook invented and transferred surveillance capitalism into "a new logic of accumulation". This mutation entailed that both companies were massively gathering data points about their users, with the core purpose of making profit. By selling these data points to external users it has become an economic mechanism. The combination of the analysation [analysis] of massive data sets and using those data sets as a market mechanism has shaped and changed the concept of surveillance capitalism.

> Note: The only legislative solution to this hideous form of capitalist (private) and state (public) infringement upon an individual's personal data and quasi-subliminal coercive activities directed at unnecessary consumption, is the introduction of laws that allow the general public full access to all personal data relating to the individual requiring it of himself/herself, wherever it may be, at any time, with an automated up-date of this information at reasonable frequencies at the choosing of the individual concerned. This would be a requirement placed upon the social media company or other, in order to procure a license to trade or operate in the jurisdiction that the law applies to.

Chapter Summary

To refresh the reader's memory, this chapter is entitled 'Chapter 6 - Climate Change, Potential Tragedy of Emerging Technologies - The Forces of Implosion'. Let's look at the Forces of Implosion further.

The forces, or vectors of implosion are the causes of climate change and potentially the emerging technologies listed: 5G, Internet of Things, Robotics and Artificial Intelligence 'AI', Quantum Computing, Bio-Technology, Blockchain, Nano-Technology, Big Data.

Climate change can be seen, as above from studies, to be the result of human activity to the tune of 75% of net increase in global ambient temperature. – see 'Chapter 6 – Climate Change'.

The study of capitalism above reveals that it bulldozes it way to its myopic 'destiny' irrespective of the very real potential for unfore-seen, as well as foreseen, problems. From global maldistribution of wealth to modern slavery, from nicotine to asbestos to encouraged gambling addiction, from asset stripping to gross unpreparedness (UK Covid-19 'strategy' etc.), from over-consumption to school playground peer pressure on parents, crass stupidity is everywhere and capitalist avarice encourages it.

In the 1960's when Mankind nearly blew itself off the planet with the USA-Kennedy Russia-Khrushchev stand-off over the Cuban missile crisis;

Bertrand Russell was asked, words to the effect of, how was it possible that Mankind in the 1960s, after two millennia of 'civilisation', had come to the brink of global self-annihilation using thermo-nuclear warheads. His reply was words to the effect "Because world leaders are wicked and stupid."

I stopped watching television many, many years ago, the reason being that television communicators intellectually atrophied exponentially a few years after the Russell interview. Russell's presence in a television studio over half a century ago was the last time, to my knowledge, that an intellect higher than an invertebrate's laid forth discourse using such a medium. It appears to be the noblest ambition of most present-day parliamentarians, 'leaders' and their 'advisers' to appear on a television programme entitled 'Strictly Come Dancing'. Whatever that is.

Now with the 'benefit' of the World Wide Web and Internet social media, global cretinism is the order of the day. Those of us trying to initiate a global, intellectual, cultural, ethical, moral, spiritual Renaissance, have our work cut out. However, regarding homo sapiens, where there is Hope there is Life. Without Hope there is Nothing.

In the post-industrial revolution we appear to have a western society that has:
lost its sense of identity,
lost its sense of purpose,
lost its humanity,
lost its sense of oneness [if it ever had one],
lost its sense of family and community,
lost control of its destiny,
lost its sense of culture,
lost its freedom for free speech.

Western Society is lost in a lowly moral, intellectual, cultural, emotional, spiritual quagmire of its own making.

Post-industrial technology is the Great Unperceived Driver; driving in multiple, unconnected but related multifarious channels simultaneously but in separate, independent unconnected directions.

In industrial capitalism the change could be readily anticipated. A simple sketch could explain the principle workings of a 'spinning jenny', simple diagrams could explain the ideas behind Watt's

Steam Engine or Richard Trevithick's 'Pen-y-derren' locomotive. Furthermore although the changes were, in their time radical, their effects were spread over a relatively long period of time compared to changes today. Also these industrial innovations affected directly, only a small proportion of the population in terms of their work.

Today, the great issue of the survival of Humankind is truly at stake.

The agents of change - the 'forces of implosion', are far greater in inherent magnitude of total global effect, far greater in number, have far greater simultaneity, are far greater in global reach, are happening at a far greater speed, so that society has difficulty keeping abreast of them, and legislative structures simply cannot keep up with, and do not have the cross-border powers, to legislate effectively these all powerful pan-global corporations and the implementation of their technologies. Some of today's corporations are global reaching networked monopolies with business units hidden in tax heavens but trading all over the world: Google, Facebook, Amazon. They practically are beyond the Tax Laws and Monopoly Commissions [of the disparate, 'local' countries and regions that they trade in].

These emerging technologies, these forces of implosion, are 'attacking' simultaneously and globally on many fronts:

5G – information technology transmission protocol, 4G liability is minimal, fuelling geo-economic one-upmanship, not fully tested as safe for human use, what liability is there on untested 5G?;

Internet of Things – connectivity of every home, car, office, factory, retail outlet, warehouse, library etc. [every electro or electro-mechanical device that one can place a sensor in], privacy issues, human beings reduced to robots, over-reliance upon technology, de-humanisation;

Robotics and IA – with the possibility of robot/AI automation right through the supply chain from design, prototyping manufacturing, storage, distribution and home delivery (drones), with massive redundancy in human labour, deliberate strategy of decimating the human labour market, mass unemployment, break-up of human to human communications, destruction of the family and communities, de-humanisation of humans to the position of sub-robots;

Quantum Computing – calculations that take 10,000 years on super-computers reduced to less than four minutes by quantum computing, security issues, military issues, first past the post in Quantum Computing gains world domination through cyber spying, world peace under enormous threat;

Bio-Technology – exploitation of biological processes for industrial and other purposes, genetic engineering of babies, food engineering genes into plant genomes by using methods such as particle bombardment, huge potential for violating Natural Law with potentially irreversible consequences;

Blockchain – database security, huge energy requirement when global resources are at a premium, cryptocurrencies with the unashamed gambling potential and addiction;

Nano-Technology - manipulation of matter on an atomic, molecular, and supramolecular scale, significant health risks with Nano-technology, grow human organs for transplant, loss of identity, ethical considerations, potential violation of Natural Law;

Big Data - treats ways to analyse, systematically extract information from, or otherwise deal with data sets that are too large or complex to be dealt with by traditional data-processing application software, with attending surveillance capitalism with state collaboration for consumer exploitation, and 'Click bait' – the process of enticement attention grabbing of the on-line user may be a form of subliminal, or semi-subliminal consumer manipulation, privacy issues with huge data sets unknowingly surrendered by the consumer to the big-data harvester, exploitative semi-subliminal advertising and consequential unnecessary over-consumption, cynical exploitation of social media dopamine addiction – peer approval 'Like' flags;

All of these disparate, multifarious technologies in simultaneous development coming together eventually to fruition, perhaps by 2030 or thereabouts, has impending disaster written all over it.

If we look at Mankind's achievements so far in the area of post-industrial technology, the primary driver being the World Wide Web and Internet then we see great errors. The most significant was the Dot Com Crash.

The dot-com bubble (also known as the dot-com boom, the tech bubble, and the Internet bubble) was a stock market 'gambling' bubble caused by **excessive speculation** in Internet-related companies in the late 1990s, a period of massive growth in the use and adoption of the Internet. In 2001 and through 2002 the bubble burst, with equities entering a bear market. The crash that followed saw the Nasdaq index, USA which had risen five-fold between 1995 and 2000, tumble from a peak of 5,048.62 on March 10, 2000, to 1,139.90 on Oct 4, 2002, a 76.81% fall. In principle regarding trading, the Internet was a single dimensioned straight forward new means of trading, its advantages facilitated by the global reach of the Internet and its capability for remote purchase and remote delivery of products and services. It was initially particularly prevalent in 'non-touch and feel requirement' products such as books, videos and compact discs for music and films where attendance at a retail outlet for product perusal was not an essential pre-requisite.

High-Tech start-ups complete with 'catchynames.com' promised venture capitalists and other investors, quick returns on their investment with hopefully 'minimum' risk. Although the principles behind on-line trading were relatively straight forward, there was massive hype and induced over-speculation founded on the human weakness of greed.

If the world cannot handle something as simple as trading on-line on the Internet how is it possibly going to handle the simultaneous greed/avarice motives for investing in, and the simultaneous roll-out of:

5G, Internet of Things, Robotics and AI, Quantum Computing, Bio-Technology, Blockchain, Nano-Technology, Big Data?

A total of eight disparate and complex new technologies coming to fruition at perhaps much the same time. How are these technologies that impinge on a global manner to be regulated and controlled by the current country-specific legislative structures?

Who will manage, the **management of human change** that this most extraordinary phenomenon of these eight simultaneous, disparate super-technologies, plus others that will no doubt emerge soon, will require. Who will manage the management of the enormous global human change; the separate capitalist corporations all paddling their own canoe(s) whether it is Robotics, 5G, Big Data individually or anything else combined, the independent governments, the electorates, the UN, the local councils, 'Black Lives Matter', Think Tanks, Tony Blair, John Bercow, The Klu Klux Klan, The Pope?

Recent history shows that we cannot even manage something as benign, one-dimensional and straight forward as the Dot Com Internet phenomenon. That was trivial compared with what is going to happen in the next thirty or so years. The ostensible truth is that there is no recognised body, perceivable today, that will be responsible for the management of human change throughout this most extraordinary all-encompassing global revolution.

The present incumbents in government in the UK could not even manage the relatively trivial matter of Covid-19 that would require little more than a telephone call with the South Korean health authorities and follow their advice to the letter. One telephone call, if acted upon intelligently, would have resulted in a prompt, short and efficient UK Lockdown and no temporary 'dole queue' of almost one third of the UK's working population. The long term economic and social effects of the UK government's handling of Covid-19 are yet to unfold.

Furthermore, the current incumbents 'running' the UK government had a school meal policy overturned by a twenty-two year old professional footballer, with presumably some experience of school meals, but certainly no experience of government. These government geniuses did much the same thing with another sports personality – this time it was cricket. Indicating that they do not even have the balls [pun intended] to believe in, and carry through to completion, their own polices. Such extraordinary and utterly bungling incompetence has not been experienced in UK government, in my view, since 'Lord North' 1732-1792 'lost us' America.

Irrespective of Covid-19, [and school dinners] between 2020 and 2050, a period of barely more than a generation may result in:

The potential for unknown problems and illnesses emanating from:

1. **Untested 5G** – respiratory issues and immunity reduction have already been mooted [I am still awaiting a reply from the UK Government under the Freedom of Information Act 2000 for all independently peer reviewed, with fully blind 'nil' effect placebo groups if required, scientific studies demonstrating the complete safety to humans when subjected to 5G emissions. No such thing exists for 4G].
2. **A dysfunctional robotisation** of humans from over reliance on the mass connectivities of anything and everything by IoT

3. **Mass unemployment** and/or mass underemployment courtesy of Robotics/AI
4. **World domination through cyber spying** and world peace under threat via Quantum Computing
5. **Human genetic engineering moral dilemmas** and potential irreversible errors of judgment by the use of Bio-Technology
6. **Enormous energy consumption via Blockchain** when energy resources are at a premium
7. **Human organ transplant disasters** from Nano-Technology
8. **The encroachment of civil liberties and privacy** through surreptitious manipulation by Big Data harvesting by Global Social Media companies
9. **10. 11. + Add your own observations here! Please forward your 10. 11. + to: saveyourselfsaveusall.com – copyright retained by the original forwarder as/if applicable**

Some of the inherent dangers of these technologies have been listed above but perhaps the most galling is that of Quantum Computing. If a state power of aggressive military intentions achieves global dominance in quantum computing ahead of others, then it may quite well use quantum computing to hack into the 'secure' data of its rivals with relative impunity. If as reported, super-computing tasks taking a theoretical 10,000 years can be achieved in less than 4 minutes with quantum computing, then so-called existing 'secure' data will probably be accessed in seconds and transmitted to the data bases of the militaristic power and stored in a further few seconds. All this perhaps unbeknown to the cyber-attacked power.

As stated above, all of these disparate, multifarious, complex technologies, each with their own known dangers and hidden dangers, in simultaneous development coming together eventually to fruition, perhaps between 2030 to 2050, has impending disaster written all over it, when you consider that the world could not even handle the comparatively simple task of DotCom and the UK government could not handle the relatively straight forward Covid-19 pandemic, similarities of which, the South Koreans have much previous experience. Picking up a telephone and calling the South Korean health authorities is not difficult.

Chapter 7

Family of Humankind

The Nature of Man

TRUTH begins at Infinity and ends at Eternity

The Puppet 'Masters' pull the Strings of the Puppets
but the 'Masters' have No Control over Themselves

Why is the world in such a mess? Why oh, why is the world in such a mess?

The world's mess is caused almost entirely by the Will of Mankind, since the Will of Mankind caused it, then Mankind's Will can and must resolve it. Nothing else can, nor will.

What genuine progress has Humankind made in 2,000+ years of western 'civilisation'?

2000+ years of 'civilisation' and what does the Family of Humankind have to show for all its hard work and sacrifice? What true progress have we made? We have today:

List 1. Endless war(s), global starvation, global modern slavery, global self-imposed slavery; a few very, very rich people, many many very, very poor people, many in-between people without very much – "just getting by", human stupidity creating climate change, over exploitation of natural resources, global terrorism, corrupt international businesses, world-wide international crime, world-wide drugs crime as a self-sufficient industry in its own 'right', global human trafficking, global corporations ostensibly beyond the reach of domestic government legislation, governments 'ruled' by the social media masses and their hysteria, technological advances outstripping legislation that cannot keep up-to-date with the technology and its social effects and consequences, internationally lead violations of domestic country democratic processes, polluted over-crowded cities, city crime and city violence, city depravation, child criminality, institutionalised paedophilia, humankind's unnecessary self-inflicted suffering, religious segregation, religious antagonism, racial tensions and antagonisms, racial sectarianism, people losing their jobs for holding perfectly intellectually valid and rational views, UK police non-impartiality publically showing racial/ethnic bias, crass stupidity of mainstream media, intrusive surreptitious surveillance capitalism, global financial market collapses owing to capitalists selling property market junk to people who have as much chance of repaying the property 'loan' as flying to mars on a 'Boris Bike', total Covid-19 incompetence and unpreparedness particularly by the UK government, unprotected elderly in Care Homes resulting in their deaths owing to UK government Covid-19 total incompetence, 'inverted' moral values in favour of over-represented minorities at the expense of the genuine numerical majority, some of the finest minds in the UK losing their jobs because they spoke their truth, some career politicians and some civil servants [ostensibly intellectual light-weights and moral light-weights both] who have the vanity to call themselves leaders when they could not lead a starving man to a bread stall and have never had any real authority or responsibility in their entire lives, a UK politician leading the world into a morally repugnant war declared illegal by the United Nations, so called 'world leaders' aiding and abetting the global criminal activity of human trafficking gangs, mass intellectual atrophy, mass cultural atrophy, idiotic minority fringe 'values' violating rational discussion, gender identity horse-shit.......the list of contemporary human idiocy must be infinite, if it is not infinite then it must be greater than infinity…..I have to stop here because there is not enough ink in my printer to complete the list…

> Note: The reader may reasonably enquire of the author's position of authority under which he declares "…ostensibly intellectual light-weights…". Although Intelligence Quotient 'IQ' is only an indicator of intellect, the author passed a one-hour Mensa UK IQ Test in 44 minutes gaining a position in the top 1% of the world's population. He took another, far more demanding, untimed, creative problem solving test and self-adjudicated a higher IQ – IQ170 with Standard Deviation 16, is 1 in 164,571 of the population and in the top 99.9993923584% (percentile) i.e. residing in the top 0.001% of the population rounding to three significant figures.

List 2. In our post-industrial revolution we appear to have a western society that has lost its sense of identity, lost its sense of purpose, lost its humanity, lost its sense of oneness [if it ever had one], lost its sense of family and community, lost control of its destiny, lost its capacity for rationalism, lost its sense of culture, lost its sense of ethnic proportional representation, lost its freedom of free speech….. the list is as endless as human stupidity is infinite…..

So far in this essay, for brevity and ease of communication, capitalism has been occasionally denoted as a potential 'causation'. Although done for brevity and ease of communication, however it is not truly deemed to be so. The reality is explained below:

It would be unwise to claim that capitalism, in itself, was the root cause of the two horrific lists of total, abject failure above - List 1 and List 2. In the same way it would be unwise to claim that religion, in itself, caused religious dissent and religious wars. Capitalism, religion and any other similar concepts are not, in themselves, agents of causation. They are nothing more than concepts of mind. These concepts have no actual existence or a communicative causal existence in the empirical, physical world.

Therefore, in themselves they cannot have deterministic causation. In themselves they are not the cause of anything. What does exist in the empirical world is the implementation of these concepts. Capitalism as empirical entity was not caused by capitalism; it was caused by the actions of Humankind. Empirical Capitalism is an effect; the causation of capitalism's effects and its follow-on effects are caused by the actions of Humankind.

Perhaps in excess of 99.9% of all the problems on this little planet are caused by Humankind. If Humankind's Will has caused the world's problems then the Will of Humankind can resolve them. All is within our Control. All that is needed is the Courage, Honesty and the Will To Do It. Your choice!

As counterpoint, Humankind is capable of great self-sacrifice that accompanies Great Belief. This comes in two forms. There is instinctive self-sacrifice that attends Great Belief and conceptualised self-sacrifice that attends Great Belief.

A typical example of the former might be a case of a child, when with its parents, recalcitrantly runs into a busy road or jumps off a low-walled bridge into a strong river. There are many stories in the press and media of passers-by, indeed often completely total strangers; without a moment's thought for their own safety and/or well-being, running into the road in front of on-coming traffic in both directions and scooping up the youngster into their arms of safety; or stripping down to one's underwear and jumping into the strong river swimming against the torrent to bravely save the child, hold him/her aloft the waves and return the child to the safety of its parents. Herein lies, within the inherent Nature of Humankind, its essence of Instinctive Greatness. Herein lies Humankind's Instinctive Greatness of Spirit – the instinctive willingness to put one's own right to Life in jeopardy and huge risk, without a second moment's thought for the Higher Ideal of saving a Young Life that without one's intervention may be extinguished before its due time.

This is Humankind's Instinctive Noble Spirit. A Transcendental Instinctive State of Being.

An example of the latter, the conceptualised self-sacrifice that attends Great Belief, would be for instance, a case of when a person's beliefs are so at odds with their socio/politico/economic environment, or more accurately perhaps, their socio/politico/economic environment is so at odd with their beliefs, that they are prepared to undergo lengthy imprisonment and/or other deprivations in an attempt to implement change in that socio/politico/economic environment that they consider, in certain ways, to be unjust.

This is Humankind's Ethical and Moral Noble Spirit. A Transcendental Ethical and Moral State of Being.

Of these two examples the former is completed, hopefully successfully in a matter of minutes or perhaps hours. The latter may take years or in some instances almost, or even an entire, lifetime. It also very unfortunately, may carry enormous risk to one's own safety and even one's very life may be permanently at risk. Indeed, one may lose one's life in such a venture.

If certain persons can achieve such Greatness as described in the examples above, why has Humankind reduced itself to the two horrific and pathetic lists, List 1 and List 2 detailed a few pages above?

Why are the Transcendental Instinctive State of Being and the Transcendental Ethical and Moral State of Being not the norm?

The reason primarily rests in the fact that all living creatures strive to continue their existences to perpetuity. This is the Nature of Life. This is the Nature of All Life. It is non-negotiable. The True Meaning of Life will be dealt with in later volumes, a subject that has forsaken Humankind for the entirety of its existence but it is not as complicated as others may believe.

No one may reasonably deny each individual within Humankind their striving for the perpetration of their existence. However, it is in the manner of such striving where the faults appear.

By the very definition and nature of striving for the perpetration of the individual's existence, the individual would tend towards, de facto, negating all other persons' same and equal right. If I have eaten a meal, that meal cannot be eaten by another person. The other person has to go without that particular meal. If I have, someone else must go without. However, it must be such that there is sufficient for all. Which there is. In the animal kingdom there is sufficient for all, so it must be in the Kingdom of Humankind.

Capitalism is an individuality driven method. It encourages greed, avarice, stupidity and laziness. It is 'easy'. It is not that difficult to rip up the raw minerals and materials that exist just beneath the planet's surface and turn these materials into motor cars, mobile phones, jet planes, speed boats, swimming pools and other false 'symbols' of 'success'. In fact it is very easy indeed. It has been shown to be the apogee of Humankind's 'genius'. It is right in front of your face – its 'genius' cannot be denied. It is the Holy Grail of the Greatest and Profoundest of All Humankind's Thought and Action. It must be, for by and large, that is all that Humankind has been striving for since the birth of Leodamas of Thasos c. 380 B.C. and the only primary achievement of 'success' and 'recognition' by the Capitalist Ethos and the Establishment. Indeed, in the UK, the Monarchy has the inclination to honour such earth moving and metal/mineral/fossil fuel reformation expertise by endowing upon the endowable worthy, a little piece of metal and coloured ribbon that was created by the very same mechanism. In the distant past, these pieces of metal and coloured ribbon were primarily endowed upon those who killed other people. In some cases, large life-like statues of the endowable, by extension, again created by the same process, are erected in solemn, noble civic squares. From each his own/to those bestrewn.

How is it possible that Spinoza, Kant, Hume, Schopenhauer, Goethe and Wittgenstein all, to the very man, missed it? They must therefore all have been complete blockheads! There can be no other explanation.

Under the false marketing, false advertising and false peer group pressures that people allow themselves to be manipulated by, entire populations come into line by falling prey to the puppet 'masters'. There are perhaps about 0.005% of the global population who genuinely believe in the capitalist lies that those who own the most are intrinsically happier than those who own less, and that those who own the most are intrinsically superior to those who own less. In any large number of statistical samples there will always be a very small number that pertains to its own peculiarity, adverse to the majority. The issue with the true avarice believers is that they are typically the ones driving the lie because their avarice has got them to the position they need to be in in order to enslave the masses in their idiocy. The greater the voluntary self-slavery of the masses, the greater the 'avaricists' potential for satisfying their own personal unquenchable avarice. Before I wrote the sentence above, the word 'avaricist'(s)' was not in the English language – it now is. However, unfortunately for the 'avaricists' they will never satisfy their avarice, it is not in the nature of avarice to be able to do so. It is an unquenchable thirst. Consequently, they are condemned by their avarice value judgments, to be enslaved to them for their entire mortal existences. In their mortal physical state they will remain slaves until the time comes for their death. There are no physical objects in a higher world beyond this one. This matter will be dealt with in subsequent volumes. However, for the remainder of Humankind, to their benefit and potential salvation, their false slavery is purely voluntary. How this remainder of Humankind may rid itself of its voluntary, self-inflicted slavery, is dealt with in the next chapter. Whilst the avaricists in their sad, almost child-like understanding of Life, remain in inexorable condemnation until only Nature exercises its reprieve, and expunges the avaricists Lowly Life Longing and Lowly Purpose.

Chapter 8

Family of Humankind

The Moral Imperative

I am only for TRUTH, any Man who is not, must be a LIAR

Modern self-inflicted slavery – how does it come about?

Some of the characteristics of Humankind, as previously explained, are that they have the base tendencies of greed, laziness, stupidity, selfishness and cowardice. This greed, laziness, stupidity, selfishness and cowardice has caused far too much self-inflicted suffering, Man inflicting unnecessary suffering upon himself but perhaps more importantly, inflicting far too much unnecessary suffering upon his fellow man. There is also a strong tendency towards conformance and there is comfort in conforming. A comfort in a sense of belonging.

However, why would one want to conform to the base values of greed, laziness, stupidity, selfishness and cowardice? What comfort is there in that? Why would one want to feel comfort in belonging to a herd of idiots? Where is the individual's value of SELF? Why are people so imbued with FEAR?

Are we all not greater than this?

Dear Reader, YOU are greater than this!

266

There have been many scientific studies on the subject of human coercion. In the extreme, how much can the manipulator manipulate a person so that that person behaves in a manner that defies the principle of the person's instinctive obligation to the perpetuity of that person's own life? Once we have designed the principle to achieve this severe form of coercion, we may apply it to an entire country's population and indeed to the entire acquisitive global population who believe that they have disposable income. Advertising and marketing achieve this by exploitation of people's weaknesses to such an extent that they put their future livelihood of their entire immediate family at risk for the benefit of the false god of present 'ownership'. This phenomenon is called the Unnecessary Burden of Grossly Excessive Debt.

There are many, many examples of peer-reviewed scholarly articles on this subject available on the World Wide Web. However this example experiment is presented as an illustration. This is typical of how people will allow themselves to be manipulated against their will and against their natural instincts for self-preservation.

A traveller (the experimental subject) is sat on a crowded train in an 'open' seating carriage. A man (the experimenter) approaches the subject and asks him politely to surrender his seat to him. No explanation is given. In excess of 65% of the subjects gave up their perfectly valid right to the seat that they chose to use in exchange for the price of their rail ticket. Why give up one's paid-for seat, a seat provided under the terms of the contract for the duration of the person's travel, for which one has already paid, to a completely unknown stranger with no explanation as to why the stranger wants your particular seat? The mind boggles.

How much easier must it be then, to manipulate people in compliance with their baser instincts of greed, laziness, stupidity, selfishness and cowardice? Where the result of the manipulation is seen to be of significant benefit to the manipulated? It is as easy as taking sweets from a five-year old child! The only difference is that the child may cry. As explained earlier:

Inherent in the capitalist structure and myths described above is a form of self-inflicted slavery and consequently unnecessary suffering. Before one can contrive a mass of docile producers it is necessary to produce a docile mass of consumers. Consumption is a pre-requisite to production. Once you have the nation enslaved by consumerism and consumption, the job is done. For if one is coerced to consume, then one is de facto obliged to produce. One cannot consume unless one or someone produces that that is to be consumed. The payment for production (work) is used for one's acquisitive consumption.

The populace is thus held in a perpetual state of enslavement where the artificially created 'desires/must haves/to die for' false values being perpetual and ever-increasing; the individual never reaches satisfaction for there is always a bigger house, larger, faster car, larger yacht, younger mistress etc. to strive for. This system filters from the 'top' down to the working man who is ever longing a BMW or Mercedes Benz car rather than a Ford. Everything else and much more besides.

This can only result in perpetual unnecessary suffering as the entire nation and nations continually strives for false 'gods' and false goals that bring no true meaning to people's lives. It brings nothing other than a very brief and temporary false release when one false goal is finally 'achieved'. Only for the self-inflicted slavery to almost immediately recommence, once the novelty of the current bauble wears off and disappears forever, rather like a child's toy soap-bubble upon rising, disintegrating into thin air. The consumer then re-enters the vice-like grip of the capitalist manipulator and his or her next tempting bauble of false desire.

However, the tragedy does not end there. Like Covid-19, this perpetual unnecessary suffering is a global pandemic. Those people in the poorer countries, often termed the third world, observe the wonders of the people in the first world's bigger house, larger, faster car, larger yacht, younger mistress etc and want to join, in their mistaken lack of wisdom, the 'Big Party'. However, because for whatever reasons specific to the country where they reside, more often than not they cannot join this senseless madness because their country's production rate does not create sufficient disposable income for the individual. Perhaps this is their unknown good fortune? However, it is probably the case that these poorer people experience unnecessary suffering in their desire for that that they cannot procure, completely oblivious to the fact that if they could procure that that they cannot, they would be obliging themselves to unnecessary suffering of a different form. They would join the first world's herd in its perpetual unnecessary suffering as they and presumably their entire country continually strives for false 'gods' and false goals that bring no true meaning to people's lives. This ever increasing spiral of 'consumerist barbed wire' tends to entangle all.

Humankind has a moral imperative to rid itself of these self-inflicted chains. A moral imperative inherent to the very survival of our species. Out of a new moral imperative there must become A New Paradigm.

Chapter 9

Family of Humankind

A New Paradigm

2020 – Global Capitalism on Hold
The Post Covid-19 Global Opportunity

*HISTORY is a moving TARGET. If you have to do SOMETHING,
do it at the RIGHT TIME and do it FAST.*

The biggest existential threat to Humankind, as I write these words is Climate Change – Global Warming. If you seriously consider Climate Change – Global Warming is not the biggest existential threat to Humankind then please provide your peer-reviewed research study links and citations to 'Contact Us' on http:// saveyourselfsaveusall.com

As stated in 'Chapter 6 – Climate Change, Potential Tragedy of Emerging Technologies

– The Forces of Implosion':

[The] World hits record high for heat-trapping carbon dioxide in air.

Chief greenhouse gas averaged record levels in May [2020] *despite reduced emissions amid coronavirus* [Covid-19] *pandemic.*

The world has hit another record high for heat-trapping carbon dioxide in the atmosphere, despite reduced emissions because of the coronavirus pandemic.

Measurements of CO_2, the chief greenhouse gas, averaged 417.1 parts per million at Mauna Loa, Hawaii, for the month of May, when carbon levels in the air peak. That's 2.4 parts per million higher than a year ago.

Source: National Oceanic and Atmospheric Administration (NOAA) – 4th June 2020

Countries work together on climate change under the umbrella of the United Nations Framework Convention on Climate Change (UNFCCC) which has near-universal membership. The goal of the convention is to *"prevent dangerous anthropogenic interference with the climate system"*.

However, the situation and intention is clear. After over one hundred years of the abuse of the planet by the advocates of the false goals and false beliefs of capitalism; the capitalist practitioners, belatedly recognising the errors of their ways, are setting about methods contradictory to the core beliefs in capitalism, in order to correct capitalism's and their, catastrophic errors.

Catastrophic errors so profound and far-reaching, that without urgent effective dramatic radical changes, brought about immediately on a concerted and globally coordinated program to correct these errors, will in themselves, cause significant detriment and frustration on the western worlds need to satisfy its greed, that one dreads to think what life would be like, in the fourth quarter of this century for our grandchildren.

The Intergovernmental Panel on Climate Change IPCC has stressed the need to keep global warming below 1.5 °C (2.7 °F) compared to pre-industrial levels **in order to avoid some irreversible impacts.**

With current policies and pledges, global warming by the end of the century [2100 - Eighty years off!] is expected to reach about 2.8 °C (5.0 °F). At the current greenhouse gas (GHG) emission rate, the emissions budget for staying below 1.5 °C (2.7 °F) would be exhausted by 2028.

2028 is only eight years away! There are another 72 years to go to 2100! That won't work! We will all be cremated maggots long before the end of the century.

Multiple independently produced instrumental datasets confirm that the 2009–2018 decade was 0.93 ± 0.07 °C (1.67 ± 0.13 °F) warmer than the pre-industrial baseline of 1850–1900.

Currently, surface temperatures are rising by about 0.2 °C (0.36 °F) per decade.

> **Note: If this continues then we hit the 1.5 °C** in 70 years i.e. 2095. **Therefore irreversibility starts in 2095 and then it is only a matter of time before its lights out!** Why should I worry, why should I care? I won't be here! Well, for better or worse, I do care. That is the reason for writing this book.

This phenomenon of 'Global Warming', the mean temperature rise of the Earth's climate system, has been demonstrated by direct temperature measurements and by measurements of various effects of the warming. It is a major aspect of climate change which, in addition to rising global surface temperatures, also includes its effects, such as changes in rainfall or precipitation. While, it is understood that there have been prehistoric periods of global warming, observed changes since the mid-20th century have been unprecedented in rate and scale. The increase in global surface temperature from 1880 to 2020 has been observed to be approximately 1.2 deg. Celsius, with natural 'drivers' contributing 0.1 deg. Celsius, with the 'human drivers' contributing approximately 0.9 deg. Celsius, with the remaining 0.2 deg. Celsius increase caused by other, unspecified factors. The 'human drivers' therefore represent the great majority of the global warming causes at 75% of the total.

If we want to leave a world to our children, that is a world worth living in, then ALL of us have to make our personal contribution. This is non-negotiable.

IF WE WANT TO LEAVE A WORLD TO OUR CHILDREN, THAT IS A WORLD WORTH LIVING IN, THEN ALL OF US HAVE TO MAKE OUR PERSONAL CONTRIBUTION. THIS IS NON-NEGOTIABLE.

I have repeated this sentence and capitalised it, to ensure the importance of the point being made.

The old capitalism paradigm has been shown to be strewn with flaws; we must correct those flaws and correct them now, before it is too late!

All this stupid over-consumption to the pipe-tune and 'benefit' of the sociopathic few is leading us like lemmings over the Abyss Edge, never to return to Nature's beauteous hills and valleys, lakes and woodlands, beaches and seas.

However, the greatest successes can be built upon the greatest failures.

Covid-19 – Capitalism on Hold – A Brief Breath of Fresh Air

As described above Covid-19 was a global disaster, particularly in the UK and USA where the governments were literally criminally under-prepared. In particular the democratically elected UK government that over-turned some policy decisions on the basis of the singularly undemocratic 'genius' of two individuals in the 'sports' business. A 'sports' business that makes more money out of advertising and media coverage than it does out of the sport. However for better or worse, hopefully for better, world capitalism was essentially put on hold for a quarter of a year. The second quarter of 2020, essentially April to June 2020. It is interesting to note the quotation given at the beginning of Chapter 4 – The Failure of Capitalism:

"On the face of it, shareholder value is the dumbest idea in the world" Jack Welch CEO General Electric USA. Source: 'The Financial Times' 13th March 2009.

Jack Welch, the most successful Global Corporate Chief Executive Officer in the world in the 20th century and who is regarded as the father of the "shareholder value" movement that has dominated the corporate world for more than 20 years, **has said it was** *"the dumbest idea in the world"* **[for executives to focus so heavily on quarterly profits and quarterly share price gains…]**

By perhaps some simple twist of fate, the relentless march of capitalism, the endless, relentless, pathetic pursuit of tomorrow's fictitious greater material 'gain' has been put on hold by an agent other than Humankind – Covid-19. This agent could never have been Humankind, because Humankind is always 'within' its own self–imposed slavery. It perhaps does not perceive its own self-inflicted slavery and that that you cannot see, you cannot know. That that you do not know, you cannot change.

It is always difficult to revolutionise from within. Indeed, if a consciousness is wholly 'within', it cannot readily perceive itself because the change of social environment is such that the consciousness changes and adapts with it. One has to have the 'freedom' of the time, the energy, the intelligence and the intellect of perception to perceive change as it goes on around us in the social environment. When the individual and therefore entire societies are continually chasing their own tail of the false 'god' of consumerism then they will perceive nothing of any significance.

Indeed, the last thing that the Puppet 'Masters' want is for society to perceive its self-imposed consumerist manacles, to see its foolishness and stupidity and consequently break free of its manacles and run high, wild and singing in its new found ecstasy across Nature's beauteous hills and valleys, lakes and woodlands, beaches and seas.

History has given Humankind a Second Chance.

By a 'Simple Twist of Fate', by a 'Fluke of Nature', by 'The Diktat of Destiny', Humankind is graced with a Second Chance. The second chance must be taken, we may not get another.

This second chance, this temporary break in the relentless march of global, capitalist consumerism, involuntarily inflicted upon us by the external force Covid-19, must be utilized as a potential for good. A potential for reflection; calm reflection upon change for the Greater Good. This break gives Humankind a unique opportunity for Self-Reflection upon our Self-Realisation - to think upon where we are now and in what direction we should really be going in the future. We must turn a temporary abeyance into Truly Long Term Success.

Out of the Dust and Ashes there must come a New Paradigm, A New World Order.

History has given Humankind a Second Chance.

Chapter 10

Family of Humankind

A New World Order – Post Covid-19

To Fully Live LIFE, you must first release your Fear of DEATH.

If you have no fear of DEATH, you have no need to fear ANYTHING

WORK must become PLAY, PLAY becomes work

From Time beyond Time there has been far too much unnecessary suffering, some self-inflicted, some inflicted upon others by others. This must stop. There is no true long-term happiness in the acquisition of objects. There is perhaps at most, a few moments pleasure but that soon fades and becomes a distant, forlorn memory. Dawn into Dust. Dust unto Dust.

If re-shaping the earth's sub-strata into mobile phones, bigger wall-televisions, bigger cars, self-cretinising 'gadgetery'etc does not secure true long lasting happiness for Humankind, then where does true happiness lie?

Why are we here? What does each individual person bring? What is the direction of Humankind?

Within the constraints of our Ethics and Morals we are here to perpetrate Humankind the best we can by achieving individual self-realisation. In achieving the individual particular self-realisation, we contribute to Humankind achieving The Universal Self-Realisation.

How can we achieve true Self-Realisation if we are incessantly strapped inside the Eternal Hamster's Wheel of False Acquisitive Toil? The individual's Self-Sealisation has nothing to do with objects, it is nothing to do with your colleagues, it is nothing to do with 'success', it is nothing to do with what the neighbours will think.

It is to do with YOU.

One of the most inexplicable things about Humankind is that, although all driven by the will to survive and live this Life, all made of the same materials and of the same construction, all essentially looking similar in shape, height and form, all possessed of similar consciousness.

However we are all Unique. Similar, but ultimately Unique.

There are no two identical people in the world. No two people who have exactly the same ideas, exactly the same likes, exactly the same dislikes, exactly the same logic systems, exactly the same sense of aesthetics, exactly the same tastes, exactly the same desires, exactly the same sense of humour, exactly the same Lives.

We are all Absolutely Unique. 7.8Bn people and not two Lives the same.

It matters not a jot whether your skin colour is black, brown, white, pink, yellow, polka dot orange on indigo or Bridget Riley multi-coloured patterns. **It matters not a jot** whether you believe yourself to be Atheist, Agnostic, Christian, Buddhist, Muslim, Sufist, Hindu, Sikh or if you believe yourself to be orange peel.

The only Human value of any true worth is **Virtue**.

Are you a good person, good to yourself, your family, your friends, does your existence on the surface of this planet make the world a better place for all? You know what is good, it is within us. Truth is Within. You need only yourself; you need only to ask yourself. We are All One.

The Unique YOU: Self-Realisation, and True Happiness

Self-realisation and true happiness comes in discovering The Unique You. Who are You? Who is The Unique You? Where is the Unique You? What is the Unique You?

To find true happiness one must first find Yourself. In some quiet moments you must think only of yourself, for yourself and only of that, that is you. Take a Holiday from Life once a year, say the day before your birthday. Travel away for the day. Go to your favourite spot, perhaps a mountain, lake or sea-shore preferably on your own or perhaps with a friend. Take a notebook and pencil and make notes. Sign and date them. Make this your Life Journal. Take it with you whenever you think that you are likely to want to jot down some notes. On your Holiday from Life, step 'outside' yourself, briefly 'transcend' your own consciousness and contemplate your last year and how you can improve your next.

This is not some Corporate Annual Review. You may take your 'Holiday from Life' as frequently and briefly as you wish, to fit your needs, whenever you wish, wherever you wish. A quiet moment in your bath, a walk with your dog, a quiet moment of peaceful rest before you go to sleep. Always have a little notebook and pencil with you, and another at your bedside, so that you can at any time write your thoughts. You can transcribe them to your 'Life Journal' later.

Take some time to think about your natural abilities, your strengths, your weaknesses, your aptitudes, the things you love to do, your family, your friends – the ones you love, and how you can bring all your strengths of the different facets of you into a 'synergistic whole'. For the betterment of all.

Your Synergistic You is The Unique You.

Once you "know yourself", set out your plan and Go! Do not bother to compare yourself to others. You have your life to lead, they have theirs and never the twain shall meet.

Devise a flexible plan to achieve your own personal Self-Realisation: your work, your career, your family, your partner, your children, your leisure pursuits, your loves, your likes, your dislikes.

How can you, in becoming who you really are, contribute to the greater good?

Think of yourself as you wish to become, and you will become. Think of yourself as you wish the world to be a better place, how your Unique YOU can make its greatest contribution where, in becoming Yourself, you are becoming a better person, and contributing to making a better world. In becoming your Self-Realisation you will help the World to Become Itself. You will be helping your fellow Humankind become what it should become. There can be no greater contribution to the Betterment of Humankind than that.

Once we have released ourselves from our self-inflicted slavery to become our true selves we are no longer slaves to the capitalist method and capitalism is no longer a 'method', it becomes a system. The system which is designed for the self-realisation of the people, not for their self-infliction.

This Truth is applicable to everyone, from the Banker on Wall Street USA, to the Eskimo of the North, from the Farmer in Norfolk UK to the Maasai Tribesman in East Africa.

The Particular becomes The Universal. The Universal becomes the Particular. The Eternal Cycle of Wonder and Mystery. The Eternal Cycle of Life.

Chapter 11

The Challenge for You, World Leaders and All Humankind Alike

Have you ever wondered how miraculous it is that tomorrow will begin a virgin day untouched by a reality yet to be? Life itself, the very Existence of Anything is such a Miracle - it is completely beyond YOUR comprehension, YES I said, YOUR comprehension.

Man, Woman, Child; Mankind, Womankind, Childkind we are all of Humankind. We are all of Soul. We are all Souls in the particular; we are all Of Soul in the Universal. We are One. From Now until all Eternity Returns, we are One. This is how it is, this is what we are. This is how it will always be.

To Hell with differentiation, to Hell with greed, stupidity, laziness and cowardice. We are Greater than that. YOU are greater than that. President or Pauper, Attorney or Apprentice, Carpenter or Table-Thrower, Beard-Wearer or Warrior, we are all greater than that. It does not matter who you are: Donald Trump, Angela Merkel, Boris Johnson, Emmanuel Macron, Xi Jinping... They are Greater than that. We are Greater than that. YOU are greater than that.

You are not the sum total of your suit, your job title, you are not the sum total of your Bentley car, Patek Philippe watch, your swimming pool or your overalls, Ford motor car, Citizen watch or your snooker cue. You are not the sum total of your wardrobe, your jewellery, or perfume. We are Greater than that. YOU are greater than that.

We are ALL ONE. The challenge rests with us ALL. The challenge rests with ME. The challenge rests with YOU. The challenge rests with Humankind – to build a better Home, to build a better World. FOR ALL.

For All of us, when we are Born, Nature gives us Love, Peace and Joy from then on all we may do, if we are not very careful, is lose them. We must keep them and treasure them. They are all that we have that is TRUE LIFE. They are all we have that is TRULY OURS.

The pen is mightier than the sword, Actions speak louder than words. As Nature gives, so the Pen may also give, as Nature gives, so may our Actions also give: Love, Peace and Joy. The sword ultimately gives only Death and often a premature, painful and unnecessary one. History wearing its windswept Crimson Cloak is hurriedly walking past your door; seek the vision and the courage to walk with it.

Here are some words that came from One Voice:

Live your Life Through the Happiness of Others, Nothing more

and Nothing Less

HOPE

VIRTUE

LOVE

LIFE

WORK must become PLAY, PLAY becomes work

Nothing Exists that may not exist, all of it may not be good, but it is a part of an ever evolving Greater Whole. Give your Love to The World, to those who deserve it, to those in most need of it. For There are Many.

This morning at my local supermarket, a lovely little girl four or five years old, hair full of bouncing golden ringlets, was running around the shop in great joy, so pleased and full of life to be helping her mother with the weekend family shopping. At the check-out till she was in a form of joyful ecstasy, loading it with delicious food and then decanting the food into Mum's shopping bag. Such an innocent, endearing, joyful delight to watch!

As I watched her I thought "What sort of planet is this gorgeous, life-loving, little girl going to inherit from us? We cannot forsake her, can we? Surely not. She deserves better from us. As all our children do."

Our clock is ticking on your mantelpiece!

Ooops! Here's my bus. Quick! Got to hop on! Life waits for no man!

This particular subject will be dealt with in greater detail later…

LW-96

Officium est

About the Author

Lawrence Wolfe-Xavier - Mystic Genius

Wit/Aphorist/Philosopher/Writer/Lyricist/Polemicist
Literary Historian/'Socratean' Dialectician/Photographer/Hunter

Lawrence Wolfe-Xavier previously a Designer, Project Engineer/ Product Manager working for US global blue chip companies based in UK, Europe and Africa, had his fill of the corporate world and its inhabitants. From CEO to salesman, technician to shop-floor worker he had the usual fill of corporate middle-management but being an Independent Managerial-Technical Consultant helped to keep them at a pre-covid 19, social distance.

He has travelled the world and spent two and a half years working and travelling in Africa, Indian Ocean, the Far-East and photographing people of little known places. He now produces a book of photographs/images a year. When travelling, some twenty years ago through the Maasia Savanna Grasslands of Africa he was inspired to write verse which he continues to do. The author, for over ten years, is the Chairman of a Literary Society, that encourages creativity and self-improvement amongst youngters. He writes answers to questions on Life & Living, World Events, Philosophy, Literature and other subjects on the Internet with more than 1.4 million personal readers and with circa 40,000 readers per month. A 'most viewed' writer on many occasions.

"Not all of the writer's Genius was used in the writing of this book, rather, just enough to get it done".

The author of this book has created a **'must-read'** for anyone concerned for, or confused by, today's world and our future.

Reader Reviews

If you would like to review this book or make any comments about it, please use the 'Contact Us' page on the website: http://saveyourselfsaveusall.com

Reader Email Listing Sign-Up

If you would like to join the email list, please make your request on the 'Contact Us' page on the website:

http://saveyourselfsaveusall.com

or Email:

lawrence_wolfe_xavier@yahoo.co.uk

The author has 1.4M readers and circa 40,000 per month on an Internet Q&A forum.

Regular Emails, prizes, 'freebies' will be sent personally by Lawrence Wolfe-Xavier on a wide range of topics of interest to readers. Advice will be provided if required, provided that I am qualified to do so. Any and all personal information, if any needs to be provided, will be treated as Strictly Confidential, not disclosed to any third parties and will be treated in accordance with all General Data Protection Regulation GDPR legislation.

Lawrence Wolfe-Xavier
2020

Index